MEMOIRS OF THE LIFE OF
SIR SAMUEL ROMILLY

The Development of Industrial Society Series

MEMOIRS OF THE LIFE OF SIR SAMUEL ROMILLY

with a Selection from His Correspondence

Edited by His Sons

Volume 3

IRISH UNIVERSITY PRESS
Shannon Ireland

First edition London 1840
Second edition London 1840

This I U P reprint is a photolithographic facsimile of
the second edition and is unabridged, retaining the
original printer's imprint.

All forms of micropublishing
© *Irish University Microforms Shannon Ireland*

ISBN 0 7165 1784 1 Three volumes
ISBN 0 7165 1785 X Volume 1
ISBN 0 7165 1786 8 Volume 2
ISBN 0 7165 2062 1 Volume 3

T M MacGlinchey Publisher
Irish University Press Shannon Ireland

PRINTED IN THE REPUBLIC OF IRELAND BY
ROBERT HOGG PRINTER TO IRISH UNIVERSITY PRESS

MEMOIRS

OF

THE LIFE

OF

SIR SAMUEL ROMILLY.

VOL. III.

London :
Printed by A. Spottiswoode,
New-Street-Square.

MEMOIRS

OF

THE LIFE

OF

SIR SAMUEL ROMILLY,

WRITTEN BY HIMSELF;

WITH A SELECTION FROM

HIS CORRESPONDENCE.

EDITED BY HIS SONS.

IN THREE VOLUMES.

VOL. III.

𝔖𝔢𝔠𝔬𝔫𝔡 𝔈𝔡𝔦𝔱𝔦𝔬𝔫.

LONDON:
JOHN MURRAY, ALBEMARLE STREET.
MDCCCXL.

CONTENTS

OF

THE THIRD VOLUME.

1816.

1817.

LETTERS TO C.

1801.

1807.

MEMOIRS

OF

SIR SAMUEL ROMILLY.

DIARY OF HIS PARLIAMENTARY LIFE — *continued.*

1812.

Jan. 6th. I attended a meeting at Stephen's Slave trade.
with Wilberforce, Brougham, and Babington, to
consider what measures it would be necessary to
take, to make effectual the Act which has passed
for the abolition of the slave trade. The most
effectual measure appeared to all of us to be the
establishing a registry for slaves in all the islands,
and a law that every negro not registered should
be free; and it was determined that an attempt
should be made to procure an Act of Parliament for
this purpose.

7th. Parliament met.

The state of Bristol I find is this: It has been Bristol
long agreed between the leaders of the Whig and election.
Tory parties in that city not to interfere with each
other in the election; but that each party should
have its own member, who should be the person proposed by each of the two great political clubs which
have been formed there. Mr. Bathurst is the Tory
member, and it is intended that he should be re-
elected. In the place of Mr. Baillie, it has been

proposed to choose me. Some other candidates, however, have been, within a few days, talked of. Admiral Berkeley has been named by some of his friends, but, on finding that he had no chance of success, his pretensions have been withdrawn. Another candidate, who may, I understand, very probably have a large party in his favour, is Mr.

Edward Protheroe, a Bristol man, who lately was a banker there, though he now resides in London. He professes to be a Whig, though he seconded at a public meeting a motion for an address of congratulation to the King on dismissing his ministers in 1807. At the club of the Whig party, which met 7th of January, this gentleman was proposed, and supported, I understand, by some of his friends with much eagerness. His claims, however, were rejected by a very large majority; and the follow-

ing resolution was adopted: — " Resolved, that Sir Samuel Romilly is a fit person to represent the Whig interest of the city of Bristol in the ensuing Parliament, provided he can assure this club through their chairman, that his professional duties are not of such a nature as to prevent his attendance in the committees of the House of Commons, and other duties attendant on the representative of the city of Bristol."

In answer to the letter of Mr. Claxton,. the chairman of the club, who transmitted this resolution to me, I said, " I have lately endeavoured to ascertain the nature and probable extent and frequency of such attendances and duties; and, from what I am able to learn, I have no hesitation in assuring the club that, if I should have the honour of being returned to represent the city, I will give these attendances and discharge these duties."

Mr. Protheroe, or his friends, disregarding the determination of the club, are very actively canvassing Bristol; and both the candidate and his brother, Sir Henry Protheroe, have published in the newspapers addresses to the electors. Another gentleman, a Mr. Hunt, has also advertised that he is a candidate, and that his principles are those of Sir Francis Burdett; and he asks the electors whether it is right to elect as their representative a man who voted against an amendment to the address to the Regent, proposed by that Baronet on the first day of the session. He took for granted that I had so voted, though, in truth, I was not in the House at the time of the division. If I had been there, I certainly should have voted against it. My Bristol friends have pressed me very much to publish an address to the electors; though very unwilling to do so, I have yielded to their wishes, and have this day, 17th January, sent them an address, in these words: —

Candidates set up at Bristol.

    " To the Gentlemen, Clergy, Freeholders, and Freemen of the City of Bristol.

My address to the electors.

    " Gentlemen,

        " A stranger to the city of Bristol, and having scarcely a personal acquaintance with any of its inhabitants, it would have been very great presumption in me spontaneously to have offered myself as a candidate to represent you in Parliament. I had not the vanity to imagine that my humble endeavours faithfully to discharge my duty as a member of the

House of Commons could have attracted your notice. It has, however, been represented to me by some highly respectable electors of Bristol, that the manner in which I have sought to discharge that duty has been looked upon by many of you in so favourable a light, that they are desirous that I should be proposed to be one of your representatives. By this intimation alone it is that I am encouraged to say, that to be returned to Parliament by your free and independent suffrages is an honour which I should prize more highly than any other that could be conferred upon me. The very circumstance of my being known to you only as I am known to all the other electors of Great Britain would, in my estimation, greatly enhance the value of so enviable a distinction; and I should proudly exult at being able to enter the House of Commons with such authority for the opinions I have maintained, and the principles on which I have acted, as they would derive from your unsolicited and honourable choice. After saying this, it is hardly necessary for me to observe that I am not about to commence a personal canvass for your votes. If my past conduct has in your judgment rendered me worthy the high honour of being your representative, it is unnecessary for me to go about soliciting your suffrages; and if it has not, I know of no ground upon which I could presume to make such a request, for I have ever found that those who are most ready with professions are most tardy in performance."

Bad police of the metropolis. 17th. There has of late been a very great increase of crimes in the metropolis; and some of the

outrages which have been committed are marked
with a character of savage atrocity which is without example in this country. Mr. Ryder, the
Secretary of State, has, in consequence of these
enormities, moved this day that a committee should
be appointed to inquire into the state of the nightly
watch. I expressed on this occasion (as I felt)
great surprise and disappointment that for such an
evil such a remedy should be thought of. Crimes
had multiplied, and this, too, in a time of war
(during which crimes have generally been observed
to be comparatively few in number) to a most
alarming degree.* Two whole families, one consisting of four and the other of three persons, had,
at a very short distance of time, been murdered in
their houses [1]; and the Minister proposes nothing
more than to inquire into the state of the nightly
watch. I suggested that the inquiry should be
into the causes of the late increase of crimes, or
into the state of the police. I stated that I believed
that amongst the foremost causes of this increase
would be found the mode of punishment now in
use, that of imprisonment on board the hulks, or of
promiscuous imprisonment in gaols ; which turned
loose upon the public the convicts, at the end of
their terms of punishment, much more hardened

---

* The number of persons committed for trial at the Old Bailey for the
last six years, for offences of all descriptions, have been as follows : —

In 1806	-	- 899	In 1809	-	-	- 1242
1807	-	- 1017	1810	-	-	- 1214
1808	-	- 1110	1811	-	- 1252

Vid. infra, June 22. 1815.

---

[1] The murders of the families of Marr and Williamson : the first took
place on the 7th, and the last on the 19th of the preceding month.—ED.

and profligate than they were before. I spoke of the system, now in use, of giving rewards for the apprehension and conviction of offenders of some descriptions, such as burglars and robbers on the highway, as extremely pernicious ; since it gave a direct interest to the police officers and thief-takers that crimes of great atrocity, but extremely profitable to them, should greatly multiply. After the debate had continued for some time, Abercromby moved as an amendment, that the inquiry should also extend to the state of the police of the metropolis, which Ryder at last agreed to; and the committee has been so appointed.* Perceval, in the course of the debate, said, he doubted whether it would not be expedient, if any alteration were made with respect to rewards, to extend them to all crimes (proportioning the amount of the reward to the enormity of the crime), rather than to take them away as to any.

Abuses in Ecclesiastical Courts.

23d. Lord Folkestone moved for a committee to inquire into the state of the inferior Ecclesiastical Courts. What led to this motion was a petition presented by a young woman [1] not of age, who has been confined two years, having been arrested on a writ *de excommunicato capiendo*, for not paying costs in a suit for defamation. Sir William Scott defended the Spiritual Courts with great

---

* This committee has since made a report, the object of which seems to have been to suppress all information as to the present state of the police. It contains no evidence, and does little more than refer to some old Acts of Parliament.

---

[1] Mary Anne Dix ; her case, as stated in her own petition to the House of Commons, will be found in Hansard's *Parl. Deb.*, vol. xxi. p. 99. — ED.

adroitness. I spoke after him, and strongly endeavoured to impress on the House the mischiefs
of this power of excommunication which the Spiritual Courts possessed.* I took advantage of
what Sir William had said upon excommunication,
as being a very inexpedient mode of enforcing
obedience to a judgment; and I pressed him very
strongly, as being the person best qualified for it,
to undertake himself the task of reforming this by
a statute; and I represented to him how few difficulties he, as a friend to the Administration, was
likely to encounter in such an attempt, and what
good he might do by such a measure. Several persons who spoke afterwards adopted this idea, and
the matter ended by Sir William Scott undertaking
to prepare and bring in a Bill for the purpose.[1]

31st. I moved for some returns of convicts.

Having been told by some of my Bristol friends Bristol
that my address had been understood to mean that election.
I would not, even when an election should take
place, go near Bristol; and that it was very important that they should be undeceived in this respect,
and that they should have some public assurance
that I was not unwilling to undertake their business; I wrote a letter to Mr. Edge at Bristol, and
gave him permission to publish it as he might
choose. My letter was in these words: —

---

* I mentioned that the evil had been stated to Parliament in King
James's time, by a message from that prince, delivered by the Archbishop
of Canterbury. — *Vid. Lords' Journals*, 1st April, 1606. No remedy,
however, had ever been applied.

---

[1] This bill was brought in, and it passed into a law in the next Parliament. See *infra*, July, 1813. — ED.

" Sir,   Lincoln's Inn, January 31st.

" I have learned with much surprise that the declaration in my address to the electors of Bristol that I was not about to commence a personal canvass for their votes has been construed to mean, that I intended, whenever an election might take place, to remain in London, as if I were little interested in the event of it. Nothing certainly could have been farther from my meaning ; and I really should have hardly thought it possible that such an interpretation could have been put upon my words. It is, and always was, my intention, upon a dissolution of Parliament, to hasten to Bristol, and there offer myself to the choice of the electors, and to express to them my gratitude for the honour which I have been led to believe they would confer upon me. But I entertain too high an opinion of the public spirit of the citizens of Bristol, to believe that at any time, and much less in such times as those we live in, their votes are to be gained by the personal attentions, and individual flatteries, and the other little artifices which are so often resorted to at elections. I am at this moment canvassing for their votes, and I shall continue to canvass for them, by a close attendance in Parliament, and by an anxious care not to neglect my public duty. These are the only arts I am practising, and which I shall continue to practise, to obtain their suffrages. Another opinion which I am told has been propagated is, that, as a Member for Bristol, I should be either unable or unwilling to give that time to the local and particular interests of my constituents which they would demand.   This opinion is just as unfounded as the former.   As I would never consent to be placed in any situation in which I should be unable to discharge the duties which might justly be expected from me, it was not till I had ascertained, as well as I could, the nature and extent of the business which usually devolves upon the representatives of Bristol, and found that I could well undertake it, that I presumed to address the electors.   I have presumed, Sir, to trouble you with this letter, in the hope that you would have the kindness to endeavour to remove these misconceptions, if they really exist. I am, &c."

This letter was printed in all the Bristol newspapers.

Feb. 7th.   On the second reading of the Bill to prevent the granting places in reversion, Perceval, without giving any previous notice of his intention, opposed it; although on former occasions the Bill had passed the Commons almost without opposition. I spoke in support of the Bill.   It was rejected in a thin House by a majority of two.[1]

Reversion Bill.

On the same day I moved for, and obtained leave to bring in a Bill to repeal the Act of 39 Eliz. c. 17., which makes it a capital offence for soldiers or mariners to wander and beg, without a pass from the magistrate or their commanding officer.   (*Vide infra*, p. 19.)

Bill to repeal 39 Eliz.

12th.   I moved for a committee to inquire into the manner in which sentences of transportation have been executed, and into the effects which

Transportation to New South Wales.

---

[1] The numbers were — for the second reading of the Bill, 54 ; against it, 56.— Ed.

have been produced by that mode of punishment. The Ministers did not oppose it, and the Committee was appointed.*

The Regent's determination to keep Perceval as his minister.

18th.   On this day the restrictions imposed by Parliament on the Regent cease ; and this is the period which he has been pleased for some time to mention as that at which he should think himself at liberty to call into his service such Ministers as he approved of.   Why this period was fixed on for that purpose it is not easy to say.   That, as long as any hope was entertained of the King's recovery, the Prince might think the reasons which induced him to continue the present Ministers ought still to operate, is intelligible ; but why, when all hope was gone, the exercise of his own judgment, on a point so important to the people he is called upon to govern, should still be postponed, was incomprehensible till within these few days, which have unravelled the mystery.   His Royal Highness, it seems, notwithstanding all his professions, in spite of his letter of last year to Mr. Perceval[1], and in spite of the hopes and expectations which he has held out to the Catholics of Ireland, had determined to retain the present Ministers, or at least such of them as would remain in his service ; and the longer the avowal of that determination was postponed, the greater chance there was that something or other might happen which might afford a decent apology for a step which must to the whole nation appear so extraor-

* See a Report of this Committee ordered to be printed, 10th July, 1812.

[1] See vol. ii. p. 359. — ED.

dinary.   No such event, however, has happened.
The large minority which appeared upon the question respecting Ireland frustrated a plan which
had been laid to get the House of Commons to
adopt some resolution that should seem to set the
question of Catholic Emancipation at rest, at least
for the present ; and it was with a view to this that
Sir John Nicholl was induced to put himself forward in the debate, as the opposer of the Catholics.   The turn, however, of the debate and the
numbers[1] on the division defeated the project;
and the Prince has been obliged in a letter to the The
Duke of York, written for the purpose of being Regent's
letter to
communicated to Lord Grey and Lord Grenville, the Duke
to avow his intention.   He has proposed, indeed, of York.
a coalition with Mr. Perceval, a proposal which he
knew must be rejected.   The very proposal, indeed, imports that a total sacrifice of honour and
of character was a necessary qualification for entering into the Prince's service.   He says in the letter
that he has no predilection to indulge and no
resentment to gratify : a most dangerous statement
at the commencement of his reign, considering his
past conduct and his past professions.   It will be
understood to mean that there are no injuries he
will not forgive, and no services he will not forget.
A declaration better calculated to estrange from
him all his friends, if he has any remaining ; and
to invite the most violent personal opposition to
his government (since every thing at a convenient

[1] The debate took place on the 3d and 4th February, on Lord Morpeth's motion that the House resolve itself into a committee of the
whole House, to take into consideration the present state of Ireland ;
and the numbers in favour of the motion were 135, against it 229.—ED.

time may be forgiven), could hardly have been invented. In the beginning of the letter, he seems to affect to consider the question of Catholic Emancipation as disposed of by the fate of the late motion in the House of Commons. This was intended, undoubtedly ; but, as I have already observed, the scheme was frustrated. The newspapers in the pay of Government, finding how ill the idea of a coalition with Mr. Perceval has been received by the public, pretend, and some of the Prince's immediate dependents pretend, that this was not his Royal Highness's meaning. But what doubt can be entertained of it ? The Prince, after pronouncing the highest panegyric on the conduct of his present Ministers, says, that he cannot conclude without expressing the gratification he should feel, if *some* of those persons with whom the early habits of his public life were formed would strengthen his hands, and constitute a part of his government ; and he adds in a postscript, that he should send a copy of the letter immediately to Mr. Perceval. The proposal was immediately rejected by Lord Grey and Lord Grenville. Lord Wellesley, it seems, had before tendered his resignation, and Lord Castlereagh is to succeed him. What other changes are to take place is not yet known, and perhaps not determined.

The Prince does not pass a day without visiting Lady Hertford.[1]

Colonel M'Mahon's sinecure.

24th, *Mon.* In the course of the last summer, the Prince appointed his secretary, Colonel M'Mahon, to the office of Paymaster of widows' pensions,

[1] See Vol. II. p. 152. — ED.

which had become vacant by the death of General Fox. The office produces about 2700*l.* a year to the holder of it, but it is a complete sinecure, and the propriety of abolishing it has been stated in several reports of committees of the House of Commons. The House this day, on the motion of Mr. Bankes, refused to vote the money to pay the salary of the office. The numbers on the division were 115 and 112, so that the Ministers were in a minority of 3.[1]

26th, *Wed.* Michael Angelo Taylor renewed his motion for a committee to inquire into the causes which have delayed the decision of suits in Chancery. Perceval did not oppose the motion ; but he has prevailed on Taylor to let him make such changes in the members of the committee, that I expect no good from any report they will be disposed to make. At Perceval's suggestion, Master Simeon has been added to the committee. When his name was read, I opposed his being upon it, and moved to substitute Mr. C. Williams Wynn. I did not, however, divide the House, as there were hardly forty members present, and I had no chance of success. I said that I thought that neither Mr. Simeon nor Mr. Edward Morris ought to be on the committee, not on account of any objection that could possibly be taken to either of them personally, but because they were Masters in Chancery. The Master of the Rolls, who had been on the committee appointed in the last Session, had desired that he might not be again placed in that situation ; there being, in his opinion, an

Delays in the Court of Chancery.

Masters in Chancery not fit members of a committee to inquire into the delays of the Court.

---

[1] Sir S. Romilly voted in the majority.— ED.

impropriety in a Judge of the Court sitting upon a committee to inquire into that which might possibly implicate himself. His name was accordingly omitted; and the objection was certainly a very just one in point of principle, though there was no person at all acquainted with the Court who did not know that it never could enter into the imagination of any man that any part of the delays complained of was imputable to the Master of the Rolls. The same objection applied with equal force to the Masters in Chancery, who were subordinate Judges of the Court. I said that, in my opinion, the committee would ill discharge their duty, if, amongst other objects of their inquiry, they did not endeavour to ascertain the cause of suits being so many years, as it was notorious they were, depending in the Masters' offices. I added, that I did not believe that the Masters were at all to blame in this; that they gave all the attendance in their offices which was necessary to go through the business brought before them; but that, probably, the defect was in the modes of proceeding, established according to the constitution of the Court, and that the proper remedy would be an alteration of the present practice : that this however remained to be ascertained ; and, although improbable, it might possibly happen that, in the progress of the inquiry, abuses might be suggested to exist in some of the Masters' offices : that in such an event it would be extremely invidious for the Masters who were on the committee to prosecute inquiries tending to criminate their colleagues, and that, if any abuse should by chance be said to exist in their own offices, it would be a very strange situation that solicitors and other witnesses would be placed in, who would be called upon to give evidence before the committee against some of its own members; and a still stranger situation in which the Masters would be placed, whose duty it might be to make a report against themselves.

March 5th, *Th.* Benjamin Walsh, a member of the House of Commons, was this day expelled the House. I was one of a very small minority, consisting only of eighteen persons, who voted against his expulsion. He had certainly been guilty of most dishonest conduct; but I thought the expelling him would establish a precedent of which very dangerous use might be made hereafter. As I did not speak, I am the more desirous of preserving the reasons for my vote. Walsh had been tried at the Old Bailey for felony, in stealing bank notes to a very great amount from Sir Thomas Plumer, and he was convicted; but a case was reserved on the conviction for the opinion of the Judges, who were unanimously of opinion that what he had done did not amount to felony, and therefore that he ought to have been acquitted. It was clear, too, that the facts of the case did not constitute a misdemeanour, or any offence whatever, cognizable before any criminal tribunal; but they amounted to a private and fraudulent breach of trust, committed with very aggravated circumstances. I thought it extremely dangerous that the House of Commons should assume to itself a power of expelling any of its members, merely on the ground of their having been guilty of gross

Expulsion of Walsh from the House of Commons.

immorality. Such a censorial power cannot be entrusted to a popular assembly, acting, as it often necessarily must act, under the influence of political prejudices, without being liable to the greatest abuse. There was a further, and, as it appeared to me, a very solid ground which decided my vote. The house, I thought, had no evidence of the fact, whatever might really be its character, on which it could proceed. It had before it only the record of the conviction, a letter of the Chief Baron to the Secretary of State, containing the opinion of the Judges, and a private letter from Walsh to his brother, which had been produced in evidence upon the trial. This letter had been put into the post-office, and had there been opened and delivered to Sir Thomas Plumer, to be used as evidence against Walsh.* Nothing could justify the opening this letter, or putting it into the hands of any other person than the individual to whom it was confidentially addressed, but that the author of it had been guilty of felony or some other crime, and that without the production of it there would be a failure of justice. The moment it was decided by the Judges that no crime had been committed, the letter ought to have been considered as under the seal of the public faith to which it was entrusted. The facts which the jury had found upon the evidence of this letter alone, ought to have been considered as unproved; and it appeared to me to be inconsistent with the honour of the House to take as original evidence produced before its own body a letter which had

* I have since been informed that this letter was not intercepted at the post-office, but that it was obtained by some other surreptitious means.

been opened in violation of the trust which men are invited to repose in the post-office, upon a pretence which turned out to be false.   The minority consisted, on this occasion, with the exception of a single individual, of men who always vote with the Opposition.   Walsh, however, had never in any one instance, while he was in Parliament, voted against the Ministers.

13th, *Fri.*   On occasion of a Bill for building a workhouse and making regulations for the management of the poor in the parish of Stroud in Kent, I again called the attention of the House of Commons to the evil of passing these local Poor Bills, which make a different state of the poor laws and the criminal law in each particular parish which chooses to apply for such a Bill.*   In the Bill now before the House, and which stood for the third reading, I objected, first, to a power given to the trustees to bind poor children apprentices at any age, and I proposed to fix the earliest age at which they might be bound at ten years ; secondly, to a power to bind children apprentices to persons residing in Scotland ; and thirdly, to a power in the trustees to let out the poor to any persons, to labour of any kind, and for any term.   Sir Edward Knatchbull, the Member for Kent, who brought in the Bill, opposed my amendments ; but on a division, I carried my first proposed amendment ; and the opinion of the House appearing to be strongly against him on the other two, he conceded them to me ; and all the passages I objected to were struck out.

Local Poor Bills.

Stroud Poor Bill.

* Vide *suprà*, Vol. II. p. 381.

VOL. III.

Military
punish-
ments.

On the same day, on the third reading of the
Mutiny Bill, Sir Francis Burdett proposed a clause
to abolish the punishment of flogging in the army.
I was one of only eight[1], including the tellers, who
divided with him in support of the clause. I spoke
too in support of it; and in the course of my speech,
I vindicated my friend Brougham, who had been
accused of making a most extravagant and exaggerated statement, because he had said, on a former
occasion, that, for very serious offences, it would
be better to punish soldiers by shooting than by
flogging them; and I mentioned what I had read
a few days before in the *Transactions of the
Missionary Society*. In the journal of one of the
missionaries at the Cape of Good Hope are the
following passages : — " July 14th, 1810. A soldier
belonging to the Cape regiment had been tried for
desertion, and was condemned to die." It then
proceeds with an account of his being attended by
one of the missionaries, and his conversion previous
to his being shot. " Another, who had been also
guilty of desertion, and who was to receive 1000
lashes, appeared more impressed. He received but
224 lashes, the surgeon judging that he was not
able to bear more, and thus he was for this time
freed. Being brought to the hospital, he remained
there some weeks, and died. Brother Read, visiting
him before his dissolution, gave us likewise hope
of his salvation." (*Transactions of the Missionary
Society*, vol. iii. p. 392.) The facts are here mentioned without any observation, and are preserved
only incidentally, and as necessary to state what is

[1] The numbers against the clause were 79. — ED.

the business of the journal, the successful spiritual labours of the missionaries.

We have here for the more aggravated crime, a criminal simply deprived of life; and for the slighter offence another put to death with exquisite tortures; and by his sentence doomed to suffer four times as much misery as God had given him a capacity of enduring. Who can doubt that in this instance, and in many more which have occurred, a sentence of death would have been a sentence of mercy?

18th, *Wed.* The Bill which I brought into the House of Commons to repeal the Act of Queen Elizabeth, which punishes with death soldiers and mariners who are found begging, passed the House of Lords to-day [1]; but with the amendment of leaving out one word, which Lord Ellenborough made a point of having struck out of the Bill. The Bill, as it passed the Commons, recited that it was *highly* expedient that the Act of Elizabeth should be repealed; and this word "highly" it was which gave offence to his Lordship. The Lord Chancellor this morning in Court sent me down a note in these words: — "The Bill about sailors and soldiers will pass our House to-day. Lord Ellenborough objected to the word *highly*, and said he would attend to move the amendment. The preamble now stands that it is *expedient* to repeal, without the words *highly expedient*. There seemed to be a notion that this statute was impliedly repealed by some other — what I know not — but I did not think it *tanti* to have discussion

Margin notes: Bill to repeal 39 Eliz. against soldiers and mariners begging.   Lord Ellenborough.

[1] The Act is the 52 Geo. III. c. 31. — Ed.

upon it. A statute inflicting death may be, and ought to be, repealed, if it be *in any degree* expedient, without its being *highly* so. We, therefore, so settled the matter with the Chief Justice."

Abuses of
charitable
trusts.

20th, *Fri.* Mr. Lockhart has brought in a Bill similar to one he brought into the House last session, to compel the registering of all charitable trusts. On moving for leave to bring it in, he stated that he should adopt the suggestion thrown out by me last year *, and provide by his Bill a more summary remedy for the correction of the abuses of such trusts. He afterwards applied to me, and I drew such clauses as I thought would answer the purpose, which he has since incorporated in the Bill. It accordingly provides that, in every case of a breach, or supposed breach of any trust created for charitable purposes, it shall be lawful for any two persons to present a petition to the Lord Chancellor, Master of the Rolls, or Court of Exchequer, who are required to hear such petition in a summary way upon affidavits, and make such order as shall be just; which order shall be final, unless the party who thinks himself aggrieved shall within two years appeal to the House of Lords, to whom it declares that an appeal shall lie. The petitions are to be signed by the persons preferring them, and attested by their solicitor, and are to be first allowed by the Attorney or Solicitor General; and none of the proceedings upon such petitions are to be liable to any stamp-duty. To-day, before the House went into a committee on this Bill, the House resolved, on my motion, that it should be an instruction

* Vide *suprà*, Vol. II . p. 385.

to the Committee, to separate the Bill into two Bills. My clauses, therefore, now constitute a separate Bill.*

31st, *Easter Tuesday.* My friends at Bristol have for some time pressed me very much to make them a visit, not for the purpose of canvassing, but merely to show myself there, which they think will be of great service to my cause. Those gentlemen who have been canvassing for me have, therefore, determined to have a public dinner, to which they have invited me, and I have accepted their invitation. It was fixed for this time, as being the Easter holidays, when it was known I should have a few days of leisure. I accordingly set out this day for Bristol, and slept at Reading. Mr. Vizard, the solicitor of Lincoln's Inn, who has many friends at Bristol, accompanied me in my journey.

April 1st, *Wed.* I arrived at Bath.

2d, *Th.* Three of the stewards for the dinner came over to Bath, for the purpose of accompanying me into Bristol. We arrived there about half after one o'clock. A great number of persons came out on horseback to meet us. The crowd assembled at the distance of about a mile from the city was immense. A phaëton was brought that I might enter the city in it; and the people took off the horses, and insisted upon drawing me themselves. The weather was extremely unfavourable, and at intervals there fell a good deal of rain. An immense multitude, however, was assembled, and

My reception at Bristol.

* This Bill was suffered to pass without alterations, and is the statute 52 Geo. III. c. 101.

thronged all the streets; the windows and the tops
of the houses were crowded, and all the shops were
shut.   In this manner I entered Bristol, amidst the
repeated huzzas of the people.   Nothing could be
more unpleasant to me than all this parade, and I
had done every thing in my power to prevent it.
But it was unavoidable; and I was assured that if
I were to come into the city unexpectedly, so as
to prevent such a reception, it would be attended
with great dissatisfaction, and might do me much
harm.   I can most sincerely say that my unwilling-
ness to disappoint and give pain to the persons who
have been zealously exerting themselves in my
behalf has greatly contributed to induce me to
submit to these ceremonies, which are to me so
disagreeable.   On my arrival at the Bush Tavern,
where my committee meet, I had, as is usual on
such occasions, to address the people.   I told them,
amongst other things, that I had no professions to
make them, except that I would persevere in that
line of conduct which had obtained for me their
approbation.   I gave them, too, my reason for not
canvassing them; I said that it was out of respect
to them; that votes which were not asked for acquired a value from the very circumstance of their
being unsolicited; that, as such votes could only
be given from public motives, they were always
honourable both to the giver and to those for whom
they were given; and I earnestly exhorted them
not to suffer the peace of the city to be interrupted
by any disturbance. No disturbance did take place
in any part of the city; and before night the whole
crowd had quietly dispersed.

The dinner was very numerously attended. After dinner, on my health being drunk, I addressed the meeting at considerable length, in a speech which was very favourably received. Its merit consisted more in what I omitted than in what I said.*   I

Speech at Bristol.

* A tolerably accurate account of this speech ¹ appeared in the Bristol newspapers, and was copied from thence into most of the London papers, particularly the *Times* of Tuesday April 7., in which it was printed most at length.

---

¹ The following is the newspaper report of the speech referred to, which is inserted at the end of the second MS. volume of this Diary.—ED.

" I return you my most sincere thanks for the honour you have done me. These, gentlemen, are terms which but faintly express the sentiments I feel on this occasion. Indeed no expressions that I can use, and, I fear, no actions I can perform, can make an adequate return for the exertions you have made, and are making in my favour. It is, indeed, only in the consciousness of the disinterested and patriotic motives by which you are actuated that you can find that return. When it was first intimated to me that my conduct in Parliament had attracted the notice of many of you, and had produced a desire that I should be put in nomination to be one of your representatives, I own that I received the information with the most heartfelt delight. Though I have never made public favour the object of my pursuit, yet I have always thought that, next to the satisfaction which every man feels from the consciousness of having endeavoured well and faithfully to discharge important duties, the best reward, in this life, of public conduct is the approbation and applause of a generous and enlightened public.

" I rejoiced at it, too, from other and higher considerations than those which are personal to myself. I rejoiced to find that the sentiments, and opinions, and principles which I had entertained, and on which I had acted, on subjects of the deepest interest to the country, were probably the principles and sentiments of a great portion of the inhabitants of Bristol, and consequently, I believed, of a large portion of my countrymen in every part of the kingdom. I looked forward with exultation to the time when, in resisting measures which appeared to me to be the fruits of pernicious counsels, or in supporting or proposing those which I thought highly conducive to the best interests of the country, I should speak, not as an humble and unsupported individual, but with the weight and authority and commanding influence of this great and populous city.

" I hailed it, too, as a most fortunate and auspicious circumstance, that, preparatory to a general election, likely to take place at a crisis more important than any that is to be found in our history since the Revolution, an example was likely to be set by the city of Bristol of looking for a representative towards men who could have no recommendation to favour but their public conduct, and in overlooking all

touched upon no topics calculated to court popular
favour.   I said nothing of a reform of Parliament,

---

personal favour and private attachment, when in competition with the
interest of the nation.   I could not doubt that such an example, set by
a city which must have such influence on public opinion, would awaken
other places of popular election to a sense of the importance of conscientiously exercising their elective rights in the return of a Parliament
on whose wise and honest, or rash and corrupt councils, will depend
every thing that is most dear and valuable in life, every thing that can
most vitally affect ourselves and our posterity.

" In the midst, however, of the satisfaction which I felt, one reflection arose which has occasioned me much pain, and which has thrown
a gloom over my mind, and has prevented my fully enjoying the splendour of the present day.   I have been unable to avoid comparing, what
it is too evident you have conceived me to be, with what I feel that I
am.   That I may not disappoint the expectations you have formed of
me, is my wish rather than my hope ; but there is no sacrifice that I
will not submit to to accomplish it.

" Every man who offers himself as a candidate for popular representation puts himself, as it were, upon his trial before his country : he
must expect the most severe inquiry into the whole of his past conduct,
private as well as public.   He must expect to hear the whole truth,
and much more than the truth.   It is not possible that, in the midst of
the rivalship and of the other passions which such occasions excite,
calumny should not often be mixed with just accusation.   I cannot,
however, consider it but as a circumstance highly honourable to this
city, and creditable to those to whom I am opposed, and with respect
to whom my pretensions may raise obstacles to their attaining the objects of their honourable ambition, that so very little has been objected
to me, of which any honest man need be ashamed.

" Some things, however, have been objected to me, on which, if I
am not trespassing too long on your patience, I should be glad to make
a few observations.   It has been said, that I once filled a public office,
and that I am desirous of being again in such a situation, and of
receiving a salary from the public money.   It is true that I had the
honour of being appointed his Majesty's Solicitor-General; and it is
also true that if office were again offered to me under such circumstances
that I could accept it without swerving in any degree from the line of
conduct which I have hitherto pursued — so offered me that, by accepting it, instead of abandoning my principles, I should acquire the means
of giving effect to them — it is true that I would accept it, and would
receive the honest emoluments belonging to it.   I should think, by so
doing, I was not departing from, but discharging my duty — that I was
only putting myself in a situation in which I could be more useful to
the country than I can now be ; but it is only by an adherence to the
principles which I have hitherto professed that I can ever be useful in
any situation.[a]   I do not, however, believe that I shall be put to this test
— I have little doubt that I am destined to pass the remainder of my

---

[a] See Vol. I. p. 215.

of pensions, of sinecures, of economy in the public
expenditure, of peace, or of any other of the sub-

---

life in privacy ; and it is a destination with which I am well contented,
for I had rather leave to my children only a name connected with measures which tend to increase the happiness, or to assuage the evil, of any
portion of my fellow-subjects, than the proudest title which the Crown
has to bestow, or the amplest possessions which the long enjoyment of
the most lucrative offices could enable me to acquire.

" It has been said, I understand, that I cannot undertake to do that
business relating to your local interest, which is justly expected from
the representatives of Bristol.   To this my answer is, that I have said
that I will undertake it.   It has been observed, that to do so, I must
give up a large portion of that time which is now occupied in the pursuits of my profession ; but I have made such sacrifices already to a
considerable extent, and I am prepared to make still greater sacrifices
in your service.

" I have seen it also stated, that I am a man devoted to a political
party.   Gentlemen, if by devotion to political party is meant the giving up my judgment, and voting, against my reason and conviction,
for measures, because those with whom I generally act, and whose
principles I approve, have adopted them, I wholly deny the charge,
and I appeal to my conduct in Parliament for my defence ; but if
attachment to party means only an adherence to those whose public
principles I wholly approve, and in whose hands I in my conscience
believe the Government can be most safely intrusted, to that charge I
have no defence to make.   I reflect with satisfaction on my connexion
with that administration of which one of the principal members was
that illustrious statesman, that strenuous asserter of the cause of religious and civil liberty — the late, and ever to be lamented, Mr. Fox ;
on my connexion with that administration which was not exempt from
errors, undoubtedly, but which carried the two measures which most
tended to improve the condition of mankind of any that have taken
place in the course of the present reign — the abolition of the slave
trade, and the alteration of enlisting soldiers for a limited period, instead of enlisting them for life ; thus preserving to those armed citizens
an interest in the blessings of our constitution, and suspending only,
not taking away from them, the trial by jury and the writ of Habeas
Corpus.   It is with satisfaction, too, that I reflect upon the union of
my name with those of the distinguished statesmen who are still preserved to us.   That I had an office under the administration of which
they were the chiefs, that I have enjoyed their friendship in retirement,
and that when they are excluded from office because they will not
abandon their principles, I have the honour to be comprehended in that
exclusion, are to me matters of pride and exultation.

" There is another matter, which perhaps does not deserve to be
mentioned ; and yet I should be glad to say a few words upon it.   It
has been published in this city that I am a foreigner, and that if you elect
me you will send a foreigner to represent you in a British Parliament.
Gentlemen, I was born and educated, and have passed my whole life, in

jects which are at the present moment generally so
favourably received in public assemblies.   I justified myself from some charges which I had seen
brought against me in the election hand-bills and
paragraphs of my opponents.   I avowed my attachment to Lord Grey and Lord Grenville ; said
that I reflected with pleasure on my having been
connected with their administration ; and admitted
that, if I could with honour be again in office I
would accept it; but that I would accept it only
if I could be of use to the public in it ; and that I
was sensible that I never could be of any use, but
by adhering steadily to the principles which I had
hitherto professed.   I vindicated myself from the

England, with the exception of a short interval which was spent in
visiting foreign countries.   My father, too, was born and educated in
England, and spent his whole life in it.   My grandfather, it is true,
was not an Englishman by birth, but he was an Englishman by choice.
He was born the heir to a considerable landed estate at Montpellier,
in the south of France.   His ancestors had early imbibed and adopted
the principles and doctrines of the reformed religion, and he had been
educated himself in that religious faith.   He had the misfortune to live
soon after the time when the edict of Nantes, the great toleration act
of the Protestants of France, was revoked by Louis XIV., and he
found himself exposed to all the vexations and persecutions of a bigoted
and tyrannical government, for worshipping God in the manner which
he believed was most acceptable to him.   He determined to free himself from this bondage ; he abandoned his property — he tore himself
from his connexions — and sought an asylum in this land of liberty,
where he had to support himself only by his own exertions.   He em-
barked himself in trade ; he educated his sons to useful trades ; and he
was contented at his death to leave them, instead of his original patri-
mony, no other inheritance than the habits of industry he had given
them, the example of his own virtuous life, an hereditary detestation
of tyranny and injustice, and an ardent zeal in the cause of civil and
religious freedom.   To him I owe it, among other inestimable blessings, that I am an Englishman.   Gentlemen, this is my origin, I trust
that I need not blush to own it.

   " Gentlemen, I am sorry to have so long detained you ; I can but
again return you my thanks.   That I may be what you already so in-
dulgently believe me to be, is the first wish of my heart, and shall be
the unremitted study of my life."

false representation of my being a foreigner, and stated what my family really was.

3d, *Fri.* I this day wrote an address to the electors to be inserted in the newspapers of to-morrow. It is in these words : — " Gentlemen,— The reception I have met with from you has far surpassed the most sanguine expectations which I had been taught to form of your kindness and fa-vour. Whatever may be the event of the election, I shall always be proud of the strong and unequi-vocal proofs of your approbation which I yesterday received. I can hardly, however, allow myself to doubt of the event; and if I do not already anti-cipate the triumph which seems prepared, not for me as an individual, but for the principles and measures which have recommended me to your favour, it is because the language of moderation seems best suited to the occasion, and is most re-spectful to you." *My second address to the electors.*

I dined this day at Mr. Castle's, at whose house I am staying, with many gentlemen who are mem-bers of the committee formed to conduct my elec-tion, and some other of his friends.

4th, *Sat.* I set out for London, passed through Devizes, and slept at Maidenhead.

5th, *Sun.* I arrived in London.

15th, *Wed.* On a motion of Mr. Bennet for a return of the sentences of Courts Martial for the last seven years, and the mode in which they had been executed, I had the satisfaction to express my sentiments at some length on those military punishments now in use, which are so disgraceful to us as a nation, and so shocking to humanity. *Military punish-ments.*

On the division there were 17 and the two tellers, in all 19 for the motion ; against it [49].

Cobbett's attack on me for what passed at Bristol. Cobbett, in his last Saturday's weekly paper, has made an attack upon me, and under pretence of correcting mis-statements in the newspaper accounts of what had passed at Bristol, has himself mis-stated those proceedings throughout. The truth is, that the account which he animadverts upon, and which was copied from a Bristol paper, is very accurate, and that Cobbett's account is false in almost every statement. As a specimen of his misrepresent-ations, he says, amongst other things, " If the report be correct, Sir Samuel Romilly not only told the company that he was willing to take *place* again, but that he should be *better able to serve them* in place than out of place ; thereby avowing, it seems to me, the corrupt principle of ministerial influ-ence." The passage in the speech thus represented by him, is, in the report he speaks of, in these words : " It has been objected to me that I once filled a public office, and that I am desirous of being again in that situation, and of receiving a salary out of public money. It is true that I had the ho-nour of being appointed His Majesty's Solicitor-General ; and it is also true that if office were again offered to me under such circumstances that I could accept it without swerving in any degree from the line of conduct which I have hitherto pursued — so offered to me, that by accepting it, instead of abandoning my principles, I should ac-quire the means of giving effect to them — it is true that I would accept it, and would receive the honest emoluments belonging to it. I should think that by so doing I was not departing from, but discharging, my duty ; that I was only putting myself in a situation in which I could be more useful to the country than I can now be ; but it is only by an adherence to the principles which I have hitherto professed that I can ever be useful in any situation.   I do not, however, believe that I shall be put to that test : I have little doubt that I am destined to pass the remainder of my days in privacy, and it is a destination with which I am well contented ; for I had rather leave to my children only a name connected with measures which tend to increase the happiness, or to assuage the evils, of any portion of my fellow-subjects, than the proudest title which the Crown has to bestow, or the amplest possessions that the long enjoyment of the most lucrative offices could enable me to acquire."   This specimen of Cobbett's fairness requires no comment.   He threatens me with future attacks ; says that he shall notice my speech more fully hereafter* ; that at the dinner the toasts given were insults on the people, for which we shall have cause to repent before the close of the next poll at Bristol ; with much more of the same kind ; and he boasts of Mr. Hunt, his patriotism and popularity.

16th, *Th.* The Committee of the House of Commons appointed to inquire into the causes which have retarded the decisions of suits in the Court of Chancery, after several meetings, at which it had merely inquired into the state of the business

Committee on the delays in the Court of Chancery.

---

* This he never did ; but in a paper published long afterwards, in September, 1813 (the 11th or 18th), he complains of the number of letters he had received, and the uproar he had excited by this attack on me.

in that court and in the House of Lords, and into
the progress which had been made in the decision
of causes since their last report, met to-day for the
purpose of determining in what course they should
next proceed.   It was suggested that the only
course we could take, was to call before us the
principal persons who practise in the Court of
Chancery, and to inquire of them what, in their
opinion, and from their observations, were the causes
of the delay.   This was very strenuously opposed
by many members of the Committee ; by the Solicitor-General, who had never attended it before ;
by the Attorney-General, by Master Simeon, Masters Morris, Leicester, Giffin Wilson, and Kenrick.
They said that so to proceed was to prefer a charge
against the Chancellor ; that it was putting the
counsel who would be examined in a very invidious
situation ; that it was destroying the respect which
ought to be preserved towards a magistrate at the
head of the judicature of the country ; and that it
was not difficult in any court to find some person
who, thinking his talents had not met with all the
encouragement from the Court which, in his own
opinion, they seemed to deserve, entertained and
would deliver a judgment unfavourable to the
Judge.   To this it was answered, that it was very
true, that counsel and attorneys, who practised in
the court, would be put in a very unpleasant situation in being examined as to what might tend to
censure the Judge of the court in which they practised ; but that there did not appear to be any
other authentic source of information which could
be recurred to, and therefore that this must be

submitted to ; that it was singular that the friends of the Chancellor should take for granted that an inquiry from the persons best qualified to give information would necessarily criminate him : it would criminate him only if he were really to blame ; and if he were, it was the duty of the Committee to ascertain the fact : that the objections now made were in truth objections to the appointment of any committee ; and, the Committee being appointed, it was too late to make them : that it was very true that some one or two persons might perhaps be found in a court of justice, who, from pique and disappointment, might be desirous to calumniate and injure the Judge ; but for one such person, it was probable that there would be found twenty who were eager to palliate the defects, to exaggerate the merits, and to seek the countenance and favour of the Judge in whose court they practised.   To bring the matter to a decision, I moved that Mr. Richards, as being the senior counsel attending the court who is not in Parliament, should be summoned to attend and give evidence.   The seven persons I have already named voted against this resolution ; those who voted for it were only six in number ; Martin, Horner, Brougham, Abercromby, Bankes, and myself.   Taylor, the chairman, had a right to vote, and then to give the casting vote ; and by this means the question would have been carried ; but Taylor did not know this, and did not vote, in consequence of which the question was lost.   This puts an end to the Committee for any useful purpose.

Catholics; disqualifying laws against them.

24th, *Fri.* Upon an adjourned debate on Mr. Grattan's motion for a Committee of the House of Commons, to inquire into the state of the penal laws of Ireland affecting the Catholics, I spoke in support of the motion.[1] Amongst other things, I stated that I supported the motion not on account of the Catholics alone, but because I considered that it would naturally lead to the removal of all those disabilities under which dissenters of every description from the established church now labour. Hitherto, I have always given a silent vote on this question; but I was very glad on this occasion to take a more conspicuous part: because reports have been by some persons very industriously circulated, that I have been paying my court to the people of Bristol, where the Catholic cause is supposed to be very unpopular, by agreeing to abandon it.

May 4th, *Mon.* I voted for Mr. Bankes's Bill to abolish many sinecure places. The Ministers opposed the Bill, and were in a minority.[2]

Delays in the Court of Chancery.

6th, *Wed.* In consequence of what passed in the Committee upon the delays of the Court of Chancery, Taylor moved to-day in the House, that it should be an instruction to the Committee to examine barristers and solicitors practising in the court upon the subject of the delays. The motion was rejected by a majority of 84 to 20. The two Masters in Chancery, Morris and Simeon, alone spoke against it. I said nothing, nothing

---

[1] The motion was lost by a majority of 85; the numbers being, — for the question 215; against it 300. — ED.

[2] For the Bill 134; against it 123; majority 11. — ED.

having been advanced in argument which deserved an answer; but I voted in the minority.

7th, *Th.* Creevey moved several resolutions respecting the Tellerships of the Exchequer, now held by the Marquis of Buckingham and Lord Camden, the profits of which have, in consequence of the immense issues of public money which the present expensive war renders necessary, risen to the enormous amount of 26,000*l.* or 27,000*l.* a year each. The last of these resolutions was, " That, in the present state of unparalleled expenditure and distress, it was the duty of Parliament to exercise its right over the fees of these offices, so as to confine the profits to some fixed and certain sums." Mr. Brand moved as an amendment to leave out all the words; and to substitute the following : — " That a committee should be appointed to inquire into the precedents which exist as to the reduction or suppression of fees payable to the Tellers of the Exchequer, from monies issuing out of the same." The Ministers opposed both the original motion and the amendment ; and upon the amendment a division took place, upon which I voted in the minority and for the motion. The minority consisted of only 38 and the two Tellers.[1] The original motion was lost without a division. On this occasion, Ponsonby, Tierney, and the greatest part of the Opposition joined the Ministers. Lord Grenville, indeed, had said that he considered the motion as aimed personally at himself, his family, and his friends; and most of the firm adherents to the

Marginal note: Tellerships of the Exchequer held by Lords Buckingham and Camden.

---

[1] The majority consisted of 146, exclusive of the tellers. — ED.

Opposition party voted accordingly, or stayed away. In the minority, however, were Whitbread, General Fergusson, Lord Tavistock, Lord Archibald Hamilton, and Brougham.

Reform of Parliament.

8th, *Fri.*   Mr. Brand's plan for a reform of Parliament came to-day before the House. His motion was merely for leave to bring in a Bill to give copyholders a right to vote at county elections. He gave notice, however, that, if that were carried[1], he should propose to abolish some of the close boroughs, and increase proportionably the number of members returned by counties. I spoke and voted for the motion. Amongst other things, I said that this Parliament was bound to take some steps towards a reform of the representation; because otherwise they would leave the influence of the Crown over the representation greater than they found it; the Act of the 49 Geo. III. [2] to prevent the sale of seats, having in effect nearly secured to the Treasury the exclusive purchase of seats.

Mr. Perceval most inhumanly murdered.

12th, *Tu.*   Yesterday afternoon, as Perceval was going to the House of Commons, he was most barbarously murdered by a man of the name of Bellingham. The assassin shot him with a pistol through the heart just as he was entering the lobby of the House, and he expired in less than ten minutes. No adequate cause can be discovered for so atrocious a crime. The wretch who perpetrated it had presented memorials to the Treasury

---

[1] The motion was lost by a majority of 127; the numbers being, — for it 88; against it 215.— ED.

[2] See Vol. II. p. 292.

soliciting a compensation for wrongs which he had suffered in Russia; but which, not having been incurred in the course of any public service, really afforded him no title to compensation. Perceval had, as was his duty, refused to listen to these applications; but he could hardly have accompanied his refusal with any harshness, for few men had ever less harshness in their nature than he had; and yet this seems to have been all that has provoked this most savage act. The assassin appeared, I understand (for I had left the House myself about a quarter of an hour before the event happened), perfectly cool and collected. He did not attempt to escape, went calmly to the fire, and laid down the pistol on the bench beside him; acknowledged to every one that he was the person who had done the act, and said that it was perfectly justifiable. There does not appear to have been any person concerned with him, or any mixture of political feeling in his motives. Among the multitude, however, whom the news of so strange and sudden a catastrophe had soon collected in the street, and about the avenues of the House, the most savage expressions of joy and exultation were heard; accompanied with regret that others, and particularly the Attorney-General, had not shared the same fate. Sentiments so horrible as these, together with the recent assassinations and attempts at assassination which have taken place at Nottingham and in the North of England, are well calculated to excite the most lively alarms in the minds of all thinking men. The English character seems to

The
murderer
convicted.

have undergone some unaccountable and porten-
tous change.

16th, *Sat.* Bellingham was yesterday brought
to trial at the Old Bailey, and convicted of the
murder of Mr. Perceval. His counsel applied to
the Court to put off his trial, in order that witnesses
might be brought from Liverpool, where he had
resided, and where his family now are, to prove
that he is insane. As, however, he had been for
the last four months in town, and, if he had been
disordered in his mind, must, during that period,
it was supposed, have given proofs of it, the Chief
Justice (Mansfield) and the rest of the Court rejected the application. No person can have heard
what the conduct and demeanour of this man has
been since he committed the crime, or can have
read his defence, without being satisfied that he is
mad; but it is a species of madness, which probably, for the security of mankind, ought not to
exempt a man from being answerable for his actions. There certainly has been no acting in that
calmness and steadiness of opinion uniformly manifested by him, that what he has done was perfectly justifiable, and that he has set an example,
which will be highly useful to mankind.* The
application, however, to put off the trial was
surely very reasonable, and it might well have been
postponed, though but for a few days. It was not
possible that a letter giving information of his
crime and his apprehension could have reached

---

* This extraordinary infatuation continued unaltered to the last
moment of his existence; and he seems to have died in the firm conviction that he had done nothing wrong.

Liverpool, where his family and all his friends reside, and an answer to it have been received by
the day of his trial.

The House of Commons has been employed, Provision for Perce-val's fa-mily, and a public monument.
since the murder of Perceval, in little else than
voting money to his family, and a monument to his
memory, at the public expense. I was present on
Tuesday, when an address was voted in answer to
the Prince Regent's message, assuring His Royal
Highness that the House would concur in making
a provision for the family, and in that vote I concurred. To what has since been done; — to the
extent to which the provision has been carried, by
granting a pension to the eldest son, in addition to
the pension to the widow, and the 50,000*l.* voted
to all the children, and by voting that a public monument should be erected, I certainly should not
have agreed if I had been present; but I have not
been in the House since Tuesday. As a private
man, I had a very great regard for Perceval. We
went the same circuit together, and for many years
I lived with him in a very delightful intimacy. No
man could be more generous, more kind, or more
friendly than he was. No man ever in private life
had a nicer sense of honour. Never was there, I believe, a more affectionate husband or a more tender
parent. It did not proceed from him that of late
years our intimacy was totally interrupted. He
would, I have no doubt, have been glad to have
obliged me in every thing that I could have wished;
and that without any view of detaching me from
my political friends, but from personal regard to
me. It was I who refused his repeated invitations

and shrunk from his kindness and friendship :
but I could not endure the idea of living privately
in intimacy with a man whose public conduct I in
the highest degree disapproved, and whom, as a
minister, I was constantly opposing. I cannot indeed reconcile to my way of thinking, that distinction between private and public virtues which
it is so much the fashion to adopt. It may be
called liberality, or gentlemanly feeling, or by any
other such vague and indefinite term ; but it is
not suited to any one who is really in earnest and
sincere in his politics.

Projected change in the Ministry. 20th, *Wed*. A negotiation has been depending
between the present Ministers and Lord Wellesley
and Mr. Canning ; but it has gone off, and it seems
those two personages are not to form any part of
the Administration. Vansittart has accepted the
office of Chancellor of the Exchequer ; and a new
writ has been moved for this day for Old Sarum
(the place he represents), in consequence of his
promotion.

21st, *Th*. In some of to-day's newspapers, the
letters and conversations which have recently passed
between Lord Liverpool, Lord Wellesley, and
Canning, on the subject of their coming into office, have been published. According to Lord
Liverpool's statement, the overture was made to
them in consequence of the Regent being desirous
of continuing his administration on its present
basis, and of strengthening it as much as possible
by associating to it persons who agreed most nearly
in the principles on which public affairs had been
conducted. On the Catholic question it appeared

that the sentiments of the present Ministers were unaltered, and upon this Lord Wellesley and Canning refused to join with them in an administration.

In the House of Commons to-day, Stuart Wortley (a man who supported Mr. Pitt's, and afterwards Perceval's, administration uniformly) moved, pursuant to a notice he gave yesterday, that the House should address the Regent, praying that he would take such measures as would enable him, under the present circumstances of the country, to form a strong and efficient administration. This motion was carried against the Ministers by a majority of four (174 against 170). Lord Yarmouth, George Rose, Bragge Bathurst, and some more friends of Ministers, happened to be out of the House at the time of the division, and came in the moment the doors were unlocked. On seeing this additional strength which they had acquired, Charles Yorke and Lord Castlereagh endeavoured to defeat the address, by opposing the motion that it should be carried up by such members as were Privy Counsellors. On this division the Ministers had a majority of two (176 to 174). But they were soon ashamed of this kind of victory; or, I believe, some other friends of ours had come into the House, and they saw that ultimately they should be beaten, and they therefore consented to a motion that the address should be carried up by the mover and seconder, Wortley and Lord Milton.

Address of the House of Commons to the Regent.

22d, *Fri.* All the Ministers have tendered their resignation to the Regent.

30th, *Sat.* No administration has yet been

formed. Lord Wellesley and Lord Moira have several times seen the Prince on the subject, but nothing has been settled or seems likely to be settled immediately. In the mean time, the resigned Ministers have translated Dr. Sparke, Bishop of Chester, to the Bishopric of Ely * ; and yesterday, being the first day of term, Sir Vicary Gibbs, the Attorney-General, was sworn in a Judge of the Common Pleas, in the place of Lawrence, who has resigned.

Petition respecting abuses in Lincoln gaol.

I this day presented to the House of Commons a petition from Thomas Houlden, who was lately a prisoner for debt in Lincoln Castle, complaining of his having been confined by Dr. Illingworth, a magistrate, eleven days and nights in solitary imprisonment, in one of the cells appropriated to convicts condemned to die; and I gave notice of a motion which I shall make upon it on a future day.

Attempts to form a new administration.

June 4th, *Th.* Although the address of the House of Commons was presented to the Regent the day after it was voted, and although the Prince said, in answer to it, that he would take it into his immediate consideration, it was not till last Monday, June 1st, that he gave authority to any person to submit to him the plan of a new Ministry. The interval was spent in audiences given to Lord Moira, to Lord Wellesley, to the Lord Chancellor, and to others of the present, or more properly the late, administration. On Monday, however, the Prince authorised Lord Wellesley to form an administration, and yesterday that nobleman said, in

* *Vid.* Vol. II. p. 304.

the House of Lords, that he had resigned the commission with which he had been honoured into the Regent's hands, without having been able to effect the object of it. I understand that the proposition made by Lord Wellesley to Lord Grenville and Lord Grey was this (and it was so proposed under the Prince's commands), that Lord Wellesley should be first Lord of the Treasury; that the Prince should name four members of the Cabinet; that four more should be named by Lord Wellesley; and four by Lords Grenville and Grey. Or if, upon further consideration, it should be thought expedient that the Cabinet should consist of thirteen members, then that five should be named by those Lords; and, at the same time, the members named by the Prince were stated by Lord Wellesley to be, himself Lord Wellesley, Lord Moira, Lord Erskine, and Canning. The Lords Grenville and Grey rejected this proposal.

Since the failure of Lord Wellesley's commission to form an administration, a similar commission has been given to Lord Moira, but that too has failed; Lords Grenville and Grey having very properly refused to be members of the Cabinet, unless the offices in the household usually appointed to by Ministers were to be at the disposal of the new Ministers. Lord Moira then in vain attempted to make a ministry without them; but failing in this too, it has been to-day announced in both Houses of Parliament, that Lord Liverpool has been appointed First Lord of the Treasury; or, in other words, that the Prince will try, notwithstanding the late address of the House of Commons, to go on with the old Ministers.

11th, *Th.* The House of Commons has this day acted in direct opposition to what they did on the 21st of *May.* They then addressed the Prince to form a strong and efficient administration. The same administration as was then forming now continues, and yet the House of Commons has rejected an address moved by Lord Milton in the spirit of the former address. The numbers were, for the address 165 [1], against it 289.

The whole of the negotiations for a new ministry have been conducted, unquestionably, with a previous determination on the part of the Prince and of those who enjoy his confidence, that they should not end in Lord Grey and Lord Grenville and their friends being in power. The Lord Chancellor has never, from the moment of the address of the House of Commons being carried, shown the least symptom of apprehension that he was to resign his office. During these three weeks that the Ministers have been represented by themselves as holding their offices only till their successors should be named, he has given judgment in none of the numerous causes, petitions, and motions which have been long waiting his decision; though there never before was an instance of a Chancellor about to resign the Great Seal, who did not hasten to clear away all the arrears of his court. Instead of this, Lord Eldon has been every day closeted with the Duke of Cumberland; and, during several

---

[1] The number of the minority is stated in the Journals of the House to have been 164. — ED.

days in the term, the court has been entirely shut up, while his Lordship was employed in some way never known to the suitors of his court, or to the public. We have even had the Duke of Cumberland coming down to Westminster Hall, and sending for the Chancellor out of court. The whole matter has ended pretty much as I expected. It might have been much worse, if Lords Grey and Grenville had not been deterred from taking office by the obstacles which were purposely thrown in their way. They would have been suffered to remain in the Ministry but a very short time; some pretext would have been anxiously watched for, and eagerly seized, to turn them out with loss of character; or a new cry against popery would have been raised, and they would probably have been the victims of it.

19th, *Fri.* A Bill brought into Parliament by Henry Martin, to regulate the office of Registrar of the Court of Admiralty, came on to-day in the House of Commons.* It was opposed by Sir William Scott, Sir John Nicholl, and Sir Thomas Plumer, and was rejected.[1] I supported the Bill. The principle of it was to prevent the registrar from making profit for his own use of the suitors' money deposited in his hands; and to establish regulations similar to those adopted in the Court of Chancery when the office of Accountant-General was created. Having no doubt that an officer of a

Bill to regulate the office of Registrar of the Admiralty Court.

---

* Vide *antè*, Vol. II. p. 341.

[1] By a majority of 38; the numbers being, in favour of Sir W. Scott's amendment, that the Bill be read that day six months, 65; against it 27. — Ed.

court intrusted with the suitors' money cannot legally make interest of it for his own benefit, I stated this to be my opinion. I observed that one of the articles of impeachment against Lord Macclesfield (the 18th) was, that he had permitted and encouraged the Masters in Chancery to make profit of, and traffic with, the suitors' money : and I added that, if the House rejected this Bill, they would themselves be guilty of that crime of which they had formerly accused Lord Macclesfield ; they would permit and encourage the registrar to employ and traffic with the money of the suitors. No one of the three lawyers who opposed the Bill ventured to assert that the practice was legal. It appeared that Lord Arden, the registrar, whose fees amount to about 12,000*l.* a year, has made 7000*l.* a year more by interest and profits of suitors' money, and that he has sometimes employed above 200,000*l.* of such money at interest.

Lincoln gaol.

25th, *Th.* I this day moved in the House of Commons for a committee to inquire into and report to the House what has been and now is the condition and treatment of prisoners confined in the Castle of Lincoln, and the state and management of that prison. The Committee was granted, and I am upon it ; but I shall not be able to attend it.

A subscription has been set on foot to defray the expenses of my election at Bristol. This I greatly disapprove of ; but the matter has been managed by Whitbread, Lord Folkestone, and some other friends of mine, who have acted from the best and kindest intentions ; and I know not how publicly to disavow the proceeding, without offering an insult in return for great kindness and friendship. I have, however, privately expressed to some of them, particularly to Horner and Abercromby, how extremely unpleasant this proceeding is to me. I know not what else I could do; but the matter has proceeded too far to be abandoned.

29th, *Mon.* Sir William Scott moved for leave to bring in his long promised Bill respecting the Ecclesiastical Courts. He a few days ago communicated it to me; and as far as it goes, it will, in my opinion, remove much of the evil arising from these Courts. I stated this in the House, and at the same time observed that I lamented that the Bill was not to be extended to Ireland. I observed, too, that I saw no reason why the whole of the jurisdiction of the spiritual Courts in cases of defamation should not be abolished.[1] *Ecclesiastical Courts.*

July 2d, *Th.* I moved for returns of convicts in Ireland more particular and detailed than those which have been already made.

Bragge Bathurst having been appointed Chancellor of the Duchy of Lancaster, and by that means having vacated his seat for Bristol, Mr. Hart Davis, the Member for Colchester, has accepted the Chiltern Hundreds, that he may be a candidate. He is opposed by Hunt, who has very few of the freemen with him, but who has excited the populace to commit great excesses, by telling them that, if he is elected, he will bring about a peace, and lower the price of bread. *Bristol election.*

12th. Hunt continues to keep the poll at

[1] See *suprà*, p. 6. — ED.

Bristol open. He polls very few votes, but has an opportunity, which appears to be all he wishes, of making speeches every day, and endeavouring to gain popularity. It seems, however, that he has little success with any, but the very lowest orders of the people. Cobbett, in his weekly paper, espouses his cause, and represents him to be a much more fit man to represent Bristol than I am.

Bill to suppress the disturbances in the counties of Lancaster and York.

16th, *Th.* In consequence of the outrages which have lately been committed in Lancashire and a part of Yorkshire, the Ministers have brought a Bill into the House of Commons, which is founded on a Report made by a secret committee appointed to inquire into the evidence which Government had received on the subject. There seems little doubt that the riots and acts of violence which have been committed were caused solely by the stagnation of the manufactures, and the scarcity and consequent high price of provisions. The rioters, however, have endeavoured to possess themselves of arms, with a view undoubtedly to render themselves more formidable, and to enable them to carry on their depredations. They have broken into houses and carried arms away; they have sent threatening letters to many persons, and there have been some attempts at assassination. All this is very horrible, and requires a vigorous execution of the existing laws. But there is nothing in these outrages which calls for such a law as the Ministers have proposed; a law to disarm every person from whom the magistrates shall choose to take their arms away, and to enable them to enter houses in the night to search for arms. I was not present at the second reading of the Bill; but there being to-day a committee upon it, I objected to several parts of the Bill, and endeavoured, but in vain, to mitigate some of the harsh and dangerous powers which it gives to the magistrates. The Bill enables any justice, or constable, having a warrant from a justice, to search for and seize any stolen or concealed or secreted arms, in any house or place in which the justice making or granting a warrant for making such search *may suspect* any stolen arms to be, or any arms to be concealed or secreted; and, in case admission shall be refused, or not obtained within a reasonable time after it shall have been demanded, to enter by force, by day *or by night*, into such house or place, and to carry away such arms. On this clause I moved to leave out the words *"may suspect,"* for the purpose of inserting words which would have enabled justices to search or to grant search warrants only when they *had reasonable grounds of suspicion*, which are the words in the Act, passed in 1807, to authorise search for arms in Ireland; and the same words are even in the Act passed by the Irish Parliament in 1796, notwithstanding all the rage and violence of party which dictated that most atrocious act. The amendment, however, was rejected; and the justices are left at liberty to act on any suspicions they may entertain, or say they entertain, without the necessity of ever showing that there were any grounds for such suspicion. I moved, too, to leave out the words *" or by night,"* so as to give this power of entering private houses

only in the day time; and on this amendment I
divided the Committee, and was in a minority of
only sixteen.   Giles also moved, as an amendment,
that the warrant should be signed by two justices;
but this amendment too was rejected.*

Bill to
create the
office of
Vice-
Chancellor.

On the same day, after this Bill had gone
through the Committee, and after midnight, the
Masters in Chancery brought down from the House
of Lords the Bill which Lord Redesdale, with the
concurrence of the Lord Chancellor, has brought
into Parliament for the appointment of a Vice-
Chancellor. The effect of it is to enable the King
to appoint a person, being a barrister of fifteen
years' standing at the least, to be an assistant to
the Lord Chancellor, and to be called Vice-Chancellor of England.   His office is to be held during
good behaviour; himself to have power to hear
and determine all causes and matters depending
in the Chancery of England, as a Court of Law or
of Equity, or which should be submitted to the
jurisdiction of the Lord Chancellor, by the special
authority of any Act of Parliament, in such manner and under such restrictions as the Lord Chancellor should, from time to time, direct. His orders
are to be subject to be reversed by the Lord Chancellor; but he is to have no authority to reverse the
orders of the Lord Chancellor or of the Master of
the Rolls; and he is to sit for the Lord Chancellor
whenever the latter should require him so to do,
and to sit in a separate court, either at the same

* Similar amendments were afterwards moved by Lord Holland in
the House of Lords, and were there rejected; and the Bill passed in
the form here stated.

time when the Lord Chancellor or Master of the Rolls should be sitting, or at any other time, as the Lord Chancellor should from time to time direct ; and in such separate court to despatch such business only as the Lord Chancellor should from time to time direct, and in such manner and form, and subject to such restrictions and regulations, as to the Lord Chancellor should from time to time seem fit. I immediately objected to this Bill, and particularly to the time when it was brought in, quite at the close of the Session, when there were very thin attendances, and when all the lawyers were upon their circuits ; and I asked, if it was seriously intended to carry such a Bill through in the present session? On being informed by Lord Castlereagh that such was his intention, I entered into the objections which I had to the Bill; and I also stated, that if any measures were to be taken for relieving the office of the Lord Chancellor from some of the duties now belonging to it, there were other plans which had been proposed much less objectionable than this ; such as separating the office of the Lord Chancellor from that of Speaker of the House of Lords, or taking from the Lord Chancellor the business in bankruptcy : that the principal objection to these appeared to be, that, by either of them the Lord Chancellor would lose part of the present emoluments of his office ; whereas, by the present scheme, part of the duties were taken from the office, but all its emoluments left.   Amongst other things, I mentioned an alteration which might well be made in the Equity Court of the Exchequer, by letting causes be heard by one Judge ; and a project which had lately been suggested of having an additional Baron, who should sit in the same manner as the Master of the Rolls in Chancery. I mentioned, too, the rendering the Chancellor of the Duchy of Lancaster an efficient judicial office, and assigning to it some of the present duties of the Chancellor.

Bankes, Wilberforce, and several other Members also objected to the Bill being entertained at such a period of the Session. The Bill, however, was read a first time.

The next day Lord Castlereagh said, that the Bill would not be persevered in now, but would be brought in early in the next Session.

I presented a petition to the House of Commons from a man of the name of Eaton, a prisoner in Newgate, lately convicted of a profane libel, complaining of exactions of money made from him by the keeper of Newgate. I presented the petition, and merely moved that it lie on the table. I conceive it to be the duty of a Member of Parliament to present such a petition.

30th. Parliament was prorogued.

Aug. 18th, *Tu.* The Lord Chancellor sat in the morning for the last time before the long vacation. In the evening I left town.

Oct. 31st, *Sat.* The Master of the Rolls held the first seal for the Lord Chancellor.

The foregoing diary[1] shows where I have been during the long vacation. The first part of it was spent very pleasantly and very profitably, in reco-

---

[1] This and similar portions of the Diary, which consist of a mere enumeration of towns and places visited, have been omitted, as being devoid of interest. — ED.

vering myself from the effects of a very close attendance on business, and in laying in a stock of health to enable me to encounter another winter of professional and parliamentary fatigue. But the latter part of it has been sadly broken in upon by the Bristol election, and has passed very disagreeably. My visit to Edinburgh had for its principal object to see once more my excellent friend George Wilson. At Durham, where my Chancery sittings obliged me to be, I had performed nearly two thirds of the journey, and I could not resist the temptation of going on to see him. An attack of palsy compelled him two years ago to quit the bar and retire to Edinburgh, from whence there is no prospect that he will ever return to London. An intimate private friendship has long subsisted between us. A man of a stronger understanding, of a sounder judgment, of a warmer heart, of a nicer sense of honour, of stricter morality, or of better political principles, hardly exists ; and to all these valuable qualities, he adds much general knowledge and great learning in his profession. He was universally beloved and respected while he continued to attend in Westminster Hall, and was universally regretted when he quitted it. His uncommon clearness of expression, and the remarkable correctness of his understanding, qualified him in the most eminent degree to fill the office of Judge ; and on that point there was but one opinion in the profession. If the office had been elective, and the Bar had been the voters, he would probably have been unanimously elected to it. But as he never paid his court to those in power, and as his politi-

George
Wilson.

cal opinions, though· he never obtruded them on
any one, and always expressed them with moderation, were not favourable to the Ministers of the
day, he was passed by ; and men greatly his inferiors in every qualification of a Judge were promoted over his head.　Even the silk gown, which
late in life he received, he owed solely to the private friendship of Lord Ellenborough.　They were
certainly men very different in their natures, and
opposite in their political opinions ; but yet they
lived in great habits of private friendship ; and that
friendship probably served, as long as Wilson was
near his Lordship, to temper and restrain his Lordship's violence.　Wilson had undoubtedly much
influence over him ; so much that he even prevailed

Lord
Ellen-
borough.

on his Lordship once to endeavour to read Adam
Smith's excellent and very celebrated work on the
Wealth of Nations.　This, however, went no farther than an endeavour; and, after some unavailing
efforts, Lord Ellenborough returned the book, with
a declaration that he found it impossible to read it.
I doubt very much whether any other of the
Judges, with the exception of Mr. J. Heath and,
perhaps, Mr. J. Leblanc, have ever made a greater
progress in the study of political economy than the
Lord Chief Justice.　But not to digress any longer,
we found (for my dear Anne and William accompanied me) — we found Wilson rather languid, but
in the full possession of his faculties ; having two
charming young women, his nieces, to keep his
house for him, and living in a small but very delightful literary society.　Playfair, Jeffrey, Dr.
Gregory, Thompson, Murray, and, occasionally,

Dugald Stewart, were among the principal orna-
ments of it. We passed a very happy week with
him. The rest of our journey proved the means
of great enjoyment to us, as well on account of the
beautiful scenery which it presented to us, as of the
visits which, in the course of it, we paid to a great
variety of persons : amongst others, to our old
friend Mrs. Gally Knight and her son, who is just
returned from visiting Greece, Egypt, and Pales-
tine ; to Sydney Smith ; to Lady Haddington; to
Lady Minto ; to my good friend George Philips ;
to Lord Grey, who to be properly known must be Lord Grey.
seen, as we saw him, in his retirement, surrounded
by his family, his servants, and his tenants, and appearing to be an object of love and admiration to
all who are about him ; to the Duke of Roxburgh, The Duke
just put into possession of his title and of his mag- of Roxburgh.
nificent domain, but having unfortunately obtained
possession of them only in the full maturity, or rather in the rapid decline, of life, and whom we
found surrounded with enjoyments only when the
sense of enjoyment seemed to be fast wearing out ;
to my old and excellent friend Dugald Stewart, Dugald
whom we had the satisfaction to see in the full vi- Stewart.
gour of his great talents, and in the lively enjoyment of every thing about him, of the enchanting
country in which he lives, of the society of his very
sensible and amiable wife and daughter, of his books,
of his leisure, of his philosophical retirement, and,
above all, of the delight he experiences in the
pursuit of his metaphysical researches, and in continuing and completing his own admirable writings.

During my journey I had received frequent in-

telligence that Parliament was to be speedily dissolved; and the information given me during the
latter part of it was such as left me no doubt that
that measure was resolved on. When I reached
town I learnt that it was to take place in two or
three days, and I found letters from Bristol exhorting me to hasten to that place. I determined,
however, before I proceeded thither, to take Anne
to Eastbourne, in Sussex, where our children have
been from the beginning of the vacation. We
accordingly went thither, and I stayed at Eastbourne Saturday and Sunday. On Monday I
returned to town, and proceeded the next day to
Bowood, to Lord Lansdowne's, where I passed the
night; and on the following day (Sept. 30th), I set
off for Bristol. I arrived there about five o'clock
in the afternoon, some hours only after the news

Parliament
dissolved. of the dissolution, which had taken place the preceding evening. I found my friends sanguine,
nay, certain of success. In all the different parishes
committees had been formed of persons in my
interest, who had canvassed all the voters; and

Bristol
election. from the different returns made by them, it appeared that more than 3000 votes had been promised me. If these promises were performed,
there could be no doubt of my success. It was
thought expedient by my friends that I should go
round to as many of the electors as the short time
which would elapse before the election would admit
of. I reluctantly consented to this. I consented
to wait on the electors, not to ask their votes, but
to thank those who had promised to vote for me,
and merely to show myself to the others. In this

tiresome and most fatiguing way I had to pass four days, walking about from house to house, from ten o'clock in the morning (and one day from nine) till half after four. The appearance of things, upon my making these visits to the electors, very much corresponded with what the committees had reported; and I appeared to have a very flattering prospect before me.

It was obvious, however, that in the election I should have a difficult part to act, and that great caution on my part would be necessary. The Tories, inflamed with resentment against all popular candidates, on account of the tumults and acts of violence which only two months ago had disgraced the last election, would be very eager to seize on any unguarded expression that might escape me, to raise a cry against me with their party; and on the other hand, Hunt, the friend of Cobbett, and a friend worthy of him (that is, a most unprincipled demagogue), would be ready to misinterpret and misrepresent whatever I might say, in order to accomplish the object of his faction, which is to destroy the characters of all public men, and to excite jealousy and distrust of them. It was obvious, too, that Protheroe and Davis might in the course of the election find it mutually their interest to unite, and by making common cause against me, to secure their own election. The election was fixed for Tuesday, 6th of October. On that day, the Mayor, Mr. Castle, proposed me, and Sir Abraham Elton, a baronet, and a clergyman of the Church of England, whose ancestors had in several instances represented Bristol in Parliament, seconded the nomination. They did this, as is usual upon such occasions, in speeches in which they spoke of me in terms which were much too flattering. I then addressed the electors in a speech which was published in the newspapers with tolerable accuracy.*

* The following is the speech alluded to : —

" Gentlemen, — I appear before you to offer you my services as one of your representatives in Parliament. If you should repose that important trust in me, I shall consider it as the highest honour that could be conferred on me, and as the best reward I could receive for my past endeavours to serve the public. It is not, however, merely as an honour and a reward that a seat in Parliament ought to be considered, but as an office of great difficulty and fatigue, of deep responsibility, and one which no person in my situation can properly and honestly fill, without making many and almost constant sacrifices of his time, his ease, and his comforts, perhaps of his health, and certainly of his emoluments. These sacrifices I am willing, nay I am anxious to make in your service, and I shall be proud of having those duties imposed upon me. If, however, you shall, in the contest which is about to take place, decide against me, I shall submit to your decision with perfect cheerfulness; and if I am to retire into private life, I shall, while I am enjoying those domestic comforts which I have the happiness to possess in as large a portion as falls to the lot of most men, and while I am devoting my time to the occupations of a lucrative profession, have the satisfaction to reflect, that my doing so proceeds from no mean or selfish motive of preferring my own private advantage to the public good, but from my fellow-citizens having rejected the services which I had tendered them.

" It has been usual for persons who stand in the situation of candidates to make professions of their political opinions, and to give promises of their future conduct; and this is undoubtedly proper in those who have not yet been tried, and who have no past conduct to refer to; because with such persons what is it you can have to trust to but the professions which they make, and their private characters, which afford you security for the sincerity of those professions ? But with those whose public life is already before you, such professions and promises can be of little avail ; for either they are consistent with what they have already done, and then they are unnecessary, or at variance with it, and in that case they are entitled to no credit. I shall therefore, on this occasion, neither promise nor profess, nor shall I presume to remind you of what I have attempted to do; but I may with propriety tell you what are the qualifications which, in my opinion, you ought, at the present crisis, to look for in a representative.

" He ought to be a man firmly attached to those principles of our Constitution which were established at the Revolution, and which have seated and maintained the present Royal Family on the throne. He should justly appreciate, and be ready at all times to maintain the

Hunt, who a few days ago had published hand-
bills as hostile to me as to any other of the can-

---

liberty of the press and the trial by jury, which are the great securities
for all our other liberties.　He should be a sincere friend to peace, and
anxious to seize on every opportunity of securing all the blessings
which it must bring with it, whenever there is a prospect that it can be
permanently obtained.　He ought to be determined, whenever the men
with whose political principles he in general agrees, and with whom he
therefore generally acts, propose or support measures which, in his conscience he disapproves, to oppose them just as if they were the measures of his political adversaries.　He should be an enemy to that
influence of the Crown and of the Ministers of the Crown which has
been so fatally exercised in the House of Commons, and consequently
a friend to parliamentary reform.　He should be a constant advocate
for economy in the public expenditure, and a determined enemy to
corruption and peculation; and if he thinks he discovers them in persons of the highest rank, he should not be deterred from censuring and
arraigning them, by any apprehension that by so doing he may incur
their high displeasure, and blast for ever all the prospects of honourable
ambition in which he may at some time have indulged.　He should be
ready, when he sees evils arising from any of our present institutions,
to inquire into the causes of them, and to suggest a remedy, notwithstanding the reproach of being an innovator, which he may incur from
those who have an interest in perpetuating abuses; and, above all, he
should be a man incapable of being swerved from his duty by the threats
of power, the allurements of the great, the temptations of private
interest, or even the seduction of popular favour; and who should
constantly recollect, that all the toil, the pain, and the fatigue of his
office, must be his own; and all the advantages which are to result
from his labours must be for the public.　These are the qualifications
which, in my opinion, you ought to look for in your representatives.
Perhaps it is not prudent in me to state them.　Perhaps in this enumeration, I have been pronouncing my own condemnation; and in pointing out to you what is requisite in a Member of Parliament, I have
only been reminding you of what is wanting in myself.　Of this you
are the judges; but whatever be the consequence, I shall rejoice in
what I have done; for this I can with perfect sincerity declare, that I
may be elected by you is only the second wish of my heart.　The first
is, that Bristol and other places of popular election may send to Parliament able, honest, disinterested, and patriotic members.

　" Gentlemen, amongst the qualifications which are, in my opinion,
requisite in a Member of Parliament, I have not said that he should
be determined, under no circumstances, to accept an office under the
Crown.　I have not said so, because that is so far from being my
opinion, that I think there are circumstances in which it may be his
duty to accept of such an office.　I should be sorry to be misunderstood by you upon this subject, and I am glad of this opportunity of
avowing what my opinion upon it is; and, indeed, in appealing to my
past conduct, I have told you that was my opinion, since I formerly
myself held an office under the Crown.　If a man barters his principles for office, if in office he acts upon different grounds from those

didates, or, indeed, rather more so, now entirely
altered his tone ; and, being undoubtedly desirous
to avail himself of some of that popularity which
he saw me possessed of, spoke of me in terms of
high approbation, and made no other objections to
me than that I was King's Counsel, and that I had
avowed that I was not unwilling to accept an office
under the Crown. The hall was full of my friends,
and the show of hands was greatly in favour of me
and of Hunt. A poll was demanded, but the day
had been spent in speeches, and three or four votes
only were taken. The next day the Hall was again

which he professed to act upon before he obtained it, and if his official
conduct is a constant violation of those rules which he had, when in
opposition, prescribed for others, there are no terms which, in my
opinion, are too strong or too severe to stigmatise such political apos-
tasy; but if in office, his views and his principles are the same as when
he was in a private station, he deserves, in my opinion, no reproach for
accepting it ; and if it be, as I conceive it is, the duty of every man to
use all the means which he possesses of being useful to his fellow-citizens
and his fellow-creatures ; and if, by accepting office, he may become eminently useful to them, it is his duty to accept it.   In enumerating what
is in my opinion requisite in a Member of Parliament, I have omitted
to say that he ought to be a friend to toleration, and an advocate for
religious liberty to persons of all persuasions, but more especially to all
descriptions of Christians, and that he ought to be a zealous supporter
of that which is I think truly called Catholic emancipation[a], as being
of vital importance to the security and happiness of this country, and
which consists only in removing disabilities and disqualifications to
which the great majority of the people of Ireland are subject, only for
professing and adhering to that religion in which they sincerely believe,
and in which they have been brought up by their fathers.

"After saying so much of the duties of a Member of Parliament,
permit me to remind you of the importance of that duty which you are
now to discharge.   One more important never can devolve upon you.
On the Parliament which is about to be elected will depend every
thing that is dear to you and to your posterity ; the happiness, the prosperity, the safety, perhaps the existence, of this country.   You are to
exercise an important trust, not for yourselves only, but for that large
description of your fellow-subjects who, in the present state of the representation, have no voice upon these occasions."

[a] This alludes to a declaration just before made by Mr. Davis, that
in his opinion, this was falsely called Catholic emancipation.

crowded with my friends, and, in consequence of this, the partisans and agents of Protheroe and Davis determined to prevent as much as possible any votes being taken. They disputed about the mode of polling, although that had been already settled. They proposed that the candidates should poll by tallies, which would have been extremely advantageous to them, as it was probable they would each poll double votes while I polled only single ones; and this of course was not acceded to by me. They still, however, insisted upon it, and made long speeches on the subject. They then objected to every vote; and, as there was only one polling place, this manœuvre was very successful, and at the close of the day the numbers were for me only twenty-eight, for Davis only eighteen, for Protheroe only sixteen. After two days of unavailing attendance and the useless sacrifice of so much time, my friends could not be prevailed on to attend again, till there should be a certainty that their votes would be received. On the third day, therefore, on which four places were established in the Hall for taking the votes, Protheroe got sixty a-head of me. This advantage gave effect to the coalition which had been projected between Davis and Protheroe; and from the moment of that coalition being openly formed, it was evident that I could not be successful. Davis pretended to be no party to such a coalition, and perhaps he was at first a stranger to it, but his friends entered warmly into it; and as to Protheroe, he so avowedly entered into it that his committee, as Davis himself informed me, gave

Coalition of Davis and Protheroe.

Davis's cockades to Protheroe's voters, and they all crowded to the hustings with an ostentatious display of these united colours.

On the seventh day of the poll it had become quite clear that I could not succeed, unless the voters resident in London were brought to Bristol; and though they were very numerous, it was very doubtful whether even they could insure my success. The expense of bringing them would be much greater than the subscription that had been entered into could defray, and I therefore determined on the next day formally to give up the contest. I did so in a speech in which I designedly avoided taking any notice of the many very mean election tricks which had been practised against me by the supporters of Mr. Protheroe. I contented myself with merely stating my reasons for retiring. I returned thanks to the different descriptions of electors who had supported me, and expressed the good will I felt towards the city. A tolerably correct statement of the topics on which I touched was given, though very shortly, in the newspapers.*

I gave up the contest.

* The speech mentioned above was given in the newspapers as follows : —

" Sir Samuel Romilly said, that as long as there remained any prospect of success, however faint it might be, he had thought it a duty which he owed to the gentlemen at whose invitation he had offered himself as a candidate, and to those who had given him their zealous support, to persevere in the contest ; but that, upon considering the state of yesterday's poll, and making the most accurate and anxious inquiries respecting the electors who had not yet voted, he was sensible that he had now no hope whatever of success; and that though the out-voters might undoubtedly greatly diminish the majority against him, there was no chance of their overcoming it ; and he therefore thought it right to declare that he did not wish any further exertions to be made in his favour. That he had once intended to persevere in the contest as long as any of the voters would honour him so far as to

There was certainly nothing in this speech at all
calculated to excite the passions, and I know not

---

add their names to the long list of those who had declared in his
favour; but upon reflection he thought he should not be justified in
doing so, since it would only be to gain honour for himself at the expense of trouble and inconvenience, and perhaps most serious loss, to
the families of those who were desirous to serve him. That as far as
he was concerned, therefore, he considered the election at an end, and
that he retired from the contest defeated but not humiliated, disappointed but in no degree mortified, with gratitude to thousands of the
inhabitants who had shown their warm attachment to him, and without
resentment to a single individual. That he was far from questioning
that the gentlemen who were likely to be returned would discharge the
duties of a Member of Parliament with much more ability than he
could, but he would not admit that they would discharge them more
zealously or more honestly than he should have done.

"That it was now, perhaps, of little consequence to the electors of
Bristol what his political opinions were, but yet he could not refrain
from making a single observation upon doctrines which he had heard
advanced, within the last four and twenty hours in that Hall, as those
which recommended a candidate to the electors. If they really were
approved by them, it was fortunate that he was not to be their Member; because in that case the opinions of the electors and their representative would be completely at variance with each other. It might
indeed happen, and often did happen, in cases of contested elections,
that the two successful candidates were of directly opposite political
principles; but that such candidates should be chosen for that very
reason, and by a regular system, such as it had been said had long
prevailed, and ought to continue to prevail, at Bristol, was a doctrine
to which he never could subscribe. It was one by which, upon all
great and momentous questions, such as peace and war — an inquiry
into the conduct of Ministers — an investigation into political abuses —
parliamentary reform — or any important alteration in the Constitution,
this great city was at once to say Yes and No : the voice of one of its
Members was always to control the other : — it was to avoid doing
wrong, by taking care never to do what was right; and was, in effect,
to strike Bristol altogether out of the popular representation. In a
system so absurd as this, he never could concur : he should dwell, however, no longer on it, for the reason he had already given.

"Though he was unsuccessful in the contest, he was proud of the
support which he had received, and he considered it as a most distinguished honour that at that moment he had more than 700 single
votes. He had to return his most grateful thanks to those who had voted
for him; he had to thank the numerous freemen who had assured him
that he had their best wishes and their hearts, though their votes *must*
be given against him; he had to thank those, too, who had told him
that he should have not their wishes only but their votes, but who had
afterwards found it impossible, without ruin to themselves, to perform the
promise they had given; he had to thank those various sects and denomi-
nations of Christians who had united in his support; he had to thank those
numerous Friends whose quiet habit of life, and whose love of peace and

to what cause is to be ascribed the effect which it produced; but it is certain, that before I got to the conclusion, I saw the tears streaming down the cheeks of many of my hearers.   From the Guild-

---

tranquillity, made them averse to mingle in the bustling and tumultuous scenes which contested elections generally present, but who had nevertheless submitted to the pressure and noise and uproar of the crowded Hall, to give a public testimony of their honourable and valuable approbation of his conduct; he had to thank the city of Bristol for the warm and generous manner in which it had declared itself in his favour.   Though he should not have the honour of representing Bristol in Parliament he should always have in grateful remembrance the kindness and attachment which had been shown him.   He should always take the deepest interest in its success; that it might always flourish, that it might increase in prosperity, in public spirit, in virtue, and in happiness, would be his fervent prayer; he would lose no opportunity that might present itself of serving them, and though before the election, and while he was a candidate, he had made no promises, now that the election might be considered as at an end, and that nothing could be gained by his promises, he assured them that he should be always anxious to promote their interests and to advance their prosperity.

"There was one topic more to which, before he concluded, he wished to advert.   The election had hitherto been conducted with uncommon order, regularity, and tranquillity; and notwithstanding the noise and the shouts, which were unavoidable on such occasions, he could say that Bristol had set a most laudable example to other places; and he doubted, whether at this, or at the last general election, there had been in any large and populous town any contested election carried on with more tranquillity than this.   He hoped that they would persevere in the same line of conduct to the end.   He would say more than that he hoped, he earnestly entreated, them to persevere.

"If he had gained (and what had passed proved that he had) any place in their affections, he most earnestly entreated them to consider what might be the consequence to themselves of disturbance and tumult.   It is true, that tumults were often provoked by the conduct of the opposite party; but they should be more cautious not to yield to such provocations, or to take upon themselves to be the avengers of their own wrongs.   It was persons in the humble ranks of life who were in truth always the greater sufferers by tumult.   The injury done to the property of the wealthy was a small calamity compared with what was endured by the imprisonment of men who had their wives and their children depending upon them for support, and who drew down such calamities on themselves by their intemperate zeal.   Riot and popular outrages had often been the cause, but much oftener the pretext, for invading the liberties of the people; and in every light it was the persons who themselves were the authors of such violations of the peace, who were the greatest sufferers by them.   He concluded by again expressing the warm sentiments of gratitude and attachment with which he took leave of the city."

hall, I retired, as usual, to the Bush Tavern, and there in a very few words addressed the electors. I then returned thanks to my committee, and immediately proceeded to the Mayor's house in his carriage, which was waiting for me. The people pressed round me to shake hands with me, and to take leave of me. They took the horses from the carriage, and drew me home, and again as I came out of the carriage, a hundred hands were held out to be pressed in mine, and the eyes of many were suffused with tears. I am aware, while I am writing this, of the ridicule which it may provoke ; but yet it really contains nothing more than a plain and unexaggerated statement of the fact.

My giving up the contest was made matter of some reproach to me by Hunt, who reminded the electors that I had in the course of the election pledged myself, as he was pleased to express it, that I would stand the poll as long as any freeman would be found to vote for me. He did not, however, he said, complain of my conduct in this respect. I had spoken undoubtedly figuratively ; but for himself, he desired to be understood, in a strictly literal sense, when he assured them, as he then did, that he should continue the poll as long as it could possibly be kept open. It is proper to observe on the subject of this reproach, that I certainly never gave any such pledge as Hunt mentioned. I did say once during the election, at the Bush Tavern, that it was my intention to continue the poll, even after a majority of the electors might have voted against me, if it were only that I might have the satisfaction of seeing the names of those

electors who were disposed to vote for me added
to the long and honourable list of those who had
declared in my favour.   There was no resemblance
in this to a pledge.   I entered into no engagement
with the electors, and it was not for their sakes,
but as a matter of personal gratification to myself,
that I had professed an intention to keep the poll
open.   With all this, however, I was wrong; not
for giving up the poll, but for ever saying that I
would not give it up as soon as I was satisfied that
I could not gain my election.   I was provoked to
make the declaration by the arts which had been
practised and successfully practised against me by
my opponents, who had circulated reports that I
had determined to relinquish the contest as soon as
there was a small majority against me, and had descended to very mean artifices to give credit to
these reports, such as taking a place in my name
in the London mail coach, and paying for it.   Still
I ought not to have suffered myself to be provoked
to make such a declaration; nor should I, if I had
at the moment recollected that it was not at my
own expense, but at that of others, that the contest was carried on; and that it would be unpar-
donable in me to prolong that expense one moment after it had become apparent that the object
of it could not be accomplished.

On the day on which I gave up the contest, I
remained at Bristol to dine with some gentlemen
whom the Mayor had invited to meet me; and
the next morning I left the city, and proceeded
straight to Eastbourne. As soon as I arrived there,
I wrote a letter to the Mayor, to thank him for all

I left
Bristol.

the civilities I had received from him ; and as in that letter I stated very truly what I felt respecting the election, it may be worth while to preserve a copy of it.   It was in these words : —

" My dear Sir,   Eastbourne, Oct. 18. 1812.

"From your friendship and kindness to *My letter* me, you will, I am sure, be glad to learn that I *to the Mayor.* have found here Lady Romilly and all my children in perfect health, and that I am at this moment surrounded by countenances as happy and as much delighted as they could have been if I had returned covered with the laurels of Bristol. Lady Romilly desires me to return Mrs. Castle and you her best thanks for the excellent care you have taken of me, and which has enabled me to return in much better health and spirits than she expected, after the fatigues which she supposes I must have undergone.   I deeply regret the event of the election on many accounts ; but I do assure you that they are all of a public nature.   There are, on the other hand, many reasons why I should rejoice in my defeat, but these are all personal to myself.   I would not allow them to occupy my mind while the contest was doubtful ; but now that it is over, they certainly afford me much consolation.   Even those at Bristol, who might be least disposed to listen with favour to what I said, if they saw the enjoyments which my family affords me, and if they knew how sensible I am that, at my time of life, there cannot be reserved for me a great many years of such enjoyments, in health, and in the full possession of my faculties, without

VOL. III.

which nothing can be enjoyed, would, I am sure, be convinced of the truth of my assertion, that a person in my situation could not properly discharge the duties of a representative of your city without making great and severe sacrifices. If I had supposed that Mr. Protheroe's merits had procured him his majority of votes, it would have given me no concern ; because he had a very great advantage over me in the different modes in which our respective merits were to be estimated. To promises and professions which open an unbounded field to the hopes and expectations and imagination of partial friends, I had nothing to oppose but dry and simple facts. That, when so compared together, he should be greatly preferred, could not be to me a painful consideration. To be found unfaithful to one's own professions, would, indeed, be a just cause of shame ; but I should not have blushed at the conviction that Mr. Protheroe had promised better than I had performed. The truth, however, is (as you well know), that the merits of the candidates had less influence on the decision of the election than the colour of a riband. No person could have observed with what zeal determined Tories espoused the cause of a Whig in profession, and how keenly professed Whigs supported, and how ostentatiously they displayed the cockades of a tried and acknowledged Tory, without being satisfied that political principles and national interests were not uppermost in the thoughts of the majority who decided the election. If, however, it were by such a coalition only that success was to be obtained, I am not only contented, but I rejoice that I was not successful. I have thanked the gentlemen, who formed themselves into committees to conduct my election, again and again ; but when I recollect to what inconvenience they put themselves, and at what an expense of their ease and their valuable time they endeavoured to promote my success, I feel as if I had not thanked them sufficiently ; and you would add to the many obligations you have already conferred upon me, if you would take an opportunity, when you meet with any of them, to thank them again in my name, and particularly to say that I have been most highly gratified by my friends having shunned the means which insured success to my opponents. It would, indeed, have been extremely painful to me to have owed my election to the support of those who had been, at the same time, desirous of being represented in Parliament by a gentleman who, however high may be the claims which his private virtues may give him to the approbation of his fellow-citizens, entertains such different opinions on public affairs from myself, that I do not recollect that, since the dismissal of the Whig administration in 1807, we have ever been found in any one division voting on the same side. There is one thing, however, which I own gives me much concern : it is, that the public should be so ill-informed of the history of the late election, as they are likely to be from only a few paragraphs, and those very incorrect ones, in two or three news-papers. I have a very strong interest, and so have the honourable and public-spirited men who supported me, that the real facts should be accurately known. So much honour, indeed, do they reflect on us, that, if it were not for the trouble and anxiety which I have caused my kind friends, and the other sacrifices which they have made (and to which I was always most averse), I should at this moment greatly rejoice that I had been a candidate, though an unsuccessful one. But for that occurrence, I should have remained ignorant of the esteem in which I am held by your fellow-citizens, which has been to me a source of greater and purer satisfaction than could have been the highest dignity which the Crown has to bestow."

The letter then concluded with some expressions of gratitude to some of Mr. Castle's relations, who had been particularly kind to me.

It has been observed that any person who wishes to hear what harm can be said of him, has only to declare himself a candidate at some popular election. With me the reverse of this observation has been the case ; and I seem to have been a candidate only to hear the good which, on no other occasion, could any persons have ventured to say of me. Even my opponents have during the whole of the contest spoken well of me. The moment, however, it was over, Mr. Davis, in an address to his constituents, in order to make a merit with the Ministers, and to magnify his own services in keeping me out of Parliament, represented me as a person who entertained very dangerous designs against the constitution. I felt some indignation at reading this address, and thought at first of replying to it in an address to the electors, but on reflection

Davis's address to to the electors.

I thought it better not to keep up the contest. I could not however resist the temptation of making some observations on this address, which I sent anonymously to the editor of the *Bristol Gazette,* and they were by him published. My observations on it.

The address and observations will be found at the end of the volume.[1]

---

[1] We have inserted them in the following note.—ED.

MR. DAVIS'S ADDRESS.

" To the Gentlemen, Clergy, Freeholders, and Freemen of the city of Bristol.

" Gentlemen,

" The result of the contest in which we have been engaged has proved, I trust, as well to the empire at large as to the electors of Bristol, that the glorious Constitution of our country may yet be supported unimpaired against the open as well as the insidious attacks of those who desire to subvert it.

" That I have been selected as the means by which, as your representative, that Constitution may still in all its branches be maintained and preserved inviolate is, to my personal feelings, a gratification which I alone can duly appreciate.

" Practically acquainted, as I may safely assume I am, with the commercial interests of this the second city of the empire, I am sure that although I may not contest the palm of eloquence with one of my late opponents, I shall not, on that account, be deemed the less capable of attending to your local interests ; nor however less versed I may be in the legal knowledge of our Constitution, be considered the less able to judge of and to oppose any *inroads* which may be attempted to be made, either on the just prerogatives of the Crown, or on the rights and liberties of the nobles or the people.

" I am neither ashamed nor afraid to acknowledge that the support of the reformed Protestant religion, as established by law, has and ever will continue to be the foremost object of my life ; but my constituents of other persuasions will not, I trust, imagine that I am precluded by this avowal from using every means in my power to preserve unimpaired their religious liberties.

" Although I have hitherto supported, and shall not by any means be deterred from continuing to support, the unavoidable war in which the nation is engaged, I cannot but anticipate with the highest satisfaction the period, which I doubt not will arrive, when an honourable and advantageous peace may be concluded, founded on the conviction of our common enemy, that all his efforts for the subjugation of this country and of Europe are fruitless and unavailing.

" Allow me, Gentlemen, in conclusion, to repeat to you my warmest thanks for the honour you have conferred on me, and to assure you, that however great may be the responsibility which your representation

Nov. 23d, Mon.   I had occasion to-day to see Mr.
Justice Chambre on the subject of a petition which

---

incurs, I shall on no occasion shrink from a faithful and zealous performance of the duties which that situation demands.

" I have the honour to be, with unbounded sentiments of gratitude
and respect, your obliged and obedient servant,

"RICHARD HART DAVIS.

" Mortimer House, Oct. 16th, 1812,
       Friday Evening."

" To the Editors of the *Bristol Gazette.*

" Sirs,

" After the poll at the late election was closed, and two days
after Sir Samuel Romilly had left Bristol, Mr. Davis thought proper to
publish an address to the electors, in which he is pleased to say that
the result of ' the contest had proved to the whole empire that the glorious Constitution of this country might yet be supported unimpaired,
against the open as well as the insidious attacks of those who desired to
subvert it ; and that it was a high gratification to him that he had been
selected as the means by which the Constitution might still in all its
branches be preserved inviolate.' The meaning of this cannot be misunderstood ; the election being over, Mr. Davis, who as long as the
contest was depending, spoke of Sir Samuel Romilly only to compliment him, is impatient to recommend himself to those who are in
power, by claiming to himself the extraordinary merit of having saved the
Constitution from some imminent danger, with which it was threatened
by the prospect of that gentleman's election. The event, it seems, has
proved that the Constitution *might still* be preserved, that there was a
possibility, just a possibility, of its preservation ; and that he, Mr. Davis, had
been selected (by Providence we must presume, though he has so care-
lessly expressed himself that the White Lion Club might be understood,)
as the instrument by which so great a good might be accomplished.

" This is the compliment which this courteous gentleman thinks it
decent to pay at the very moment of his election to a very large body of
his constituents, — no less than 1685, — who must have been parties to
this insidious attempt to subvert the Constitution, if any such were
really made. His constituents will probably hardly think it worth while
to ask Mr. Davis what act or what expression of Sir Samuel Romilly's,
in the whole course of his public life, could justify such an insinuation,
and it is not likely that Sir Samuel Romilly should himself condescend
to put such a question to him ; but if Sir Samuel Romilly were a man
of the worst principles of any in the kingdom, how comes Mr. Davis to
arrogate to himself the merit of having excluded him from Parliament,
since the contest lay entirely between Sir Samuel and Mr. Protheroe ?
It must surely be that gentleman, and not Mr. Davis, who can with
most truth assert that he has rendered that important service to the
State. So neglectful was Mr. Davis and his White Lion Club of the
interests of the State, that they set up only one candidate ; and though
the House of Davis could, it seems, supply two instruments for working so great a good, one of them was sent to a distance to obtain a
seat at Colchester, and, as far as he was concerned, Bristol was left
entirely open to the enemy. Or does Mr. Davis by this address mean

was transmitted to me some time ago to present to the Regent, on behalf of a man convicted of felony at the Somerset Lent assizes before that Judge. The man's sentence had been that of transportation, but he is at present confined on board the hulks. In the course of our conversation, Mr. Justice Chambre told me that the Judges frequently *Practice* sentenced a man to a longer transportation than *of some* they otherwise would do, or than they think the *with re-* crime deserves, in order to secure his being trans-*spect to* ported; it being very usual, where a prisoner is *ing felons.* sentenced only to seven years' transportation, not to transport him at all*, but to keep him for the whole term on board the hulks. Lord Kenyon, he said, almost always acted on this principle; and whenever he sentenced a man to be transported, made the sentence for life, or for the longest term

Margin note: Practice of some Judges with respect to transporting felons.

to avow, what during the election he often and solemnly denied, that the influence of himself and his friends has returned both the Members, and that Mr. Protheroe, as well as Mr. Davis, is of the nomination of the White Lion Club? Mr. Protheroe, indeed, could never, on any general ground, lay claim to much merit for having kept Sir Samuel Romilly out of Parliament, since he professes to entertain opinions quite as popular as Sir Samuel Romilly; nay, indeed, to go much farther, and to adopt the favourite doctrines of Mr. Cobbett and his friends, that a candidate for popular representation should make a solemn declaration, that he will never, under any circumstances, accept any place under the Crown; and, in truth, as soon as the election was over, though never till then, he obtained, according to the newspapers, the flattering testimony of Mr. Hunt in favour of his political principles, which that gentleman pronounced to be much better than Sir Samuel Romilly's. It is certainly a circumstance not a little gratifying to the friends of Sir Samuel Romilly that that gentleman's political principles were in one and the same day strongly censured by Mr. Davis and Mr. Hunt."

* In April, 1813, I happened to meet Mr. Justice Bailey, who had just returned from the Oxford circuit. We had some conversation about the increase of offences, which he represented to be very great. He said that he ascribed it in some degree to the hulks, which made the prisoners confined in them much worse than it found them; and he said, if we sentence a man to transportation for only seven years, he is almost sure not to be transported, but to be sent on board the hulks.

allowed by law. If I were merely to state in the House of Commons, that Judges might perhaps sometimes act upon such a principle as this, what an outcry would there not be raised against me. Lord Ellenborough would not fail to take notice of it in the House of Lords, on the first occasion that presented itself, and he would find no terms too strong to censure what he would treat as a gross libel on the administration of justice.

The Duke of Norfolk offers me a seat in Parliament. Before the Bristol election, the Duke of Norfolk offered, in case I should be unsuccessful at that place, to bring me into Parliament without any other expense than just that of a dinner to the electors, which was always usual. He said that he would either have me returned at the general election, or, if I thought that my being already elected would operate at all to my prejudice at Bristol, he would reserve a seat for me till the contest there should be over. He told me that it was to be fully understood that I was to vote, when in Parliament, just as I should think proper; and that, if I accepted his offer, he should consider it as an obligation conferred on him. This very kind and liberal offer I accepted; and Mr. Henry Howard, the Duke's relation, who was elected to represent Gloucester, was also returned for Arundel, with an intention that he should elect to sit for Gloucester, and leave Arundel open for me.

I had formerly determined never to come into Parliament but by a popular election, or upon the purchase by myself of a seat from the proprietor of some borough, and I refused an offer which the late Marquis of Lansdowne made me, to come in for

Calne, a great many years ago ; and more recently (in 1805) I declined accepting a seat which the Prince of Wales had procured for me.[1]   The alteration, however, which has taken place in the law, and the change in my own situation, have made that quite unobjectionable to which there appeared to me formerly to be the strongest objection. Since Curwen's Bill has declared illegal the purchase of seats in the manner which was formerly practised, there is no choice for a person like myself, but to come into Parliament on such an offer as is now made me, or to decline Parliament altogether, and I cannot think that it is my duty to decline it. The objection to coming into Parliament upon the nomination of some nobleman or other great landed proprietor, is, that you come in shackled with his political opinions and subservient to his will ; but, after the part that I have already acted in Parliament, no doubt can be entertained that the Duke of Norfolk is quite sincere in telling me that I shall be quite independent of him ; and no person will, I believe, suspect me of intending to speak and vote on any question merely as the Duke may wish, and not according to my own judgment and conscience.[2]

[24th.] The new Parliament met.   *Parliament met.*

30th, *Mon.*   The Regent went to the House of Lords, and opened the Session. In his way to the House and back again, he was received with a dead and most humiliating silence ; no marks of disapprobation, but no applause.   The Princess Char-

[1] See Vol. II. p. 114. — ED.
[2] See Vol. II. p. 128. — ED.

lotte, who was present as a spectator of the ceremony, was recognised by the people on her return,
and was greeted with loud and repeated huzzas.

Bill for
creating a
Vice-
Chancellor
of Eng-
land.

Dec. 1st, *Tu.* Lord Redesdale brought into
the House of Lords a Bill for creating a Vice-
Chancellor.

I supposed that it was the intention of Ministers
to carry this Bill through Parliament before the
Christmas recess, and, consequently, before I should
be in Parliament. As the only way, therefore, in
which I could give any opposition to it, I printed
a very short statement against it, and published it
in a pamphlet, under the title of, " *Objections to the
Project of creating a Vice-Chancellor of England.*"[1]
I did not put my name to this publication, but I
avowed it, and sent copies of it myself to the Chancellor and to Lord Redesdale. It seems, however,
that in consequence of some opposition given to
the Bill by Lord Holland, it is not to pass through
the House of Commons till after the holidays. In
my pamphlet I have confined my objections to the
effect which will be produced on the law and practice of the Court of Chancery by this projected
alteration in its constitution.

19th, *Sat.* I set out for Arundel in the afternoon, and got late at night to Petworth.

20th, *Sun.* Arrived at Arundel.

Election at
Arundel.

21st, *Mon.* I was elected without opposition.
An opposition, however, was threatened up to the
moment of the election taking place. None that
would have been made could have been effectual.

---

[1] The substance of these objections is stated in Vol. II. p. 403, *et
seq.* — ED.

The right of election is in the inhabitants paying scot and lot; and of 310, the whole number of electors, 195 were decided supporters of any candidate the Duke of Norfolk might recommend. After the election, about fifty of the principal inhabitants and electors dined with the Duke at the Castle. Healths were drunk, and speeches made, as is usual upon such occasions; and the Duke, in the course of one of his speeches, said that he had introduced me at Arundel, not from any private friendship he entertained for me, for he knew me but little in private, and, till the last autumn, when I passed two days at Arundel, we had never both slept at the same time under the same roof, but because he approved my political principles and my public conduct; and that all that he had required of me, when he had proposed to introduce me to his friends at Arundel, was, that I should do him the favour of dining with him once a year.

The Duke's convivial talents are universally acknowledged by all who know him. It is a great misfortune that he possesses them, as they probably have prevented his exerting talents of a much higher order with which he certainly is endowed, and which, joined to his high rank and eminent station in society, ought to have made him act a very great part in the eventful times in which he has lived. He has an excellent understanding, improved by a great deal of reading. He seems to possess a very intimate and perfect knowledge of our history and constitution. His language is correct and forcible, and remarkably perspicuous; and he has a very happy facility of applying the

Duke of Norfolk.

various knowledge he possesses. I know few persons whose conversation is more entertaining and instructive. His political principles are very good, and he has constantly and firmly adhered to them through life, though at the expense of being always in disfavour with the Court. The Prince warmly cultivated his friendship, while his father reigned; but since he has himself assumed the Regency, and laid aside the Whig principles he once professed, he has slighted and shunned the Duke, as well as all the rest of his early friends. What reason is there not to deplore the habits of dissipation which the Duke in his youth acquired, and which he has never since endeavoured, or at least never been able, to shake off!

[The following prayer is written on the last page of the second MS. volume of this Diary: we have inserted it at the end of the year in which it is dated. — ED.]

1812.

ALMIGHTY God! Creator of all things! the source of all wisdom, and goodness, and virtue, and happiness! I bow down before thee — not to offer up prayers, for I dare not presume to think or hope that thy most just, unerring, and supreme will can be in any degree influenced by any supplications of mine — nor to pour forth praises and adorations, for I feel that I am unworthy to offer them, but, in all humility, and with a deep sense of my own insignificance, to express the thanks of a contented and happy being, for the innumerable benefits which he enjoys. I cannot reflect that I am a human being, living in civilised society, born the member of a free state, the son of virtuous and tender parents, blest with an ample fortune, endowed with faculties which have enabled me to acquire that fortune myself, enjoying a fair reputation, beloved by my relations, esteemed by my friends, thought well of by most of my countrymen to whom my name is known, united to a kind, virtuous, enlightened, and most affectionate wife, the father of seven children all in perfect health, and all giving, by the goodness of their dispositions, a promise of future excellence, and though myself far advanced in life, yet still possessed of health and strength which seem to afford me the prospect of future years of enjoyment, — I cannot reflect on all these things and not express my gratitude to thee, O God! from whom all this good has flowed. I am sincerely grateful for all this happiness. I am sincerely grateful for the happiness of all those who are most dear to me, of my beloved wife, of my sweet children, of my relations, and of my friends.

I prostrate myself, O Almighty and Omniscient God, before thee. In endeavouring to contemplate thy divine attributes, I seek to elevate my soul towards thee; I seek to improve and ennoble my faculties, and to strengthen and quicken my ardour for the public good; and I appear to myself to rise above my earthly existence, while I am indulging the hope that I may at some time prove an humble instrument in the divine work of enlarging the sphere of human happiness.

1813.

Jan. 7th, *Th.* I returned to Town from Tanhurst, a house most delightfully situated upon
Leith Hill, in Surrey, which I have very lately
taken as a yearly tenant. I have been passing ten
days there with my family, and should have prolonged my stay for a few days more, if the sitting
of the Privy Council to-morrow on plantation appeals had not compelled me to return.

The day to which the House of Commons is
adjourned is now fast approaching. I think of
taking my seat immediately on its meeting, and
of bringing in without delay the Bills which I have
in contemplation for making some alterations in
the criminal law, and a Bill for subjecting the
freehold estates of persons who die indebted to the
payment of their simple contract debts. Ever since
I was turned out of the office of Solicitor-General
in 1807, I have been somewhat backward in proposing alterations in the law, because I have always supposed it possible that I might again be in
office ; and changes proposed by a person who has
the support of Government, or at least has not
their opposition to encounter, are so much more
likely to be adopted than those which come from
another quarter, that I have reserved myself for
that favourable season. There seems, however,

now to be no prospect that the time will ever come when I or my friends shall be in power ; and the only task that is likely ever to be allotted me, is, to propose useful measures with little hope of being able to carry them. Some good, however, may be done even by such unsuccessful attempts, and I shall therefore persevere in them.

15th.   Lord Redesdale has published an answer to my pamphlet on the appointment of a Vice-Chancellor, which he has entitled " *Observations occasioned by a Pamphlet entitled, ' Objections to the Project of creating a Vice-Chancellor of England.'* " It appears to me to be very feeble and very unsatisfactory. Bill to create a Vice-Chancellor.

Feb. 1st, *Mon.*   I have written and printed an answer to Lord Redesdale, under the title of " *A Letter to a Noble Lord, by the Author of ' Objections to the Project, &c.'* "

2d, *Tu.*   The House of Commons met after the adjournment for the Christmas recess, and I took my seat.

8th, *Mon.*   I moved for returns of convicts.

11th, *Th.*   The second reading of the Vice-Chancellor's Bill was carried by a majority of 79 ; 201 for it, 122 against it.   I spoke very shortly upon it, having risen late in the debate.

15th, *Mon.*   A debate on receiving a report of the Vice-Chancellor's Bill, in which I took some part.

17th, *Wed.*   In the House of Commons, I moved for leave to bring in a Bill to repeal so much of the Act of King William as punishes with death the offence of stealing privately in a shop, warehouse, Criminal Law.

or stable, goods of the value of five shillings[1] ; and
also for leave to bring in a Bill to alter the punishment of high treason ; and another Bill to take away
corruption of blood, as a consequence of attainder
of treason or felony.   I omitted the Bills formerly
brought in to take away capital punishments in the
cases of stealing in dwelling-houses and on board
vessels; because those Bills had excited much more
opposition than that relating to shops ; and some
persons had even said that they would have voted
for the latter if it had not been accompanied by

**Cruel
sentence
in high
treason.**

the two former.   The alteration I proposed to
make in the punishment of high treason was, to
omit the embowelling and quartering.   I observed
upon this horrible punishment, that it was that
with respect to which the Judges had no discretion.
In the case of Captain Walcot, who was concerned
in the Rye-House plot, after his execution his heir
brought a writ of error, and the judgment was
reversed by the King's Bench, which reversal
was affirmed in the Lords, because the judgment
had omitted to say that the bowels of the prisoner
should be taken out and burned, while he was yet
alive : " In conspectu ejus et ipso vivente." These
were the words the omission of which was held
fatal to the judgment.   (*Salk.* 632. ; *Sho. P. C.*
136.)   The Judges, it was held, had no discretion;
the discretion here is transferred from the Judge
to the executioner.   The judgment now is never
executed, it is said intentionally ; when it does
happen, it is, as Blackstone says, by accident or

---

[1] This Bill had been thrown out in the House of Lords in the Session
of 1810–11.   See Vol. II. p. 396. — ED.

through negligence. (4 *Black*. 377.) As late, however, as the rebellion of 1745, it appears to have
been executed intentionally, to make the punishment severe.   (See the case of Mr. Townley,
9 *St. Tr.* 551.)   In former times it was usually
executed.   (See as to Babington and his accomplices, *St. Tr.*, vol. i. 134, 135.; *Camd. Ann. anno*
1586 ; *Bacon's Works*, vol. ii. 57. : the case of
Harrison, one of the regicides, 2 *St. Tr.* 403. ; and
of James, *ibid.*, 274.)   It is uncertain when this
judgment was first introduced.   Luders, in his
Tracts, supposes it was in the reign of Edward I.,
in the case of David Prince of Wales ; and a passage he cites from Fleta seems to favour that
opinion.   This instance, and that of William Wal-
lace in the same reign, are the earliest accounts we
have of the existence of such a sentence.   It ought
to be abolished, as the judgment of burning in the
case of women was abolished by 30 Geo. III.
c. 48.   On the subject of corruption of blood, I
said very little, and only pointed out the distinction between that and forfeiture, which, though I
highly disapprove, I do not now mean to propose
to abolish.

There was no opposition to my motions ; but Garrow,
Garrow (the Solicitor-General) announced his in- General.
tention of opposing the Bills when they shall be
brought in.   In what he said, he proved that he
had never thought on the subject, and was ignorant altogether of the grounds on which I proceed.
He supposed my object to be, to state one certain
punishment exactly defined in its nature and degree
for each crime, and which was never to be departed

Corruption
of blood.

from; and this, he argued, was impracticable, or would be attended with pernicious effects. On corruption of blood, he only observed, that men who would not be deterred by the fear of punishment on themselves were often prevented from committing crimes by compassion for their children; and he said he believed that suicide had often been prevented in persons who had insured their lives, by the knowledge that the sum insured would not be paid to their families if they fell by their own hands.

18th, *Th.* I republished my pamphlet on Criminal Law, with some additional notes to it.

Catholics.

March 2d, *Tu.* Mr. Grattan's motion for a committee to inquire into the state of the laws relative to Roman Catholics was carried in a very full House by a majority of 40, after a debate which has lasted four days. The division took place at four o'clock in the morning of the 3d of March. I had supposed it would be at a later hour, and unfortunately got to the House just as the division was over, and was prevented from adding one to the majority.[1]

Princess of
Wales.

5th, *Fri.* Cochrane Johnstone made a motion in the House of Commons respecting the Princess of Wales. It consisted of a long resolution, arraigning the proceedings which took place in 1806, and the subsequent proceedings, and requiring a production of papers. I thought it a duty which

---

[1] When it was expected that the debate in the House of Commons would be protracted to a late hour, Sir S. Romilly not unfrequently went to bed at his usual time, and rising the next morning somewhat earlier than usual, would go down to the House to be present at the division. — ED.

I owed to the Lords who were parties to these proceedings, and to the Prince too, to state what I know of the manner in which the inquiry had been instituted, and the mode in which it was conducted; and to vindicate the legality of the proceeding.*

* The following is a tolerably accurate account of what I said upon this occasion. It is taken from the *Morning Chronicle* of Monday, 8th of March.

" Sir Samuel Romilly said, that if the motion had been merely for a production of papers, he should not have taken any part in the debate, for there were circumstances which would make it extremely improper in him to state any opinion upon the conduct of the Princess ; but the motion conveyed a strong censure on the proceedings which took place in 1806 ; and knowing what he did of those proceedings, he could not in justice to the persons concerned in them remain silent. That he believed that no impartial man who was acquainted with the manner in which that inquiry was instituted, and the mode in which it was conducted, could think that any blame was imputable to those concerned in it. That in November 1805, he received the commands of the Prince of Wales to attend him at Carlton House ; and his Royal Highness on that occasion informed him, that he was desirous of consulting him (Sir S. Romilly) on a matter of great importance to himself (the Prince), to his family, and to the State ; that it was by the advice of Lòrd Thurlow that his Royal Highness had selected him to advise with ; and his Royal Highness either said in express words, or conveyed by what he said the impression, that what had principally determined that he (Sir S. Romilly) should be advised with, was, that he was not connected in any manner with the Prince, and that he was wholly unconnected with politics.ᵃ His Royal Highness then stated the information which he had received respecting the conduct of the Princess of Wales, and the manner in which it had been communicated to him, and told him (Sir S. Romilly) that the information should be put into writing, and delivered to him, in order that he might give his opinion and advice upon it. That soon afterwards the written information, with certain other documents, were put into his hands ; that he

ᵃ On reflection, I doubt whether I did right in saying this, though it is strictly true. The Prince conveyed this idea to me, and the fact was, that I was quite unconnected with him, and with all political parties ; but recollecting what had passed between the Prince and myself a short time before, and of which a very accurate account is to be found among my papers ¹, I doubt whether the Prince considered me as quite unconnected either with himself or with the Whig party. It is certain, however, that what had passed on that occasion was of such a nature as must have prevented my being advised with in such a case, if credit were not given to the truth of it, and if it were not intended to proceed upon it only by fair and honourable means.

¹ See *suprà*, Vol. II. p. 129.—ED.

The debate was a very triumphant one for the Princess, and must have been extremely mortifying

considered them with all the attention and anxiety which their great importance demanded, and in a letter, which he addressed to his Royal Highness, he stated the impression which they had made on him, with his reasons, at considerable length : that after this he knew that the Prince had caused means to be taken to have ascertained, as far as was possible, the truth or falsehood of the statement which had been made to him ; and those means were, as he believed, adopted at the suggestion of Lord Thurlow. While those matters were depending, Mr. Pitt died; and, in consequence of his death, a total change took place in the administration. In that change he was appointed Solicitor-General, and some time afterwards he again saw the Prince on the subject of the Princess's conduct, and by his Royal Highness's command waited on Lord Thurlow, who told him that he thought the information much too important to remain without any step being taken on it; that it ought to be communicated to the Ministers; and that, in his opinion, it had already remained too long in the Prince's possession unproceeded on. On the same day he delivered this message to the Prince ; and immediately, or very shortly after, the matter was communicated to some of the ministers ; and his Majesty was pleased, under his sign-manual, to authorize the four Privy Councillors who have been named to inquire into the truth of the representations which had been made, and report their opinion on them. Several meetings then took place for the examination of the witnesses, at which no person was present besides the four Commissioners and himself; and the only office he had to discharge was to write down the depositions of the witnesses, and read them over to them before they were signed. For this office he was selected in preference to the then Attorney-General, or to any other person, merely because he was already acquainted with the facts ; and it was advisable, if it should not be therefore necessary to institute any judicial or legislative proceeding, that as much secrecy as possible should be observed. Having been present at all the examinations (except on one day, when by accident he did not receive the notice), he would say from his own observations that they were conducted with all the impartiality of judges acting under the sacred obligations of an oath. Of the report which they made, it would be highly improper for him to say any thing; he could not state any opinions without adverting to the facts, which, considering the manner in which he had become acquainted with them, it was his duty not to publish. Some observations had been made on the opinion afterwards given by the then Attorney and Solicitor-General. Of that opinion he would only say, that if they did not recommend a prosecution against any of the witnesses, it certainly was not from any doubt that they entertained of the authority of the Commissioners to administer an oath, or of the legality of the commission under which they acted. Doubt, however, had been suggested by the honourable gentleman on its legality; and, in the letter which the Princess of Wales addressed to the King in 1806, and which the honourable gentleman had ascribed to Lord Eldon, Mr. Perceval, and the present Attorney-General, the legality of all the proceedings are called in question.

to the Prince.   The Ministers, or rather Lord Castlereagh and some of his colleagues, to save them-

---

That the letter was written by those persons he never would believe
till he heard it from unquestionable authority.   It bore the strongest
internal evidence that it could not have had the sanction of such persons.   The objection, indeed, seemed to turn merely upon the forms
observed with respect to the instrument giving the authority, and yet
it was surely impossible to doubt that, on a representation of misconduct in a member of the Royal Family, involving besides a charge of
high treason, and presenting the danger of a disputed succession, the
King's verbal authority to a number of Privy Councillors was sufficient.
The letter complains that the ordinary modes of inquiry were not resorted to ; as if the Ministers ought immediately, without endeavouring
to investigate the truth of the charges, to have caused a bill of indictment to be preferred to a grand jury, and to kindle a flame in the
kingdom on a charge of such importance, when possibly there might
be no real foundation for it.   The slightest knowledge of our history
was sufficient to leave no doubt on the constant recourse had to such
inquiries, from the time of Sir John Fenwick (to go no earlier) to the
trials of Mr. Horne Tooke and Mr. Hardy.   Certain members of the
Privy Council had, on a charge of treason or treasonable practices,
always inquired into the truth of the charges before any judicial proceeding was instituted.   The legality of such proceedings is, indeed,
recorded by the whole Legislature.   In the Act passed on occasion of
Mr. Harley's life having been attempted while he was sitting as a Privy
Councillor on such an inquiry, the Act states that it was while he
was in discharge of his duty ; but it should seem, according to this objection, it should have been stated that he was acting illegally and in
violation of his duty.   That this committee of the Privy Council consisted only of four persons could afford no objection ; no one would
pretend that, by law, a larger number was necessary.   It had been said
that if they could acquit, they must have had a right to condemn; as if
an *ex parte* examination was not sufficient in all cases to justify an
acquittal, and as if it could in any case warrant a condemnation.
When Margaret Nicholson was seized in a treasonable attempt on
the King's life, and when, on its being ascertained, on an inquiry
before a committee of the Privy Council that she was disordered in her
mind, and in consequence of it she was never brought to trial, did any
person ever question the legality of the proceeding?   Surely the objection could never have been seriously entertained, and never could
have been made but to answer the most factious purposes.   The proceeding of 1806 was entirely an *ex parte* proceeding ; and upon that
alone no person could be convicted of any offence, whatever might be
the evidence on which it had proceeded.   He understood that it had
been treated by the Commissioners themselves as an *ex parte* proceeding, and that they had suggested that a copy of it should be delivered
to the Princess of Wales, in order to afford her Royal Highness an
opportunity of producing other evidence, if she should desire it.   These
matters, with respect to the form of the proceedings, he had thought it
his duty to state, and he thought it as much his duty not to say any
thing on the merits of the case."

selves from the disgrace which their factious conduct on this subject, in 1807, must draw upon them whenever the papers shall be published, concur in acquitting the Princess of all blame, and consequently throw all the odium of the neglect she has experienced upon the Prince. I cannot but wonder at the extraordinary success which has hitherto attended the bold, and what at first seemed the rash, steps which the Princess has taken. The publication of the depositions taken in 1806 would not, I think, fail to destroy her reputation for ever in the opinion of the public; and yet she has repeatedly called for the publication of them. The Ministers dare not produce them, because, by so doing, they would condemn themselves; and, as they were not produced, she has, in the opinion of the public, the advantage of having it taken for granted that they would put her innocence beyond all question. Brougham is her adviser, and hitherto it must be confessed that his advice has been completely successful. Johnstone's motion was negatived without a division.

Mr. Nash's
visit to me. 8th, *Mon.* Mr. Nash, the architect, who ever since his projected improvements of Marylebone Park, has been in great favour with the Regent, and who lives in constant habits of intimacy with Lord Yarmouth, called on me early this morning. He told me that the manly part I had taken in the debate on Friday had been very thankfully received at Carlton House; and, though he did not come with any express message to me, yet he knew with certainty that the Regent was very desirous of seeing and consulting me; and he desired me to tell him whether I should have any objection to see the Prince on the subject of the Princess of Wales. I told him that I was very sorry, but that I certainly must object to it. That the treatment of the Princess was a matter of great public concern; and that it appeared to me to be very unconstitutional for the Sovereign to advise with any persons but his Ministers, on any public matter.

9th, *Tu.* Mr. Grattan, in a committee of the House of Commons, moved for leave to bring in a Bill for the relief of the Catholics. The question was carried on a division, by a majority of sixty-seven; and I had the satisfaction of voting in the majority. The numbers were [for it 186; against it 119].

11th, *Th.* The Bill for appointing a Vice-Chancellor was read a third time, and passed. I spoke against it at more length than I had done on either of the former occasions. It was carried on the third reading by a majority of 38; for it 127, against it 89. Canning afterwards moved to limit the duration of the Bill to seven years; for this clause, upon a division, the numbers were 114, and against it 145; consequently it was rejected by a majority of 31. I have the satisfaction of reflecting that I have opposed this Bill by every means in my power: I have voted, and spoken, and written against it. There is the greatest reason to apprehend that, from this time forward, the office of Lord Chancellor will be much more a political than a judicial office; and

Bill for appointing a Vice-Chancellor.

what effect will be produced on the profession and on the administration of justice, by such a change in the highest judicial office, and in that office to which alone belongs all the patronage of the profession, with the exception of the Welsh Judges, (who, for what reason I know not, are considered as in the immediate appointment of the First Lord of the Treasury,) it is easy to imagine. In the course of the debate, and in answer to a speech of the Solicitor-General, I observed that it was generally understood that it depended on the passing or rejection of this Bill, whether he should be raised to the highest office in the profession which is not of a judicial nature. He protested that he had no knowledge who was to be appointed Vice-Chancellor*, or that he was to succeed to any office; and he declared that he had not been influenced in any thing he had said in support of the Bill by any prospect of advantage to himself.

Mr. Nash's applications to me respecting the Princess of Wales.

13th, *Sat.* Mr. Nash called upon me again. He told me that his former visit to me was made at the request of the Regent, and that he had since had much conversation with him; that the Prince was still desirous of seeing me; and said that he had a right to consult me as his counsel, and that as such I was retained for him. I told Mr. Nash that in all His Royal Highness's private concerns, he had undoubtedly a right to command my advice and assistance; but that the conduct of the Princess of Wales had become a matter of State; had been

---

* When the Bill had passed, Plumer, the Attorney-General, was appointed Vice-Chancellor; and Garrow, the Solicitor-General, was appointed Attorney-General.

submitted to the consideration of committees of the
Privy Council; had been a subject of consideration
by the Cabinet; and was as much a matter of public concern as the war with Spain or with America;
and that it was impossible for me to advise with
the Prince upon it. He said that I could surely
have no objection to see the Prince, and that my
advice to him might be of great importance to him
and to the country. To this I answered that if the
Regent commanded my attendance, I should of
course attend him; but that, if he asked my opinion
or advice respecting the Princess, I should be
obliged to tell him that I thought it my duty not
to give it him. Mr. Nash, in the course of the conversation, produced to me a letter which he had
this morning received from Lord Yarmouth, in
which was a paragraph, which, as nearly as I can
recollect it, is in these words: "It is desired that
you should tell Sir Samuel Romilly that his advice
has been followed" (or received I am not sure
which) "with all the attention and respect which
any suggestion of his deserves." On his reading
this to me, I observed that I could not understand to what it referred; that he knew very well
that I had given no advice, and had altogether declined giving any. He said this was true; but as
we had conversed together on the subject of the
Princess, he had mentioned to the Prince what he
understood to be my opinion, and particularly that
I thought the Prince had better leave the matter
as it stood, and proceed no farther upon it; and
he supposed this must be what was alluded to. I
said that he must know that this was not said as

any advice offered to the Prince. We had some more conversation, in which he said, that Lord Yarmouth had asked him whether he thought that I was so much of a party man as on that account to have any personal objection to himself: and he asked, but as entirely from himself, whether I should think it a duty to refuse the Great Seal, if it were offered me, unless all my political friends formed part of the administration. I told him that it was not by party motives that I was actuated; but that my opinion was, that no good could be done to the country unless those men who had acted upon Mr. Fox's principles were in administration; and that I should not consent to form part of any administration in which they were not comprehended.

The *Morning Herald* of to-day, which is considered as the Regent's paper, and of which the proprietor is Bate Dudley, who was created a baronet by the Regent among the last promotions, contains all the depositions taken against the Princess in 1806. A great part of them are also inserted in the *Morning Post* of to-day, the paper the most strongly in the interest of Government. They must certainly have been published by the direction of the Prince; and this brings to my recollection that, in my former conversation with Nash, I told him that, as so much respecting the Princess had been published, it seemed to be for the Prince's interest that the whole should be published. What Nash may have said or done in consequence of this I know not, but certainly I have given no advice to the Prince; and I certainly never should have advised him to publish the depositions.

14th, *Sun.* I called this morning on the Duke of Gloucester, and very unusually was let in. He was alone; and, after other topics of conversation, the Princess of Wales was mentioned. In the course of our conversation, the Duke told me that he disbelieved all the evidence against the Princess; that he thought not only Sir John and Lady Douglas, but Cole, Bidgood, and all the other witnesses who had stated any thing material against the Princess, were perjured. I did not tell him my opinion.

17th, *Wed.* Mr. Nash called upon me again this morning. He said that he came to renew the subject of our last conversation. That he was extremely anxious that I should see the Prince; that the Prince had no person who would speak honestly and openly to him; that he thought that, if I saw him, what I should say to him might lead to a total change in the administration; that he was still attached to his former political friends; and that it was ridiculous that Lord Yarmouth and Lord Hertford should be made by the opposition an objection to their coming into power; that those Lords, he was sure, cared little about any political party, and only wished to retain their situations about the Prince. He said that he did not come to me by any authority whatever from the Prince; but that, since he had seen me, he had had a very long conversation with the Prince, at which no person was present, the Prince having made some excuse for sending away Lord Yarmouth ; and that, in that conversation, the Prince had talked much about me, and of the confidence he was disposed to place in me ; and had said that, in a matter respecting his own family, he had a right to consult me as his private counsel.* The Prince, in the course of what he said, remarked, that I now never left my name at Carlton House, which is true ; since the restrictions on the Regency ceased, I have omitted to do so. Mr. Nash said that he made an excuse for me by saying that my calling at Carlton House might have the appearance of showing that I wished for some mark of his Royal Highness's favour, which, considering my political attachments, I ought not to do ; and therefore, he supposed I had omitted to do so. To all this I answered, that the more I considered the subject, the more I felt the great impropriety of the Prince taking advice relative to the Princess from any person but his responsible Ministers ; and that I could not reconcile it to any notions I entertained of my duty to offer him any advice. He spoke of the debate which was to take place to-day in the Commons upon Whitbread's motion, and seemed to wish very much that I should take a part in it favourable to the Prince, though he did not make any request of that kind : upon this I said nothing.

Debate on the Princess of Wales.

I am just returned from the House, and have taken no part whatever in the debate, except to give some explanation on a charge Whitbread

* The Prince said, that he had observed two justifications of him published lately in the *Morning Chronicle*, and he supposed that I was the author of them ; but I assured Mr. Nash, as is the truth, that I had neither written them, nor knew any thing about them.

brought against the Commissioners in 1806, of not having taken Mrs. Lisle's evidence as she gave it. Unfortunately I was not present when she was examined, which was on the 3d of July; but, unless the examinations were conducted very differently on that day from what they were on every day on which I attended, Whitbread's information could not be correct. He produced a long statement of written questions and answers, which he said constituted the examination. Now, while I attended, none of the questions were put down in writing. The information given by the witnesses in answer to the questions was alone put down, and then read over to the witnesses, and signed by them. I stated this in the House.

I brought this day into the House of Commons my Bills for taking away corruption of blood and altering the punishment of high treason.

21st, *Sun.* I dined to-day at Nash's. I and Anne had been invited some time, and we have been in the habit for some years of dining now and then at each other's houses. To my surprise, Lord Yarmouth dined there. It was his first visit, and he was introduced to Mrs. Nash as a stranger to her. I was introduced to him in the same way, though I met him once before, some years ago, at Holland House. Nothing passed between us but in the general conversation which took place. Politics were hardly adverted to; and though the Princess of Wales and the recent publications were mentioned, it was only by some common and trivial observations being made upon them. Before Lord Yarmouth came in, however, Nash took me aside

Dinner at Nash's.

to tell me that every thing was in confusion at
Carlton House; that this was the moment for
bringing about a change of administration; that he
was himself most anxious that it should be effected; and that I was the link by which the
Prince might be reunited with his old political
friends. I told him that to me this really appeared
to be quite impossible. He said that he had, however, thought it right to apprize me of this, and
that he had again had a long conversation with the
Prince last Friday.

That I make memorandums of these conversations is not because I attach much importance to
them. But it may be useful hereafter to recollect
how little of importance does pass in them, especially after Lord Yarmouth's note of the other day.

Mr. Egerton, the Member I think for Chester,
Mr. Holmes, who is also in Parliament, a Mr.
Barnston, Dr. Hughes, the principal of Jesus Col-
lege, Oxford, Anne, two other ladies, and two of
Mr. Nash's pupils, and my son William, were the
only other persons present at this dinner.

Lord El-
lenborough
and the
other Com-
missioners.

22d, *Mon.* In the House of Lords, Lord
Ellenborough and the three other Commissioners
of 1806 defended themselves from Whitbread's
accusation of having taken Mrs. Lisle's evidence
incorrectly. In substance their justification was
complete; but nothing could be less dignified, or
in the manner more unbecoming a magistrate in his
high station, than the speech of Lord Ellenborough.
He hardly omitted one epithet of coarse invective
that the English language could supply him with.

26th, *Fri.* The Bill to repeal the Act of King

William, making the offence of stealing privately in shops to the amount of five shillings a capital offence, was read a third time in the Commons and passed. On the division, the numbers were, Ayes 72, Noes 34. The principal speakers against the Bill were the Attorney-General (Plumer), Sergeant Best, Wetherell, and Frankland. Garrow did not speak, but voted against the Bill.

April 2d, *Fri.** The Bill was thrown out in the Lords to-day upon the second reading, by a majority of 26 to 15. The speakers against the Bill were Lord Sidmouth (Secretary of State for the Home department), the Lord Chancellor, and Lord Ellenborough; and amongst the silent voters against it were the Dukes of York and Cumberland, the Archbishop of Tuam (Cornwall), Bishop of Worcester (Luxmore), Bishop of Hereford (Jackson), Bishop of Oxford, and (Law) Bishop of Chester, Lord Redesdale, and Lord Liverpool. The Lords who spoke in support of the Bill were Lord Holland, Lord Grey, Lord Lansdowne, and Lord Grenville. For strength of reasoning, for the enlarged views of a great statesman, for dignity of manner, and force of eloquence, Lord Grenville's was one of the best speeches that I have ever heard delivered in Parliament. The following Lords voted for the Bill: the Duke of Gloucester, the

Bill to repeal the shoplifting Act.

---

* I this morning, as counsel, attended a committee of the Privy Council, on behalf of the inhabitants of Jersey, to resist an attempt which is making to alter their constitution, and to take from them their right of election of jurats, who constitute a part of their legislative assembly, and form their supreme court of justice. The right of election has, at least from the time of Charles II., been in all masters of families rated and paying taxes.

The Privy Council advised the Prince not to do any thing upon this application. July, 1813.

Duke of Norfolk, Lords Spencer, St. John, Saye
and Sele, Rosslyn, King, Bristol, Somers, Darnley,
Albemarle, Lansdowne, Grey, Grenville, Holland.*

Bill to take away corruption of blood.

5th, *Mon*.   The Bill to take away corruption of
blood went through the committee in the House
of Commons.   The Ministers, who opposed it,
were desirous that the debate on it should be
taken in a future stage of the Bill, and not on
the question of going into committee ; and Lord
Castlereagh, before I came to the House, taking
for granted that this would be done, told Ponsonby
that there would be no debate on it ; in consequence of which, Ponsonby and many other friends
to the Bill went away.   I said that I disapproved
very much of this arrangement ; that of course I
could not oblige gentlemen to oppose my Bill,
when they did not choose to do it ; but that it was
very desirable that I should hear what the objections to the Bill were before it was committed,
because they might be of such a nature as could
be removed in the committee ; and that it was not
quite fair to reserve their objections to the third
reading of the Bill, and then, when there might be
no time or opportunity for considering them, insist
upon them, and throw the Bill out.   All the enemies to the Bill, however, remained silent.   After
the Bill had gone through the committee, and
when I moved that the report should be received
on the next day, I said that I should take that opportunity of stating, more fully than I had done

* Against the Bill, besides those mentioned before, were Lords
Kenyon, Rothes, Poulett, Falmouth, Sandwich, Rolle, Walsingham,
Cholmondeley, Bathurst, Shaftesbury, Kellie, Grimston, Wodehouse,
and Pomfret.

on moving for leave to bring in the Bill the grounds on which I rested it ; and that I was the more desirous of doing so, because I thought that it was misunderstood ; and that, if I explained the measure, I might perhaps remove some objections before I heard them. Accordingly, I went pretty fully into the subject, and showed that it was really a consequence of feudal tenures, and not in truth a penal law. I endeavoured to show that, as a penal law, it operated to inflict punishment on the innocent for the crimes of the guilty ; and this, possibly, at the distance of a century after the offender was dead, and his crimes forgotten. That of the law of *forfeiture*, (though it appeared to me to be very unjust, since it inflicted punishment immediately on the innocent, and only by sympathy on the guilty,) yet still it might be said that the dread of that injustice falling on the near connexions of the criminal might deter him from the commission of crimes. But no such dread could result from the law which induced *corruption of blood*, since it was only in the case of the person seised dying intestate that the law could operate ; and it might always, therefore, be defeated by the party making a will. To suppose that men would be prevented from the commission of crimes by the prospect of a distant evil to befall their remote relations, and which, with a little caution, may always be avoided, seemed very absurd. I insisted on other topics, too, which it is unnecessary to detail ; and, knowing how important on such occasions the authority of writers of great name is considered, I relied very much upon what Mr. Justice

Blackstone says of this law, and upon the wish
he expresses that "the whole doctrine should be
antiquated by one undistinguishing law." (*Blackstone's Commentaries*, vol. ii. 254. 256., vol. iv.
389.)   Charles Yorke said that, as I had thought
proper to enter upon the merits of the Bill, he
should now proceed to state his objections to it;
and, that the debate might not be without any
object, he should conclude with moving that the
report be received on that day six months.   He
accordingly opposed the Bill at considerable length.
He was followed by Frankland, Wetherell, and
some others; and, while the debate was going on,
the Secretary of the Treasury sent for all the adherents to Government that could be procured;
and, on the division, the Bill was thrown out; the
numbers being for it [43], against it [55].   Both
Yorke and Frankland said that they had no objection to take away corruption of blood in cases of
felony, but in treasons they were clearly of opinion
that it should be preserved.   And yet, instead of
moving to strike out the word "treason" in the
committee, or proposing now to amend the Bill by
confining its operation to felony, they voted for rejecting the whole Bill.   As to a part, and that a
very considerable part of it, they approved the Bill
which they opposed.   Yorke was induced, I believe,
to take the part which he did on this occasion
through filial piety towards his father, who, when
a very young man, wrote his *Considerations on the
Law of Forfeitures ;* a work full of technical arguments, and of little merit, though unaccountably
of some reputation, in which he incidentally says

Yorke's
consider-
ations on
the law
of for-
feitures.

something in defence of this doctrine of corruption of blood. Charles Yorke, in the course of his speech, cited this work ; which gave me occasion to read a letter from Mr. Yorke to Blackstone on the subject, which I am in possession of, and had taken with me to the House. He says in it, " As to corruption of blood, it is one thing to explain the grounds of law, and another to wish the law altered in that respect, as being carried too far. I have done the first, but said nothing as to my opinion in the latter respect. The actual forfeiture in treason was the point of my argument ; and to show it consistent with the justice, the policy, and principles of a free government. Permit me, however, to desire that you will strike out any reference to that very juvenile treatise." * The only person who supported me in the debate was Preston, the conveyancer. The arguments used against the Bill had really no, or but a very distant, application to it : they were all in defence of forfeitures, not of corruption of blood. A circumstance which excited much surprise among my friends, and which no person could account for, was Lord Yarmouth voting in the minority. It proceeded, in truth, from a desire to show civility personally to me ; and Mr. Nash had told me beforehand that he meant to vote with me, and that he should have voted for the Shoplifting Bill if he had known when it was to come on.

9th, *Fri.* The Bill for altering the punishment of high treason passed to-day through the Committee. On my moving that the Report should

Bill to alter the punishment of high treason.

* This letter is dated Jan. 26. 1766.

be received on Monday next, Frankland moved
that it should be postponed for six months.   On
a division, this was carried by a majority of 15 ;
75 for postponing it, and 60 against it ; so that
the Bill is lost, and the Ministers have the glory
of having preserved the British law, by which it
is ordained that the heart and the bowels of a
man convicted of treason shall be torn out of his
body while he is yet alive.   In the committee, I
added to the Bill that, after execution, the body of
the convict should be at the disposal of the King.

Mr. Yorke was for preserving that part of the
sentence which ordains, that, after the offender is
put to death, his head shall be cut off, and his
body divided into four quarters.   The propriety
of retaining the severing the head from the body
was maintained by Sergeant Best[1] and several
other members, on the ground that it was the only
constitutional mode of enabling the Crown to order
that attainted traitors should be beheaded.   They
said that, by law, the Crown could not change any
sentence for another ; it could only remit a part of
the sentence ; and in these cases it, on some
occasions, remitted all but the beheading.   In
truth, however, this notion of pardoning or remitting a part of the punishment, though it is
sanctioned by the great names of Lord Coke, Lord
Hale, and Lord Bacon, seems to be a very puerile
conceit ; since the taking away the first part of the
punishment alters entirely the nature of what
remains.   It might as well be contended that the
Crown might merely remit the hanging, and by

[1] Now Lord Wynford. — ED.

that means cause the punishment to become that of tearing out the heart and bowels of the convict, while he was in full life, and possessed of all his unbenumbed susceptibility of pain ; or that, if a sentence were that the criminal should be hanged, and then buried in a particular place, or hanged in chains or burned, the Crown might remit the hanging, and send the offender to be suspended in chains, or buried, or even burned while he was alive. I contended against this doctrine, and argued, as Mr. Justice Foster has done, that the Crown had been considered to have a right by its prerogative to substitute a mild in the place of a severe punishment : that on this principle alone could be justified the many instances which had occurred of women convicted of treason being beheaded, though the judgment against them was merely that they should be burned, without any mention of severing the head from the body. Such were the cases of Anne Boleyn, Queen Catherine Howard, Lady Salisbury, Lady Jane Grey, and Mrs. Lisle. In the case of Mrs. Lisle, the matter had undergone much consideration, and James II. had it clearly ascertained that he had a right to change the sentence before he did it. In the case of the Duke of Somerset, in the reign of Edward VI., and that of Lord Audley, in the time of Charles I., though the offenders were convicted of felony, and merely sentenced to be hanged, the King changed their sentences into that of beheading. In the debate on the Bill, even those who were for getting rid of it altogether admitted that that part of the sentence which relates to the taking out the heart and bowels while the malefactor is alive, and burning them in his sight, ought to be omitted. They stated this to be their opinion ; and yet, instead of proposing any alteration of the Bill to confine it to this single object, they preferred leaving it as it was, in order to have an excuse for rejecting it. Garrow said he never would have voted for such a law originally; but, as we found it a part of the law, he was against altering it. He had come down to the House with a speech, which turned principally on the importance and necessity of leaving the body of the convict at the disposition of the King. The alteration I had made in the Bill in the committee removed these objections, and rendered his remarks quite inapplicable. He seemed, however, to think it necessary to speak ; and, therefore, delivered his speech intended for quite a different purpose. Plumer thought it important to stay and vote against the Bill, though the division did not take place till after 12 o'clock, and consequently not till Saturday

Plumer appointed Vice-Chancellor.

morning. On the same Saturday he was appointed Vice-Chancellor ; for his appointment appeared in this evening's Gazette.

A worse appointment than that of Plumer to be Vice-Chancellor could hardly have been made. He knows nothing of the law of real property, nothing of the law of bankruptcy, and nothing of the doctrines peculiar to courts of equity. His appointment to this office is the more extraordinary, as the

The Lord Chancellor.

Chancellor is fully aware of his incapacity to discharge the duties of it ; and as Richards, who is certainly the best qualified for it of any one now in

the profession, and whose politics could raise no
objection to his promotion, has been always considered as the Chancellor's most intimate private
friend.*   The Regent certainly cannot have made
it a point to have Plumer promoted, since he is
one of the avowed authors of the Princess of
Wales's defence, which abounds with the most injurious insinuations against the Prince.   The only
explanation of all this is, that with the rest of the
Ministry Plumer has a very strong interest; that
they have earnestly pressed his appointment, and
have represented that it would be a great slight
upon him, if he were to be passed by; and that
the Chancellor has not on this, as he never has
on any former occasion, suffered his sense of duty
towards the public, or his private friendship, to prevail over his party politics.

12th, *Mon.* An address of congratulation to   Princess of
the Princess of Wales, on what is called the ma-   Wales.
nifestation of her innocence, has been voted by
the Livery of London, and was this day carried up
to her by the Lord Mayor and the Livery.   The
Princess, instead of receiving it at her house at
Blackheath, appointed Kensington Palace as the
place at which she would receive it, that the procession might pass all through London; and she
fixed on a Monday, that being with a great many
inferior workmen a sort of holiday.   There was
accordingly an immense crowd of persons at Ken-

---

* Richards has since told me, that, while the measure was depending, the Chancellor gave him the strongest reason to believe that he
would be the Vice-Chancellor.   What he said on the subject was so
strong that, as Richards expressed it, coming from any one else, it must
have been understood as a direct promise.

sington and accompanying the procession. This example of congratulating will undoubtedly be followed in many other places, and meetings are already advertised in Westminster and Southwark.

17th, *Sat.* At Mr. Ponsonby's, where I dined to-day, Lord Grey told me an anecdote of the Chancellor, which, considering the part he acted in 1807, is worth remembering. A few days ago, Lord Grey was sitting by him in the House of Lords on the woolsack, and some mention being made

The Lord Chancellor.

of the Princess of Wales, the Lord Chancellor said, " My opinion is, and always was, that, though she was not with child, she supposed herself to be with child." He also said, " I do assure you (you may believe it or not as you think proper), but I do assure you that, when I had the conference with the King in 1807, which I requested, it was solely for the purpose of representing to him what mischief might follow, if Perceval was not prevented from publishing the book which he was then bent on publishing."

Case of Philip Barry.

18th. I lately entertained thoughts of bringing under the consideration of Parliament the case of Philip Barry, convicted at the Kilkenny summer assizes of 1809 of a highway robbery, and executed. Before I did it, however, I endeavoured to procure the best information possible relative to the case ; and Mr. Ponsonby and Mr. Plunket have made for me all the inquiries about it they could. The result of these inquiries is, that, although the man's trial was very improperly hurried on by

Lord Norbury.

Lord Norbury, when it was impossible for him to procure the attendance of witnesses, who had material evidence to give for him, and though on this ground alone the application to the Lord Lieutenant for mercy ought to have been attended to, yet I do not find that there is any sufficient reason for doubting that the man was guilty. I have therefore abandoned my intention of bringing the subject before the House of Commons. However culpable the Judge and the Government may have been, it is certain that the House will not think them so, or take any interest in the case, if the prisoner were really guilty. We ought to be particularly attentive to the mode in which justice is administered in Ireland; since abuse of authority and criminal neglect are more likely to take place, and, when they do, to escape observation and censure, at such a distance from the principal seat of government, than when they fall under its immediate view: but yet it is necessary to be very careful not to bring forward any charge which really can be, or can even be represented to be, satisfactorily answered; since such a step always increases the evil it was intended to remedy.

I have abandoned for the present my intention of bringing in a Bill to make freehold estates liable, after the death of the proprietor, to the payment of his simple contract debts. I could not well bring it forward while my other Bills were depending; and the fate of them proves that I could not now succeed in carrying such a Bill through the House.

May 4th, *Tu.* A Bill has been brought into the House of Commons by Mr. Holme Sumner (the Member for Surrey) to enable justices of the peace to provide proper places for depositing and preserving

Clerks of
the peace.

Fees taken
by them
upon ac-
quittals.

the public records of the counties, and to settle the fees to be taken by the clerks of the peace; upon which the House went to-day into a committee. I proposed in the committee two clauses to be added to the Bill; the one to compel the clerks of the peace to make returns every year to the Secretary of State for the Home Department, of the persons tried at the quarter sessions, of the event of their trials, and their sentences; and the other to declare that it should be unlawful for any clerk of the peace, who should be appointed after the passing of the Act, to take any fee on any acquittal, or upon a defendant pleading not guilty. The first of these clauses was lost by a majority of 45 to 40, but the second was carried by a majority of 56 to 42.*   Both the clauses were opposed by the Ministers.   Bragge Bathurst and Hiley Addington spoke against them, and Lord Castlereagh, Vansittart, and every person in the House connected with Government, voted against them. The arguments used in opposition to these clauses were not a little curious.   It was admitted to be extremely desirable that such returns as the clause required should be made, and that the fees in question should be abolished; but it was said that it would be better if I would bring in a Bill for these express purposes, and which might be made to extend to the clerks of assize who took similar fees.   To this I answered that, with the experience I had of the difficulties thrown in my way on all

---

* Most of the newspapers stated this clause to be *lost* by this majority, and probably that error will pass into the *Parliamentary Debates*.[1]

[1] Such is the case.   See Hans. Vol. XXV. p. 1133. — ED.

such occasions, I felt no encouragement to bring in such a Bill, and should not bring any in; and that it appeared to me to be a strange argument against reforming an evil admitted to exist, that, after it was reformed, there would still remain other evils of the same kind.

7th, *Fri*. Dallas was this day sworn into the office of Solicitor-General, and Richards into the office of Chief Justice of Chester, which Dallas resigned. About a week ago, Garrow was appointed Attorney-General.

June. Holme Sumner asked me, some time after the clause had, at my instance, been added to his Bill, whether I would consent to strike it out; and told me that, if I did not, he should abandon his Bill altogether. Of course I would not consent to strike the clause out, and he has since taken no step. The Bill will drop unless I carry it through, which I certainly have a right to do. But I do not know enough of the merits of the Bill, except the clause which I have added, to judge whether it is desirable that it should pass. I shall therefore take no step upon it, and the Bill will drop.

4th, *Fri*. I got out of town to Tanhurst, and was able to stay there with my family during the Whitsun holidays, and till the 10th.

A Bill for the relief of insolvent debtors came down some time ago from the House of Lords, and lingered a long time in the Commons. The object of it is to reform our present law and practice with respect to debtors; to reform the law by which a creditor has the power to keep his debtor in prison for life, notwithstanding he may be

Bill for the relief of insolvent debtors.

willing to give up every thing that he has in the
world for the satisfaction of his debts; and to put
an end to the legislative practice of having recourse,
as a remedy for these evils, to the scarcely inferior
evil of occasional insolvent debtors' acts, passed
at uncertain but never at distant periods, which for
the time abrogate the law, cancel men's contracts,
and turn loose a crowd of insolvent debtors, because
they are multiplying so fast that the prisons are
hardly capacious enough to hold them. The Bill
erects a new court consisting of a single Judge,
before whom debtors, who have been three months
confined in execution, may, on giving up all their
property on oath, claim their discharge. Their
subsequently acquired property, however, is still to
be subject to the payment of their debts; and,
on proof to the satisfaction of the Judge that
such property has been acquired by the debtor, and
is not applied to the payment of his debts, or that
a false account has been given in of his property,
or that any fraud has been practised, the Court is
to have power to recall the discharge, and to leave
the debtor again subject to the same process against
his person as he was exposed to before he took the
benefit of the Act. Lord Redesdale is the author
of this Bill. Though the principle of it is extremely
good, many of its provisions seem open to much
objection. It is, however, not a little surprising
that, such as it is, it should have been suffered by
the Lord Chancellor and Lord Ellenborough to
pass the House of Lords. Those Lords opposed
the Bills for the same object which Lord Redesdale brought in in former Sessions; and, from what

Lord Ellenborough has since said to me, I cannot but think that, when they allowed this to pass, it was very much in the hope that it would be thrown out by the Commons, or would be so altered as to afford the Lords grounds for dissenting from the amendments when it came back to them. It appeared to me, therefore, to be very desirable that the Bill should pass the Commons nearly as it came down from the Lords, and that the defects in it should be left to be removed by the act of some future session. Kenrick, who took charge of the Bill, but with no friendly disposition towards it, added several clauses in the committee, of which the most important were, one to punish with death all insolvent debtors who should give in a false account of their property, and one to limit the benefit of the Act to debtors who had been six months prisoners in execution. I prevailed on the House, on recommitting the Bill, to strike out both these alterations, and to restore the Bill very nearly to the state in which it was when it came down to us. If a debtor is to have the benefit of such a law, it is surely desirable that it should be before he has been long enough in prison to have acquired the habits, and dispositions, and maxims which are learned in those abodes of vice and misery, and while he may yet be restored as a useful member to the community. The clause creating a capital offence had been added without the knowledge of any one person in the House except the mover of it; so little account in these matters is made of human life. No one was anxious to retain it, and it was struck out at my suggestion as quietly as it had been inserted. These, however, were not alterations which would have been particularly objectionable to the Lords who were hostile to the Bill, or which would probably have been considered as affording any plausible pretext for rejecting it. It was proposed to extend the benefit of the Act to India, where imprisonment is accompanied with aggravated evils which do not in this country attend it; but this, as well as other beneficial alterations which were suggested, it was found necessary entirely to give up. The common council of London declared themselves inimical to the Bill, and appointed a committee to oppose it. A deputation of those gentlemen, consisting of Alderman Combe and Mr. Waithman, had a conference with me on the subject; which ended in undiminished hostility to the measure on their part, and unabated zeal for it on mine. Amongst other things, they were very anxious that, if the Bill were suffered to pass, it should give a power to every creditor to compel his debtor, whether he desired to take the benefit of the Act or not, to give up all his property for the payment of his debts. Such a provision I very much approve of; but to attempt it at the present late period of the Session, and with the dispositions which are entertained towards the measure by those in whose hands its fate would by such an attempt be placed, is inevitably to defeat the whole plan. To compel debtors of all descriptions to give up all their property to their creditors; to enable the taking all real estates in execution and bringing them to sale; to extend this even to copyholds; to take away the shameful means of purchasing delays which now exist, the writs of error and exchequer injunctions which are so frequently resorted to, — all this would be a great good ; but it would be a great and extensive innovation, which, as such, would have to encounter every species of obstruction from those who are, on all occasions, the defenders of long prevailing abuses.   In the mean time, however, the Bill has fortunately escaped the amendments both of enemies and of friends, and has gone back to the Lords without any important alteration.   At the Lord Chancellor's, on the first day of term, Lord Ellenborough spoke to me upon, or rather against, the Bill with no small degree of vehemence ; and declared that, if it passed, it would be indispensably necessary, in this very session, to bring in a bill to explain and amend it.

July.   When the Bill was returned to the Lords, the Lord Chancellor said in the House, that there had been a strange oversight in the Commons, in not inserting a provision for the Judge of the Court : and he intimated that it would therefore be necessary to give up the measure. When I read this in the newspapers, I immediately called upon his Lordship, and informed him (as was the fact), that it was by no inadvertence that a salary had not been provided for the Judge ; but because Kenrick, whom Lord Redesdale had desired to take charge of the Bill in the Commons, had assured me that, as it could not be ascertained beforehand what would be the extent of the new Judge's duties, it had been determined that no stated compensation should be provided for him ; but that, as had been often done in the case of commissioners appointed by Parliament, the amount of his compensation should be left for future consideration.*   The Lord Chancellor said that he really had not understood this before.   He assured me that he had no desire to throw any difficulties in the way of the Bill passing ; but that, if it were to pass in its present form, he believed that no person who was fit to be the Judge of the Court (and it ought to be filled by one who was eminently qualified for the situation) would accept the office ; and, in that case, all the odium of the measure remaining ineffectual, by no Judge being appointed, would undeservedly fall on him ; and this, he said, he was very desirous to avoid.   There cannot be any doubt who ought to be appointed to this new judgeship.   Cooke, the author of the *Essay on the Law of Bankrupts*, has pretensions to it so much superior to those of any other man, that, if the appointment depended on the suffrages of the profession, he would probably be elected without one dissentient voice.   Having ascertained from Cooke himself that, if the office were offered to him, he would not refuse it, I again went to the Chancellor, and told him that I thought he would not meet with the difficulty he had supposed ; and that I was certain that, if the place were offered to Cooke, he would accept it.   His Lordship seemed not a little embarrassed ; and he immediately turned the conversation to another subject. Not a word more, however, has been said about the objection in the House of Lords ; but the

---

* In truth I thought this, in the case of a Judge, very objectionable ; but the same reason which induced me to waive objecting to other parts of the Bill made me acquiesce in this.

amendments in the Commons have been agreed to, and the Bill has passed. That Cooke will not be the Judge, and that some man very much his inferior in every qualification for the office will, is that of which I entertain no doubt; although Cooke is so eminently qualified for the office, and although his politics have always been, in a very quiet way, on the side of Government.

Sir William Scott brought in a bill for the better regulation of the Ecclesiastical Courts, which was, in every respect, the same as that which he brought in in the last Parliament; I might say, which he very reluctantly brought in, for he has little taste for reform, and would never have undertaken such a task, if it had not been in a great degree forced upon him.[1] Among the most important clauses in the Bill was one for transferring the jurisdiction of the inferior Ecclesiastical Courts to the Consistory Courts of the Bishops; and another, requiring as a qualification for Judges in these Consistorial Courts that they should be practising advocates in the Court of Arches, or barristers of three years' standing, who had taken the degree of Bachelor of Laws in one of the English Universities; by which means clergymen would be excluded. Before the Bill went into a committee, however, Sir William told me that he had found it necessary to give up these two clauses, on account of the great dissatisfaction they had excited among the Bishops; and accordingly, they were, in the committee, both struck out upon his motion. I opposed the striking them out, but

Bill for reform of the Ecclesiastical Courts.

[1] Vide *suprà*, pp. 6, 7. — ED.

of course without success. I gave notice, however, that I should, in a later stage of the Bill, endeavour to restore the qualification clause; and accordingly, on a subsequent day, on my motion, the Bill was recommitted, and the clause restored. Sir William opposed it, but did not divide the house; and privately, both he and Sir John Nicholl told me, that it was a provision which they highly approved of; but Sir William said, that he did not choose to incur the odium of being himself the author of it. I was very indifferent about this odium; and the Bill went up to the Lords with this clause in it, and with another, which, upon my motion also, was added in the committee, to *Limitation* limit to six years the time for bringing actions at *of actions* Law, and suits in Equity, and in the Spiritual *and suits* *for tithes to* Courts, for the recovery of tithes. When the Bill *six years.* had got into the House of Lords, I mentioned to the Chancellor, that nothing had been added to the Bill, as Sir William Scott had brought it in, except the two clauses requiring qualifications in the Judges, and for the limitation of suits, for both of which I was answerable. The Chancellor said that they were both extremely proper. I apprized him, however, that it was very highly probable that the first of them would be opposed by the Bishops. Upon which he observed, " they had better not say any thing about it, I can tell them." It gave me no surprise, however, afterwards to find, upon Lord Ellenborough and his brother, the Bishop of Chester, vehemently opposing the clause, that the Lord Chancellor very patiently acquiesced in its being struck out. When the Bill had passed through the House of Commons, Sir William Scott told me, that it was a very great relief to him to have got rid of it ; and that he had felt it as a perpetual blister upon him.

7th, *Wed.* I moved for returns of convicts upon the different circuits since 1809 ; returns I have twice moved for before *, and have never yet been able to obtain.†

8th. Henry Martin's Bill for regulating the office of registrar of the Admiralty, which had been opposed by Ministers and by Sir William Scott in former sessions of Parliament, was in this adopted by them, with some alterations suggested by Sir William Scott. In the committee, however, they proposed, and strenuously supported, and of course carried, a clause to postpone the operation of the Bill till after the death of the present registrar, Lord Arden, a lord of the bed-chamber, and a constant supporter of Administration. This clause has so materially altered the Bill, that it is now converted into a sanction and an authority for the very abuses which it was originally intended to suppress. The great object of the measure was to prevent the registrar from employing at interest for his own use the suitors' money deposited in his hands. To declare that this shall be prohibited only when the nobleman who now fills the office shall be dead, is to declare, in pretty clear terms, that such an employment of suitors' money, however inexpedient it may be,

---

* I renewed this motion 8th Nov. 1813.

† On the same day William Smith moved to have the proceedings of a Court-martial on Colonel Orde laid before the House. I supported this motion.

is not illegal. Indeed, Stephen, the Master in
Chancery, though he denied that the Bill as
altered would give any sanction to the practice,
yet boldly maintained that the practice was legal
and justifiable. He was the only man in the
House who did this. The other supporters of the
measure contented themselves with saying, that
the question was doubtful, and that the Bill would
leave it so. Martin, and the other friends of the
original Bill, were desirous, now that it was thus
altered, that it should be given up. But Lord
Castlereagh would not suffer this. We were compelled, therefore, on the third reading, which took
place to-day, to oppose it, and we both spoke and
voted against it. The division, however, both to-
night and on a former night in the committee,
took place in a very thin House ; and the Ministers
had, considering the numbers present, very large
majorities. It is, indeed, on these occasions, on
Bills which, though important, do not excite any
great public interest, and which are protracted to
a late period of the Session, when the attendance
of Members is much neglected, that Ministers derive from the present constitution of the House a
very great advantage. There are thirty or forty
minor placemen, Lords of the Treasury and of the
Admiralty, Paymasters, Treasurers of the Navy,
&c. &c., who, having places only that they may
vote in Parliament, are constant and regular in
their attendance there ; or who, if they happen to
be absent, as they live very near to the House of
Commons, may be collected together in a few
minutes, while it requires as many hours to con-

vene as large a number of independent members, or of adherents to the Opposition, from their distant abodes, scattered over a great part of the metropolis. After the Bill had passed [1], Martin proposed to substitute, in place of the old title, one which would very correctly have stated its object, " A Bill to postpone all regulation of the office of Registrar of the Admiralty till after the death of George Lord Arden, and then to provide for the same."

22d, *Th.* Parliament prorogued. The Speaker, on presenting to the Regent a Bill to enable the Crown to raise five millions for the service of Great Britain, took occasion to make a speech, in which he observed upon the principal Acts which have distinguished the present Session; praising all the measures of Government, the treaties which have been entered into, our conduct towards America, the new scheme respecting India, and the new project of finance, which he described " as that which, by a judicious and skilful arrangement of our finances, would, for a considerable period, postpone or greatly mitigate the demands for new taxation, and at the same time materially accelerate the final extinction of the national debt." He then proceeded with this most extraordinary declaration: — " But these are not the only subjects to which our attention has been called. Other momentous changes have been proposed for our consideration. Adhering, however, to those laws by which the Throne, the Parliament, and the Government of this country are made fundamentally Protestant,

The Speaker's speech on the last day of the Session.

---

[1] By a majority of 36; the numbers being, for it 45, against it 9. — ED.

we have not consented to allow that those who acknowledge a foreign jurisdiction should be authorised to administer the powers and jurisdictions of this realm."

Delay in executing Insolvent Debtors' Act.

Aug. 9th.   A month has now elapsed since the Bill for the relief of insolvent debtors passed *, and the Lord Chancellor has not yet appointed a Judge of the Court, although, till that appointment is made, no person can take the benefit of the Act. There are about 3000 prisoners at this moment confined for debt in the different prisons of England and Wales.   Every day, therefore, that the Chancellor delays the appointment is an additional day of misery inflicted by him on 3000 individuals ; and of these many have wives and children to share their sufferings.†

20th.   The Lord Chancellor ended his sittings, and on the next day I went to my house of Tanhurst.

Sept. 4th.   I set out for Durham, and took my son John with me ; we slept at Baldock.

14th.   Returned to Tanhurst.

Oct. 21st.   Went to Bowood Park, and stayed there till the 31st.

Vacation spent at Tanhurst.

The whole of this vacation, with the exception of my journey to Durham, and the last ten days spent at Bowood, has been passed by me at Tanhurst.   It has been passed very delightfully.   I have had Anne and all my children (except Edward, who is at school) with me.   We have all been

* It received the royal assent 10th of July. .
† The appointment was farther delayed till the 21st of September, when Sergeant Palmer was appointed the Judge.

working four or five hours every day; my boys
with their preceptor M. Chervet, and myself in
reading, principally for my amusement, and in
putting down in writing some observations on Criminal Law, which my constant occupations in town
have long obliged me to postpone. I have been
resuming, too, an account of my life [1], which I
began seventeen years ago, and discontinued. It
is merely intended as a present amusement for
myself, and as a memorial of me for my children
when I shall be dead. I have also been answering
some cases which I could not avoid taking, and
which the press of my business had made it
necessary for me to delay writing upon till this
season of leisure. Great part of the rest of each
day we spent in riding and walking about the enchanting country which surrounded us. We have   Visiters.
had besides some agreeable visiters; my friend
Dumont for several weeks; and for two or three
days, at different times, Sharp, Bentham, Mill, Miss
Fox, and Miss Vernon, and Scarlett, our neigh-
bour. May I pass other vacations as pleasantly as
this! The last ten days we have spent very differently, but still very agreeably, in a large society
which we have met at Bowood, where Anne, and   Bowood.
William, and myself have been on a visit to Lord
and Lady Lansdowne. Madame de Staël *, her
son and daughter, the Count Palmela, Sir James
Mackintosh, Rogers (the poet), Mr. and Mrs.

---

* Madame de Staël has mentioned this visit of hers in the third volume
of her " *Considérations sur les Principaux Evènemens de la Révolution
Française*," published after her death, in 1818.

---

[1] The second part of the narrative of his life. See Vol. i. p. 40.—ED.

Abercromby, Captain and Lady Elizabeth Fielding, Mr. Hort, Mr. Newnham, Mr. Napier, Mr. Ward, and Dumont, were there, though not all of them during the whole time.

Nov. 3d, *Wed.* News arrived of the great victories obtained by the Allies over Bonaparte in the battles of Katzbach, Kulm, Denewitz, and Leipzic, and of the taking of Leipzic.

4th, *Thurs.* The Session of Parliament was opened. The Prince went to the House of Lords, and opened the Session in person. I saw him returning. A dead silence prevailed; no huzzas; very few hats were taken off.*

Lord Redesdale's Insolvent Debtors' Act.

Lord Ellenborough.

6th, *Sat.* The first day of term. At the Lord Chancellor's, Lord Ellenborough came to me, the moment he saw me come into the room, to exclaim against Lord Redesdale's Insolvent Debtors' Act; which, he said, was nonsense and unintelligible, and could not be executed. It would be proper, he said, immediately to pass a temporary Insolvent Debtors' Bill, on account of the number of prisoners whose expectations had been raised by the present Act. As for Lord Redesdale, he said, he ought to be put in a straight waistcoat. I told him that I did not consider myself as at all answerable for the Bill; that as he and the Lord Chancellor had objected to former Bills of Lord Redesdale for the same purpose, and had suffered this one to pass, I had conceived it, and had treated it in the House of Commons, as sanctioned by him. He said he had suffered it to pass because he was

* I have been told that the same thing happened when the Regent went, in last July, to prorogue the Parliament.

weary of opposing such Bills ; and he had been given to understand that all the defects in it were to be removed in the Commons.   To this, I said, that I did not believe that Lord Redesdale had communicated with any Member of the House of Commons on the subject of the Bill, except * * *. He said he knew * * *, and that he was a great fool.   I did not contradict his lordship.

11th, *Thurs.* I presented a petition to the House of Commons from the prisoners in the Fleet, complaining of the delays which had taken place in executing the Insolvent Debtors' Act.

14th, *Sun.* A weekly paper of to-day (the *Examiner*) contains a comparison between the Attorney-General and me, much too favourable to me.*

19th, *Fri.* Lord Ellenborough, in the House of Lords, intimated an intention of bringing in a Bill to repeal the late Insolvent Debtors' Act, which he is pleased to say is impracticable ; and another Bill for the immediate relief of the present insolvent debtors. Insolvent Debtors' Act.

21st, *Sun.* Intelligence arrived of the late revolution in Holland.

22d, *Mon.* I presented a petition to the House of Commons, from certain foreigners confined for debt in the King's Bench Prison, praying that the benefit of the late Insolvent Debtors' Act, from which they are now excluded, may be extended to them.   I took occasion, on presenting this petition, to notice the intention which had been

* It has been since published in a little work, entitled " *Parliamentary Portraits,* 1815."

intimated to repeal this Bill. I said that I hoped that, before any step was taken towards repealing it as impracticable, the House would be informed in what respect it was impracticable; that, however defective the Act might be in some of its provisions, I had no doubt that these defects might easily be removed : that it would be very strange if no means could be devised to make effectual a measure which only applied the principle of bankruptcy, or *cessio bonorum*, to all debtors.

24th, *Wed.* An account arrived of the old Government of Hanover being restored.

29th, *Mon.* Hiley Addington, the Under Secretary of State, brought in a Bill to continue for a year longer the Act, passed two years ago, to punish with death the offence of maliciously breaking stocking or lace frames. The Act was passed at a time when great tumults prevailed, and violent outrages had been committed in Nottinghamshire, and some of the adjacent counties; which had been produced in a great degree, if not entirely, by the declining state of the manufactures, and the distresses of the people. The causes of passing the Act having been temporary, and having now for a long time ceased, the most perfect tranquillity prevailing in every part of the country, and the manufactures being very flourishing, I opposed the Bill *, and divided the House against it : 37 for the Bill, 20 against it.†

* In the Committee on the Mutiny Bill on the same day, I again in vain attempted to obtain a declaration of the Judge-Advocate and the Secretary at War against the practice of bringing out soldiers to be flogged a second time, after as many lashes have been inflicted in the first instance as the offender could endure.

† This was the only division which took place before the long adjournment to March.

The next day Hiley Addington postponed the further progress of the Bill; and on

Dec. 3d, *Fri.*   The Attorney-General said that in the committee he should move to take away the capital punishment, and to substitute in the place of it transportation for life, or a lighter punishment, at the discretion of the Judge, and to make this new Act a permanent law. I objected to legislating permanently on the subject, without more consideration.

Lord Redesdale's Bill to amend his late Insolvent Debtors' Act was read in the Commons to-day a second time. Something having been said by a Member upon the principle of the former Act, I took this opportunity of stating that the law respecting the enforcing the payment of debts required, in my opinion, great amendment; that, while our laws were very severe as far as they gave a remedy against the person of the debtor, they were very relaxed as they supplied remedies against his property; and that there was no reason why a debtor's freehold and copyhold estates should not be taken in execution and sold for the payment of his debts, or why money in the public funds, and other property of the same kind, should not be made applicable to pay the demands of the creditors who sued him.[1]   I mentioned, too, how reproachful it was to our law, that writs of error for the mere purpose of delay should be permitted; and suggested that, before a writ of error was allowed, a certificate should be required, signed by

Law respecting debtors and creditors.

---

[1] These opinions have received the sanction of law.   See 1 & 2 Vict. c. 110. — ED.

two counsel, signifying that in their judgment there was error in the record.[1] I gave notice, too, of my intention, after the Christmas recess, to move for leave to bring in a Bill to subject the freehold estates of persons who die indebted to the payment of their simple contract debts.

Law promotions.

4th, *Sat.* In the last term there were several changes in the law. M'Donald, the Lord Chief Baron of the Exchequer, resigned on account of his sight failing him, and Gibbs was appointed to succeed him. Dallas, the Solicitor-General, succeeded Gibbs as a Judge of the Common Pleas; and the Solicitor-Generalship, after having been offered to Leach and Sergeant Lens, who both refused it, was given to Sergeant Shepherd. Sergeant Best succeeded Shepherd as Solicitor-General to the Prince.

The Houses of Parliament adjourned.

20th, *Mon.* The Commons adjourned to the first of March, on the motion of Lord Castlereagh. Sir James Mackintosh moved as an amendment, that the adjournment should be only to the 23d of January. He introduced his motion by an extremely good speech, which was, however, very coldly received by the House. I supported the amendment, on the ground that the Commons had no right to put it out of their own power, for so long a period, to do their duty towards their constituents; and that, by the sitting of Parliament being postponed to so late a period, it would be impossible that the business which came before the House could be properly done. I mentioned the

---

[1] This is now prevented, by 6 Geo. IV. c. 96., which requires bail to be given in cases of writs of error. — Ed.

press of business with which the House was generally encumbered towards the close of the Sessions; 40 or 50 orders of the day crowded into a
single night, and Bills of great importance passing
through their different stages at two or three o'clock
in the morning, when it became impossible to object to them with any hope of being attended to.
Whitbread and some others had said that they
should vote for the long adjournment, because the
Ministers had by their recent conduct entitled
themselves to such a proof of confidence : upon
which I observed, that the adjournment had not
been proposed by the Ministers on any such ground,
or on any other ground than that the state of public business made it unnecessary that Parliament
should meet earlier ; that, whatever confidence
Ministers might be thought entitled to, the Commons suspending their own functions was not the
proper way to manifest that confidence ; and that
we had no authority from our constituents to take
such a step.   If the sitting of Parliament was to
be long suspended, the constitutional mode of proceeding was for the King to prorogue it, or to send
a message to the Houses of Parliament, to desire
them to adjourn : such a measure always proceeding upon the responsibility of Ministers.   There
was no division.

24th, *Fri.* The Lord Chancellor's sittings ended.

26th, *Sun.* I went with my dear Anne and
all my children to Tanhurst, and stayed there till
Jan. 9.

1814.

Jan. 9th, *Sun.* I returned to town, the Chancellor being to commence his sittings on the next day.

For the first seven days of our being at Tanhurst, we had the finest weather imaginable, a bright sunshine not interrupted by a single cloud; while London and the country many miles around it were, for the greatest part of the same time, involved in some of the thickest fogs ever remembered. We had afterwards a very heavy fall of snow.*

24th, *Mon.* I dined at the British Coffee-house with the members of the Fox Club, it being the anniversary of Mr. Fox's birthday. This is the third year that I have been invited by the club, and that I have been present at this anniversary dinner. Previously to 1812 I never was invited to it.

Feb. 12th, *Sat.* Sir James Mansfield, the Chief Justice of the Common Pleas, has, during the whole of this term, been prevented by illness from attending in Court; and, as he is in his 80th year, there have been various reports of his intended resignation, and of the promotions which are to take place in consequence of it. Sir Vicary Gibbs, it seems

---

* This frost was very severe, and lasted several weeks; and in the beginning of February the Thames was frozen over, and many hundred persons walked across it between London and Blackfriars Bridge.

agreed on all hands, is to succeed him ; but who is to succeed Gibbs as Chief Baron seems not a little doubtful. For some time, it was considered as quite settled that it was to be the Attorney-General, and he has himself talked very confidently about it, has made inquiries respecting the probable state of business upon the different circuits, and has observed that it would be an affectation in him to be silent upon what every body else was speaking of. How well qualified he is to preside in a Court, in which all questions respecting the rights of the Crown in matters of property are decided, may be conjectured from what passed last summer in the House of Lords. On the claim to the Earldom of Airlie, which came on in last July, I, as counsel for the claimant, had endeavoured to remove the objection which had been taken by some of the Lords, particularly Lord Redesdale, that the title had become forfeited by the attainder of Lord Ogilvy in the year 1715. The question was, whether a Scotch entailed title of honour was forfeited by its devolving on an attainted person subsequent to his attainder ; or whether (as I had to contend) it was merely suspended during his life, and on his death came to the next heir of entail. Garrow, as Attorney-General, on behalf of the Crown, had to answer Adam's and my argument. Perceiving, from his observations to me while the claim was depending, how little he knew of the matter, I was curious to see how, when it came to him to speak, he would extricate himself from his difficulty. He did extricate himself, but in a way for which I certainly was not prepared. He appeared at the bar

Sir William Garrow.

of the House of Lords with a written argument,
the whole of which he very deliberately read,
without venturing to add a single observation or
expression of his own. In the Stafford peerage,
which stood for the same day, he did exactly the
same thing. He merely read an argument which
somebody had composed for him; and none of the
Lords were malicious enough to interrupt him, or
to put any questions to him on any of the doctrines which he had to maintain. I have since
been informed that both these arguments were
written by Hobhouse, one of the solicitors of the
Treasury. A very new sort of exhibition this by
an Attorney-General! Two days afterwards, in
the Court of Chancery, on a question whether a
manager of a theatre could discharge the duties of
his office without personal attendance, I, who had
to argue that he could not, said that it would be as
difficult as for a counsel to do his duty in that
court by writing arguments, and sending them to
some person to read them for him. The Lord
Chancellor interrupted me by saying, " In this
court or in any other? And after the Court rose,
he said to me, " You knew, I suppose, what I alluded to? It was Garrow's written argument in
the House of Lords." So little respect has his
Lordship for an Attorney-General, whom he himself appointed because he was agreeable to the
Prince.

26th. Sir James Mansfield has recently resigned
the Chief Justiceship of the Common Pleas, and
has been succeeded by Sir Vicary Gibbs, the late
Chief Baron of the Exchequer. Mr. Baron Thom-

son has been appointed Lord Chief Baron; and this day Mr. Richards was sworn in a puisne Baron of the Exchequer. The Attorney-General has succeeded Richards as Chief Justice of Chester.

March 1st, *Tu.* The two Houses of Parliament met, and, upon an intimation given in each House that it was the desire of the Regent, they adjourned to the 21st of March. Little opposition was made in either House, though the consequence of the Session of Parliament being postponed to so late a period is, that little more will be done than to pass the Bills brought in by Government, and to pass private Bills. Having stated my objections to this before, I did not think it necessary to say any thing now. This was not the spontaneous adjournment of the House; but it took place in consequence of an intimation for which Ministers are responsible; and, if the motion to adjourn under such circumstances had been rejected, a prorogation must have followed, which would be attended with still greater inconveniences.

Adjournment of the Houses of Parliament.

On a writ being moved for, on account of Garrow having vacated his seat by accepting the Chief Justiceship of Chester, I said that the appointment which had given occasion to the motion was one which appeared to me to be so objectionable, that I thought it my duty to draw the attention of the House to it. The independence of the Judges had, ever since the Revolution, been considered as of the utmost importance; and, early in the present reign, it had been declared from the throne, that His Majesty considered their independence as essential to the impartial administra-

Attorney-General appointed Chief Justice of Chester.

tion of justice, as the best security for the liberties of the people, and as highly conducive to the honour of the Crown. These sentiments had been applauded, adopted, and re-echoed by the House; and yet the impartial administration of justice, the liberty of the subject, and the honour of the Crown, were surely all overlooked, when a person holding a very lucrative situation, from which he was removable at the pleasure of the Crown, was appointed to the office of Judge. The offices of Judge and of Attorney-General were incompatible. The public prosecutor ought not to sit in judgment on public prosecutions; and the servant of the Crown, whose duty it was to assert the rights of the Crown against the subject, whenever those rights came into litigation, ought not to be seen administering justice between the King and the people.* I said that I desired not to be understood to make these observations with any personal hostility towards Sir William Garrow; that he had only done the same thing as two of his predecessors (Lord Kenyon and Lord Alvanley) had done before him; and that undoubtedly, when a gentleman filled the office of Attorney-General, he had a right to expect, and the public too was to expect, that he would be promoted to the highest judicial offices when they became vacant. My observations were extremely well received by the House, but not a word was said in answer to them. This is but a very short

---

* On the first circuit that Sir William Garrow went, there were four causes to be tried on questions relating to the inclosure of Delamere Forest, in which the Crown had an interest; and which, for that reason, Garrow declined to try; and after he had left the town, they were tried by Burton, the puisne Judge.

statement of the substance of my speech, but it contains every word that I said of Garrow. I was not a little surprised, therefore, to receive from him the next day the following note.

Sir Wm. Garrow.

"2d March, 1814.

" My dear Sir,

" I was unfortunately not in the House yesterday when the writ was moved in consequence of my recent appointment, but I feel myself bound, in consequence of the communications of several friends, to request your acceptance of my sincere and grateful thanks, for the very kind and handsome manner in which you were so good as to express yourself respecting me.

" I have the honour to be, with real respect and esteem, dear Sir, your obliged faithful Servant,

" W. Garrow."

I take for granted that he was not in the House, but I had seen him and spoken to him under the gallery, about half an hour before the writ was moved for.

5th, *Sat.* I had occasion to see the Lord Chancellor this morning respecting some business depending before him in his court. As I was leaving him, he said, " This is very bad news which has arrived" (alluding to the retrograde movement of the Allies, and the armistice requested by Prince Schwartzenburg) ; and he added, " This comes of people attempting too much." These words are not a little remarkable, because the Chancellor has been always supposed to be the person who, in the Cabinet, has been most eager in promoting the

The Lord Chancellor.

known wishes of the Prince, and in endeavouring to prevent the Allies from making peace with Bonaparte. Is it the expression of real regret; or was it said to disguise what have been his sentiments?

23d, *Wed.* I moved in the House of Commons for, and obtained leave to bring in, Bills to take away corruption of blood, and to alter the punishment of high treason. Charles Yorke alone opposed the motion.

31st, *Th.* I moved for and obtained leave to bring in a Bill to subject the freehold estates of persons who die indebted to the payment of their simple contract debts.

April 2d, *Sat.* News arrived of the negotiations for peace having been broken off.

5th, *Tu.* News that Paris capitulated to the Allies on the 30th of March.*

7th, *Th.* That the Emperor of Russia and King of Prussia had entered Paris; that the Parisians had appointed a provisional Government, who were to frame a new Constitution; and that the Bourbons were restored. Thus, as if by enchantment, peace seems to be restored on a sudden to Europe.

---

* *Mar.* 30th. Paris capitulated.

31st. The Emperor of Russia, the King of Prussia, and Prince Schwartzenburg, the Austrian general, enter Paris, and invite the Senate to name a provisional Government.

April 1st. Five persons are named by the Senate as such provisional government, with instructions to draw up the plan of a constitution.

2d. The Senate declare that Napoleon Bonaparte and his family have forfeited all right to the throne.

6th. The Senate adopts the constitution proposed by the provisional Government, and decrees that it shall be submitted to the French people.

On the same day Napoleon signed his abdication at Fontainebleau.

12th. Monsieur entered Paris.

I set out this day for Tanhurst; remained there during the Easter Holidays, till *Thursday, April* 14th, when I returned in the evening; the Privy Council being to sit the next day, on an appeal in which I am engaged.

I passed a most delightful week at Tanhurst, with my dearest Anne, and all my children but Edward, whom we were afraid to have home, as Frederick and Charles have lately had the scarlet fever.

From Leith Hill we saw, on Easter Tuesday, at night, the light of the illuminations of London on account of the recent events at Paris.

22d, *Fri.* Lord Morpeth moved a resolution to-day in the House of Commons, which implied a censure on the Speaker, for the speech made by him at the bar of the House of Lords, on the last day of the last Session.[1] It was perhaps a more gentle reproof than his conduct deserved. In the debate, however, which took place on it, he was treated with great severity. It was, indeed, a debate of a very novel character. The Speaker seemed fixed in his chair only to be reprimanded, for six hours together, by every Member successively that chose. The resolution was lost by a majority of 274 to 106. *Debate on the Speaker.*

25th, *Mon.* My Bill to take away corruption of blood went into a committee, in which Mr. Yorke proposed two amendments to the Bill, one to prevent its extending to treason, and the other to murder; and he carried both his amendments, *Bill to take away corruption of blood.*

---

[1] See *suprà*, p. 117. — ED.

though by very small majorities. Upon the first,
42 to 37, upon the second, 29 to 31. A debate
took place on the general principle of the Bill,
which lasted several hours.

Punish-
ment of
high
treason.

In the committee on the Bill to alter the punishment of high treason*, Mr. Yorke proposed that,
after the execution, the head of the convict should
be cut off. I expressed my disapprobation of this,
but did not divide the Committee, and the amendment was carried.

Bill to
subject
freehold
estates to
the pay-
ment of
simple
contract
debts.

29th. *Fri.* Sergeant Best, upon the motion
for the House to resolve itself into a committee on
the Bill to subject freehold estates of deceased
debtors to the payment of their simple contract
debts, opposed the further progress of the Bill, and
was supported in that opposition by Wetherell,
Sergeant Shepherd (the new Solicitor-General),
and Mr. Giddy. The Bill was defended by Preston
(the conveyancer), Sir Arthur Piggott, Lockhart,
and Stephen (the Master in Chancery), who made
an excellent speech. I also spoke in support of it.
The Bill was carried by a majority of 61 to 37.

May 12th, *Th.* I voted in the minority on the
address respecting Norway.[1]

Act of
5 Eliz.
relating to
apprentice-
ships.

13th, *Fri.* Sergeant Onslow's Bill to repeal the
Act of 5 Eliz. c. 4., which prohibits, under penalties, the exercising of trades by persons who have
not served a seven years' apprenticeship, came on
upon the second reading. There has been a great
clamour raised against the Bill. Associations have

* Vide *infrà*, p. 147.

---

[1] To rescue the people of that country from the alternative of famine,
or of subjection to the foreign yoke of Sweden. — ED.

been formed to resist it, in different towns, by the apprenticed journeymen, who are anxious to retain their monopoly.   Numerous petitions against the Bill have been presented, signed by a great many thousand persons; and as, in Bristol and other trading towns, a very large proportion of the voters are freemen, entitled to their freedom by having served apprenticeships, it is not surprising that the opposition of these petitioners should be earnestly supported in the House.   I have myself been eagerly canvassed against it by a very large body of artisans and manufacturers in Bristol who voted for me at the last election, and by a London association.   Sir Frederick Flood moved, as an amendment, that the second reading should be postponed for six months, and Mr. Protheroe, one of the Members for Bristol, seconded that motion.   In the course of the debate I spoke in favour of the Bill, and, as soon as I had concluded, Sir Frederick Flood desired permission to withdraw his amendment, and said that he should not object to the Bill going into a committee.   It was therefore read a second time.*

29th, to *June* 2.   I spent the Whitsun holidays with my family at Mr. Nash's, at Cranbourne Lodge, in Windsor Park.[1]

* There was some opposition in the subsequent stages of the Bill, but the House was never divided upon it, and it passed the Commons. It afterwards passed the Lords with scarcely any opposition.

[1] The following letter to M. Dumont, who was then at Geneva, was written from London on May 26. — ED.

" Dear Dumont,
    " I cannot thank you too much for your attention and kindness to W.   Your account of him gave us the greatest pleasure.   His attachment to you I shall always think the best security for his

6th, *Mon.* The treaty of peace recently concluded with France was communicated to the

---

doing well. Though Madame de Staël had not delivered to you the packet she took charge of when you last wrote, I hope she afterwards recollected it and gave it you. Besides my letter, it contained one from Brougham, which he was anxious you should see while you were at Paris, and another from Miss or Mr. Edgeworth (I know not which). This last was accompanied, when I received it, by a pretty thick parcel of papers, from which I separated the letter. It was lucky I did; for I soon afterwards had a note from Mr. Edgeworth, desiring me not to forward the papers to you, and telling me that they contained a critique on " *Peines et Récompenses,*" which he wished me, if I could, to get inserted in the *Quarterly Review,* without letting it be known from whom it came. I have taken steps for this purpose through Mackintosh, but I doubt whether I shall succeed. The great obstacle to its admission into the *Quarterly Review* will be, I fear, its merit. It contains a defence, and I think one of the plainest and most familiar, and therefore the best that I have seen, of what Gifford, Southey, and the other writers in the *Quarterly* hold in such horror — the principle of utility; and holds up to just ridicule and contempt Kantism and all its concomitants. The first sentence of the article is a very strange one. " When an Englishman and a Frenchman agree upon any point," says a witty philosopher, " there is a strong presumption that they are right," or something to that effect. This, I suppose, is intended effectually to conceal that the article is written by a friend of yours. For what other purpose you can be converted into a Frenchman I don't know; and neither the witty philosopher nor any other philosopher would be surprised to find that a Genevese and an Englishman thought alike on a great many subjects.

" I send you an account of the debate on my Bill to take away corruption of blood. It is more accurate than such accounts generally are; several of the speeches, and amongst others Mackintosh's and mine, having been corrected by the speakers. There is great modesty in this avowal, for mine is certainly but a poor speech; Mackintosh's is excellent. I send two copies, that William may have one; he heard the debate, and, if the variety of objects he has since seen have not driven it entirely out of his head, he will be able to judge of the correctness of the report. Nothing has passed in Parliament since you left us, except the debate on Norway, in which (as has been the case ever since the present Ministry came into power), all the argument was on one side, and the great majority of numbers on the other. The best speech made on the subject in the House of Commons was Mackintosh's; and every body says that it showed very extraordinary powers of reasoning and of eloquence. I did not hear it, and therefore speak of it only from the report of others.

" Our Prince is not quite in such high spirits as he was in a little while ago. The arrival of the illustrious visiters he expected is put off for the present, and some difficulties have arisen about the Princess Charlotte's marriage, which have made it necessary at least to postpone it. The intended bridegroom, in the meantime, is living in lodgings at a tailor's

Houses of Parliament. It contains an article by
which the King of France, after acknowledging the
slave-trade to be repugnant to principles of natural Slave-trade.
justice and to the enlightened times in which we
live, engages to unite all his efforts to those of his
Britannic Majesty at the approaching Congress, to

---

in great obscurity, and with no appearance of opulence. The Duchess
of Oldenburg has fallen into great disfavour. She is supposed to have
given bad advice to the Princess Charlotte, and she was guilty of the indiscretion of paying a visit to Whitbread at his brewery. The Prince has
since said to her, that he supposes when she goes to Paris she will make
a point of seeing Santerre. The great object of his Royal Highness at
present, is to prevent the Princess going to the Queen's drawing-room,
and being present at any of the festivals, which the different clubs are
about to give upon the restoration of peace. It is hardly credible what
pains he has given himself to accomplish this noble purpose. He has
written a letter to the Queen, in which he tells her that he has come to
a determination never to be in the same room with the Princess ; and he
therefore desires her Majesty to take care that the Princess is not at
the drawing-room. The Queen has accordingly signified this to the
Princess, and the Princess in revenge means to publish the letters. Is
not the condition of this nation a happy one when these are our most
important public events ? In the mean time, however, the war with
America still continues, and we seem to have got to be so much accustomed to war, and to consider it as our natural condition, that it is
certainly not unpopular. The *Times* newspaper, having no Bonaparte
to rail at, pours forth all its gross abuse upon the Americans, and would
fain excite the nation to conquest, and to every species of injustice and
extravagance.

Bentham is, I am afraid, about to engage in a speculation respecting
the mills at Lanark, in Scotland, which is to have the double object of
making the fortunes of those who engage in it, and of extending education and instruction among the lower orders of the people. I endeavoured strongly to dissuade him from it, thinking that, at his time of
life and in his situation, it was great folly to embark in any concern
which, by possibility, no matter how remote, might involve him in difficulty and in distress, and ultimately in ruin. All my good advice,
however, only made him very angry ; as if he did not know how to
manage his own affairs, as if he wanted advice, or was to be treated
like a child, &c. &c. I told him that the man who was engaging him
in this, though very well-intentioned, was really a little mad. To
which his answer was, " I know that as well as you ; but what does
that signify ? He is not mad *simpliciter*, but only *secundum quid*."
Finding nothing was to be done, I took my leave of him, contrived to
make him laugh, and put him at last in good humour by telling him
that, though he would not take my advice, he might depend upon it
that, when he was an uncertificated bankrupt, I would not turn my
back upon him."

induce all the powers of Christendom to decree the abolition of that trade, so that it shall cease universally; as it shall cease definitively, under any circumstances, on the part of the French Government in the course of five years; and that, during that period, no slave-merchant shall import or sell slaves, except in the colonies of the state of which he is a subject.

This article is a cruel disappointment of the hopes entertained by most people that so favourable an opportunity for the immediate and total abolition of the slave trade by all the powers of Europe would not have been lost. The address to the Regent unanimously voted by the House of Commons on the 3d of May last, and a similar address by the Lords, had greatly heightened these hopes.

8th, *Wed.* I have been much concerned at not discovering any probability of a demonstration of public opinion on the subject of the article in the treaty respecting the slave trade. Not finding any step likely to be taken, I mentioned to-day in the House of Commons to Whitbread and Horner, that it appeared to me of the utmost importance that something should be done without delay. They agreed with me, and in the House I wrote a letter to the Duke of Gloucester, as President of the African Institution, requesting that a meeting of that society should be immediately called. They together with me signed the letter, and I afterwards sent it to Stephen and Whishaw, and got their signatures to it. The next day I took it myself to the Duke of Gloucester, and he immediately appointed a meeting of the directors for Monday next.

13th, *Mon.*   The meeting of the directors of the   Slave trade. African Institution was very numerously attended. Being, at the commencement of the meeting, the only person present of those who had desired it to be called, I proposed that there should be called, with as little delay as possible, a general meeting of all the friends of the abolition, for the purpose of coming to resolutions on the subject, and petitioning the Regent or the Parliament. A few members doubted the expediency of this. Mr. Villiers, a warm friend to the abolition, but a zealous supporter of Government, and Wilberforce, who is always afraid of giving offence to Ministers, suggested that the meeting might have the appearance of a measure of opposition; that there was no saying what violent resolutions might not be proposed at it; and that it was very much to be feared that, at the present moment, when the public attention was wholly engrossed with the Emperor of Russia and the King of Prussia, and the processions, and shows, and entertainments which their visit had occasioned, few persons would be found to attend such a meeting, and that an unsuccessful appeal to the public would do much harm instead of good. A great majority of us, however, were for having the meeting called, and Wilberforce and Villiers, together with the rest of us, signed the advertisement calling it together.

17th, *Fri.*   The meeting * took place to-day

* This meeting produced a great effect. The example was followed in most of the great towns in England; and more than 800 petitions

at Freemasons' Hall, and was extremely crowded. The Duke of Gloucester presided. Resolutions were come to, and were supported in some very forcible speeches by Wilberforce, Lord Grey, Whitbread, Lord Lansdowne, and Lord Holland. Petitions to both Houses of Parliament were determined on; and it was recommended to call meetings in different parts of the country. I made a short speech on moving the thanks of the meeting to the chairman, the Duke of Gloucester.

18th, *Sat.* Was the grand dinner given at Guildhall to the Regent, the Emperor, the King of Prussia, &c. I was invited, but did not go. Instead of it, I dined with Alexander Humboldt, the traveller, at Lansdowne House; and the next morning he breakfasted with me. He is here as Great Chamberlain of the King of Prussia, and leaves this country at the same time as the King.

20th, *Mon.* Wilberforce had fixed this day for moving an address to the Regent on the subject of the slave trade. It was extremely desirable that it should come on, because the Emperor and the King of Prussia had signified their intention of going this day to the two Houses of Parliament; and it was very much to be wished that they should be present during the debates. Lord Castlereagh, however, was, or pretended to be, indisposed: and Wilberforce put off his motion for a week. The King of Prussia and his sons first, and afterwards the Emperor of Russia, with his sister the Duchess of Oldenburgh, came into the gallery of the House

---

were, in little more than a month from this time, presented to Parliament against the slave trade, signed by above 750,000 persons.

of Commons, and for some time witnessed what passed. The King of Prussia first went into the Lords, but the Emperor did not arrive till the House of Lords was up.

Lord Erskine told me on Saturday that he should certainly bring on my Bills, which he has taken charge of, on this day. He had not however given any notice of his intention, or required that the Lords should be summoned; and, though he formerly presided in the House as Chancellor for above a year, he was ignorant, till he learned from me with surprise and evident mortification, that a previous notice was, according to constant usage, necessary before he could move the second reading of any Bill.

Lord Erskine.

26th, *Sun.* Prince Radzivil and the Count de Sierakowski dined with me to-day: Prince Adam Czartoryski would have accompanied them, but he had a previous engagement. It was on his account indeed that I invited the others. I got Lord Grey, Whitbread, Lord Ossulston, Bennet, and Brougham to meet them. It was at Brougham's instance that I have made acquaintance with these persons. They justly think it very important that, in the discussions which are soon to engage the public attention, the present situation and future fate of their country, Poland, should not be overlooked; and, in consequence probably of something Brougham has said, they wished to know me.

Poles.

27th, *Mon.* Wilberforce brought on his motion on the slave trade. Before making it, he presented the petition which had been proposed at the meeting at Freemasons' Hall, and which was

Petitions against the slave trade.

signed by above 39,000 inhabitants of London and Westminster : a similar petition was presented to the House of Lords, by the Duke of Gloucester. Clarkson told me that the petition was signed by 25,000 persons in one day, and that, if it could have been delayed three or four days longer, 80,000 signatures would have been put to it. Many other petitions were presented. Wilberforce's motion was not opposed; but Lord Castlereagh took this opportunity to explain, and to attempt to justify, his conduct with respect to this article of the treaty.

In the House of Lords, Lord Grenville moved for the papers respecting this subject, which had passed during the negotiation. The motion was resisted, and negatived upon a division.

28th, *Tu.* Horner, in the House of Commons, made the same motion as Lord Grenville had done yesterday in the Lords. I supported his motion at considerable length, and expressed my strong disapprobation of this article of the treaty in a speech which was remarkably well received by the House.*

Before this debate, Sir John Newport moved an address to the Regent, to grant a commission to inquire into the fees taken in courts of justice, in the United Kingdom. Lord Castlereagh and the rest of the Ministers opposed it. The Attorney-General said, that there was not any ground whatever to suppose that any improper fees were taken in any of the law offices. Master Stephen spoke pretty much to the same effect; and the Attorney-General, amongst other things, insisted,

* I afterwards printed this speech.

that the practice of taking fees for expedition, Illegal fees
which had been mentioned, was one that certainly in courts of justice.
had no existence. I said that I was very sorry that
I could not bear the same testimony to the universal purity of the different law officers that he
had done. That, if compelled to say what I believed (though I was not prepared to prove particular instances at the bar of the House), I must
in my conscience say, that I believed that, at least
in the court which I was best acquainted with,
the practice did exist to a considerable extent.
Stephen expressed the greatest astonishment at
this; but, in consequence of my assertion, voted
for the motion which he had by his speech opposed;
and by his single vote it was carried, the numbers
being 49 to 48. A commission therefore must
issue; and, if the inquiry is properly prosecuted,
no doubt very great abuses will be brought to light.

29th, *Wed.* The treaty came under discussion
in the House of Commons. I had neither opportunity nor much inclination to say anything on
it; but I entreated Ponsonby, who was not much
inclined to speak either, to say a few words, if it
were only for the sake of drawing the public attention to the state of Poland. He did accordingly
express, very shortly, but very forcibly, his anxious
hope that this country would not neglect the interests of that unhappy nation at the approaching
congress.

July 5th, *Tu.* Lord Cochrane, having been Lord Cochrane.
convicted with several others of a conspiracy
fraudulently to raise the price of the public funds,
was expelled the House of Commons by a very

considerable majority. I took no part in the debate, and did not vote. If I had voted, it would have been against him ; but, as I arrived at the House only time enough to hear but a small portion of his speech, I did not think it right to take any part. I do not see any reason to doubt his being guilty, but great reason to doubt his having been impartially tried ; and the sentence upon him has been inordinately severe : a fine of 1000*l.*, a year's imprisonment, and the pillory. The enormity of this punishment has excited an interest in Lord Cochrane's favour, which would never have appeared if his sentence had been at all proportioned to the offence. Many persons have expressed a wish that the punishment of the pillory should be abolished ; and it unquestionably ought to be abolished. There is not, however, the least probability that, if a Bill were brought into Parliament for that purpose, it would pass into a law.

Irish Insurrection Bill.

13th, *Wed.* I opposed, with a very few other persons, the Bill* lately brought into the House by Peel (the Irish Secretary), which is to give extraordinary powers to the magistrates in Ireland, and to enable them, without a jury and without any bill of indictment found against them, to transport as felons persons who, in counties proclaimed as disturbed, shall not be found in their houses after a certain hour, and shall not be able to prove that they were absent on some lawful occasion. There has not been any committee appointed, nor any

* This was a revival of the Bill of 1807, which was repealed in 1810, on the motion of Wellesley Pole (the Secretary for Ireland), a short time before it would have expired, and had never since been revived.

evidence produced of the facts which are stated as the grounds for bringing in this Bill.*

16th, *Sat.* Lord Cochrane was re-elected to represent the city of Westminster. Many persons have persuaded themselves that he is innocent. No other candidate was put up. Sheridan had announced an intention of standing, but withdrew his claims, and told several persons that Lord Cochrane was the only man in the kingdom he would not oppose.

Lord Cochrane.

17th, *Sun.* I called this morning on the Duke of Sussex at his request communicated to me about a week ago. It was respecting the Princess Charlotte of Wales that he wished to speak to me. After his message sent to me, her Royal Highness, having all her attendants dismissed, and being told she was immediately to remove to Carlton House, had run out of her house, and getting into a hackney coach, had driven to her mother's. The Duke of Sussex and Brougham had persuaded her to go to Carlton House. The Duke told me that he had already decided what step it would be proper for him to take ; and that he had accordingly written a letter to Lord Liverpool, remonstrating upon the treatment the Princess had received, desiring to know whether it was by the advice of the Ministers, and requiring that he might have access to the Princess ; and that he was then waiting for an answer to it. He put a few questions to me respecting the time when the Princess would be of age, the Prince her father's power over her, &c. ; and related some curious facts respecting the late

Duke of Sussex and Princess Charlotte of Wales.

* *Vi.* St. 54 Geo. 3. c. 180.

intended marriage of the Princess with the hereditary Prince of Orange; but he asked me no advice.

18th, *Mon.* The Princess was removed this morning to Cranbourne Lodge in Windsor Park.

Freehold Estate Bill. My Bill to subject freehold estates to the simple contract debts of persons who die seised of such estates, was thrown out by the Lords on the third reading without a division. It was opposed by the Chancellor, Lord Ellenborough, and Lord Redesdale, and by the Duke of Norfolk. It was supported by Lord Erskine and Lord Holland.

19th, *Tu.* The Duke of Sussex gave notice, in the House of Lords, of a motion on the subject of the Princess, he having put several questions to the Ministers relating to her, which they declined answering. *

20th, *Wed.* I again opposed the Irish Insurrection Bill.

Corruption of blood. 25th, *Mon.* The House of Lords having returned my two Bills to take away corruption of blood, and to alter the punishment of high treason, with amendments, I this day moved in the Commons that the House should agree to the amendments, which was carried as of course. The alterations in the Corruption of Blood Bill are, to substitute in the place of taking away corruption of blood the taking away all the effects of corruption of blood, except with respect to the attainted person during his life only; and to prevent the Bill operating in cases of accomplices in murder.

---

* He afterwards, by the advice of Lord Grey, abandoned his intended motion.

The Treason Bill has many alterations of form, but the only substantial alteration is, to preserve as part of the sentence, that the body of the criminal after he is dead shall be severed into four quarters.[1] When I moved to agree to the amendments, I stated my strong disapprobation of this amendment. I said that either this punishment was not to be executed, and then it ought not to continue part of the formal sentence, or it was intended that in some cases it should be executed; and, if so, that, in my opinion, such horrible spectacles as that of mangling a body from which the vital spirit had just departed before a crowd of spectators tended only to deprave their minds, and to harden their hearts : that, however, I proposed to agree to the amendments, because, as the Lords had consented that it should no longer be the law that the heart and bowels of a man convicted of treason should be torn out of his body while he was yet alive, I thought that what the Lords had allowed us to pass was worth obtaining.

Punishment of treason.

The Lord Chancellor, in a note he wrote me some days ago, seemed to intimate that he should propose this alteration. He afterwards told me in conversation that it was Lord Ellenborough who meant to propose it. Who did propose it I do not know, for the whole matter passed in the House of Lords without debate, and I believe without any but the law Lords knowing what was done. The Chancellor's doubts and difficulties about this and the other Bill expressed in his note

---

[1] The law so remains in the present day.—ED.

Punish-
ment of
treason.

to me are so curious that I have thought the note worth preserving.*

26th, *Tu.* The Lord Chancellor this morning, in court, wrote a note and sent it down to me from the bench in these words: — " I was surprised to read in my paper what you said last night as to quartering. In my Bill I had left it out, and

* The following is the note alluded to.

" Upon the Treason Bill —

" Is the enactment, that 'the judgment to be awarded against any person or persons convicted or *attainted* of the crime of high treason' quite accurate? (See below. Vide 4 *Black.* 380, 381.) Attainder, he says, commences upon, and not before, judgment pronounced.

" I entertain a doubt whether the sentence should be farther changed than merely taking away the cutting down alive and drawing, without a hurdle. The King can pardon the quartering; and if he does not, the sentence, if the party is hanged till he is dead, is not more severe than in murder.[a]

" Is the last clause necessary? Cannot the King do what it is here enacted he may do, by his prerogative? If so, the clause is improper.

" Attending to the first observation, I wish to know the form of awarding execution upon attainder by Act of Parliament, to which the term *attainted* may apply. I will have Dealtry furnish this from the *Baga de Secretis.*

" In the Bill to take away corruption of blood, will the words used give the benefit of it to aiders, abettors, and counsellors of petit treason or murder — persons convicted as such, and not of the petit treason or murder? The stat. 30 Geo. 3. c. 48. has introduced these by express mention. If the blood is to remain corrupted after convictions and attainders of petit treason and murder, ought it not to be the same as to those convicted of aiding, abetting, and counselling? Is it necessary to consider this as to the High Treason Bill? I incline to think not, after reading Foster, as referred to by Blackstone, who holds, on Foster's authority, that the doctrine that there are no accessories in treason does not hold in the inferior species of high treason. The result of Foster's doctrine, that there may be accessories in treason, seems to be, that the forms of indictment must, in some cases, treat them as such, but yet that they are principal traitors.

" *Q.* Whether the words of the Act of 7th Queen Anne, c. 22. sec. 10., had not better be used in this Bill? Is it necessary or *expedient* to name Scotland?

---

a " By Act 30 Geo. 3. c. 48., *all* the sentence for murder is to be pronounced against women convicted of petit treason; and the Judges, according to Foster, soon after the 25 Geo. 2. c. 37., agreed that the like must take place where men are convicted of petit treason."

I understood that that Bill had been altered only by introducing in the recital accurately the old judgment, and I was not aware that it had been otherwise altered, though I believe upon a question, if put among us, it would have been carried." The alterations alluded to in this note were, it seems, alterations made by Lord Ellenborough.

30th, *Sat.* Parliament was prorogued.[1]

[1] The following letter to M. Dumont, is dated Russell Square, 17th August, 1814. — Ed.

" Dear Dumont,

" We are now drawing near to a close of our Chancery sittings, but, as the Chancellor always loses a great deal of time in the early part of the year, he makes up for it by extraordinary diligence at this season, and he is now sitting every day nine hours without interruption. It is with great difficulty, therefore, that I can find time to write these few lines to you; but this slavery will last for a fortnight longer and I will not remain so long without letting you hear from me.

" London has for a long time been half crazy with emperors, and kings, and shows, and illuminations, and fireworks. It has at last sunk into a dead torpor, which is very stupid to the few fashionable persons who may be still lingering in town, but which is very salutary to the lower and laborious orders of the people. The mischief which has been done to the morals and happiness of the inferior artisans by the long holidays, which they have been indulged with, is hardly to be conceived. I have been assured that several pawnbrokers have declared that, while these festivals lasted, they lent, on the pledges of the clothes, and furniture, and tools of their poor customers about ten times as much as they are accustomed to do in ordinary times. This languid season, however, has been chosen by several poets for sending their choicest works into the world. We have a new poem by Rogers, another by Lord Byron, and a ponderous quarto, in blank verse, from Wordsworth, the laborious inspiration of many years. Bulky as it is, however, it is only the fragment of a larger poem. The title explains what it is,—*"The Excursion, being a Portion of a Poem entitled ' The Recluse.'"* The scenes are in the humblest walks of life; the hero is a Scotch itinerant pedlar. Many of the verses are as prosaic as even Wordsworth ever wrote, and there is no story, and consequently nothing to give the reader any interest in the poem. There are, however, many beautiful lines, and it will certainly be praised with enthusiasm by the worshippers of the Lake-poets.

" I suppose that you see the English newspapers, and have learnt that Canning and his friends have accepted subordinate offices under the present administration. Canning, it is said, obtained these marks of royal favour by persuading the Princess of Wales to go abroad, than which nothing could be more acceptable to the Prince. Ward had agreed to accept a seat at the India Board, and to be a Privy Council-

Aug. 28th, *Sun.* The Lord Chancellor's sittings having ended last night, I set out this day for Tanhurst: Anne met me there the next day.

Speech on the slave trade published.

As soon as I had a little recovered myself from the fatigues of the many hours' attendance every day in court, which I have been obliged to give for the last month, I put down in writing the speech I had made in the House of Commons on the 28th of June on the slave trade, as well as I could recollect it, and printed and published it.

Sept. 21st, *Wed.* I set out for Durham with Anne and Sophy.

Resignation of the Chancellorship of Durham.

Oct. 5th. Returned to Tanhurst. While I was at Auckland, I mentioned to the Bishop of Durham, as I had done, indeed, a few months before in town, my wish to resign the Chancellorship. My necessary attendance at Durham breaks very inconveniently into my vacations, which I always find too short. I should not, indeed, much mind this, if I could do any good in the office; but there is scarcely any business in the court, and

---

lor, but he afterwards repented; and, perhaps through fear of the ridicule of his friends or his enemies, rejected these contemptible honours. The public attention here was for a long time engrossed with Lord Cochrane. The punishment of the pillory, so grossly disproportioned to his offence, shocked every body, and induced thousands to take a lively interest for him, who, but for that severe sentence, would never have troubled themselves respecting him. A great many Members voted against his expulsion from the House of Commons : since he was expelled, he has been re-elected by the city of Westminster, and Government has found itself obliged to remit the punishment, and Lord Cochrane is now no more thought of : a stronger instance can hardly be found of the mischief done by punishments, which are repugnant to public feeling and opinion.

" Lady R. is at Rottingdean, with Sophy and Charles. At the end of a fortnight I hope to meet her at Tanhurst. How happy it would make us if you and William could be with us!

" Sincerely and affectionately yours,

" SAML. ROMILLY."

there never can be, unless an act is passed to enable the Chancellor to enforce the process of the Court out of the County Palatine. Either this should be done, or the jurisdiction of the Court should be entirely taken away. I settled with the Bishop to resign the office in November, when he will be in town for the meeting of Parliament.

19th. An event has just happened which proves how inefficient the Court is. An infant ward of the Court, a girl of the name of Ann Wade, who has a property of about 4000*l.* a year, has been seduced, by a young adventurer of the name of Bazely, from her guardians whom she had accompanied to Weymouth, and is kept somewhere concealed by him (it is supposed in Kent), till banns can be published, and they can be married. The Court can take no effectual step to prevent this, because its orders cannot be executed out of Durham.

31st, *Mon.* I returned to town from Tanhurst, where I have spent the whole of the vacation with Anne and my children, except William, who is at Geneva, and Edward and Henry, who, during part of the time, have been at school.

Whishaw and Sharp each paid us a visit of two or three days during the vacation.

Nov. 1st, *Tu.* The Lord Chancellor held the first seal before term.

8th, *Tu.* Parliament met.

10th, *Th.* I resigned the office of Chancellor of Durham.

28th, *Mon.* I made a motion in the House of Commons that the House should resolve, that, Militia kept embodied con-

trary to the this country having been for more than five months
Act 42
Geo. III. at peace with all the powers of Europe, and in a
state of undisturbed internal tranquillity, the still
continuing a part of the militia embodied was contrary to the spirit and plain intent of the Act of
42 Geo. III. c. 90., and a manifest violation of the
Constitution.   The motion was rejected. [1]

Dec. 1st, *Th.*   Both Houses of Parliament adjourned ; — the House of Commons to the 9th of
February next.

On this 1st of December I was taken very ill. I
had a fever and an inflammation of the lungs, which
obliged me to keep my bed for ten days, and I was
unable to attend in court during any part of the
sittings.

24th, *Sat.*   I was sufficiently recovered to go
out of town to Tanhurst, where I remained till
January 11.

---

[1] By a majority of 65 :—for the motion 97, against it 32. — ED.

1815.

Jan. 11th, *Wed.* I returned to town nearly as
well as ever. A great quantity of blood was taken
from me during my illness, and I was reduced very
much ; but in the country I regained my strength.
My nephew Roget alone attended me at the beginning of my illness ; but afterwards, at his request,
Dr. Baillie was called in. He confirmed every
thing Roget had ordered to be done ; and now in
my own case, as before in the cases of several of
my children and of my servants, I had very strong
proof of Roget's great skill and ability in his profession.*

---

* During a part of my illness, my life was in some danger; and I
was fully sensible of it. I had, however, little to settle ; for, knowing how fatal would be the consequences of my dying intestate, by
which my estates would descend to my dear William, and the rest of
my children would be left very scantily provided for, I have never,
since I have purchased land, been a day without a will. There were a
few legacies which I wished to add ; and I therefore made a short codicil, which my dear Anne wrote upon my dictation. Nothing could
exceed her affectionate care and trembling anxiety for me during the
whole of my illness. While I was confined to my bed, she scarcely
quitted me day or night. In a short but most affecting conversation
which I had with her on the danger I was in, she assured me that a
sense of duty towards our dear children would, she was certain, enable
her to bear up against the calamity of losing me. This is the first
alarming illness that I have ever experienced. If it had ended in death,
perhaps, as far as concerns myself, it had been fortunate. My life had
then been one of unchequered prosperity, cheered and animated through
the whole of it by the exertion of such faculties as I have possessed,
in the pursuit of, I hope, no unworthy objects. I had then, at a mature age, but before my mind had suffered from decay, left behind me
a numerous family of children, whom I could hardly, as to any of them,
have wished, at their ages, to have seen other than they are. Healthy,
intelligent, well-disposed, and seeming to be possessed of every quali-

Feb. 9th, *Th.* Both Houses of Parliament met, this being the day to which they were adjourned.

Bill to
subject
freehold
estates of
deceased
debtors to
the pay-
ment of
their simple
contract
debts.

14th, *Tu.* I moved for and obtained leave to bring a Bill into the House of Commons to subject the freehold estates of persons who die indebted to the payment of their simple contract debts; and I immediately brought in the Bill, which was read the first time.

15th, *Wed.* A motion of Lord Fitzwilliam's in the House of Lords, on the illegality of still keeping a part of the militia embodied.

My Bill to make freehold estates liable for the payment of the simple contract debts of those who die indebted has passed the House of Commons without the slightest opposition from any one.

Militia.

28th, *Tu.* The power which the Ministers have exercised of keeping a part of the militia still embodied, notwithstanding that all the causes which can by law justify the calling them out and keeping them embodied have long ceased, appearing to me to be extremely dangerous and unconstitutional, I brought the subject again under the notice of the House of Commons, and moved this day a resolution in these words: "That nine months having now elapsed since the late definitive treaty of peace with France was signed, and this country having during the whole of that period been at peace, not

---

fication for passing through life happily for themselves and usefully for others. After witnessing the dreadful revolutions and wars which have desolated the earth during the period of my existence, I should have closed my mortal career just as peace was established throughout the civilized world; and as a new era of happiness to mankind seemed to be commencing. God grant that my life may not have been prolonged to see these enlivening prospects clouded and destroyed!

with France only but with every power in Europe,
and no cause whatever having existed or now
existing for apprehending invasion by a foreign
enemy, or any insurrection or rebellion within the
realm, it is contrary to the spirit and true intent
and meaning of the Act of 42 Geo. III. c. 90. to
continue any part of the militia force of this country still embodied." Many circumstances induced
me thus to bring this question a second time before
the House. 1st, The great constitutional importance of the question : 2dly, The opinions which
the Secretary of State had procured from the Attorney and Solicitor General in justification of the
legality of their conduct, and had circulated through
all the militia regiments ; and which opinions I had
not seen at the time of my former motion : and,
3dly, The dangerous doctrines which had been advanced on this subject by the Lord Chancellor
and Lord Ellenborough, in the House of Lords,
on the late motion of Lord Fitzwilliam. Those
two Lords had defended the present conduct of the
Ministers by the example of what had passed in
the year 1792, when, as they alleged, the militia
had been called out under the pretence of an insurrection, which, in fact, never existed ; and this
example, thus represented by them, they highly
applauded. On this question of the militia it
should seem that one of these two opinions must
be maintained : either the Crown is bound to
disband the militia as soon as it is clear, beyond
all dispute, that the causes which alone will, under
the Act of Parliament, justify the calling them out
have entirely ceased ; which is the proposition I

contended for; or, being once called out, the Crown may, without limit, continue them embodied as long as it shall be its pleasure to do so; an opinion which the Ministers and their friends had not, however, the boldness in direct terms to avow. My motion was, of course, rejected. [1]

Corn Bill. *March* 3d, *Fri.* A Bill to prohibit the importation of foreign corn for home consumption, when the price of wheat shall be below eighty shillings per quarter, was read a second time in the House of Commons. Thinking it an extremely injudicious and impolitic measure, I voted against it in a small minority. [2]

5th, *Sun.* I called this morning on Lord Grenville, to endeavour to prevail on him to take the charge, in the House of Lords, of my Bill for subjecting freehold estates to the payment of simple contract debts: for if it continues this year, as it was the last, in the hands of Lord Erskine, who does not understand the subject, and is incapable of answering any objections that are made to it, there is no chance of its being carried. Lord Grenville told me that he was at present so occupied with the Corn Laws, that he could attend to nothing else; but he promised me, that after Easter he would apply himself to the subject, and endeavour to make himself master of it.

---

[1] By a majority of 103:—for the motion 76, against it 179.— Ed.

[2] Of 44 against 215. On the 6th of March and following days, many very numerously signed petitions were presented to the House against this Bill. Amongst others, there were petitions from Manchester, signed by 54,000 persons; from Westminster, by 42,000; from Liverpool, by 48,000; from the bankers and traders of London, by 40,000; and from Leeds, by 24,000 persons. The views of the petitioners were supported by the late Sir Robert Peel, Mr. (now Sir George) Philips, Mr. A. Baring (now Lord Ashburton), and several other Members. — Ed.

6th, *Mon.* Great outrages have been committed Riots in London. against the Members of both Houses of Parliament who are supposed to be friends to the Corn Bill. The populace broke into the houses of the Lord Chancellor* and of Mr Robinson, and destroyed part of their furniture. Other houses, too, were attacked, such as Lord Darnley's, Lord Ellenborough's, and others.

7th, *Tu.* The same outrages and riots in different parts of the town, and a few persons killed or wounded by the soldiery.

8th, *Wed.* The riots continue, but to a less extent.

To-day, on bringing up the Report of the Military punishments. Mutiny Bill, I moved to add a clause to it in these words : — "And be it further enacted, &c., that it shall not be lawful for any Court-martial, by its sentence, to inflict on any offender a greater number of lashes than one hundred." It was very late at night, or rather early on Thursday morning, and after a long debate on the Corn Bill, that this business of the Mutiny Bill came on. It was the only opportunity, however, that I had of moving my clause; and, as I had long determined, on the first Mutiny Bill which should be passed after the restoration of peace, when the supposed danger of interfering with the discipline of the army would have ceased, to endeavour to diminish the excessive severity of military punishments, I would not suffer

* The Lord Chancellor was greatly affected by this attack made upon his house, and discontinued his sittings both in the House of Lords on causes, and in the Court of Chancery (in one or other of which courts he ought to have sat every day), till Monday, March 13., when he sat in the House of Lords, as usual, on appeals.

the Bill to pass without making this attempt.   Mr.
Manners Sutton, the Judge-Advocate, said, that
he wished to have time to consider the proposition,
and to consult military men upon it ; and, as the
Bill was to continue only for four months, he requested me to withdraw my motion for the present,
and to propose it again on the next Mutiny Bill.
He said that the Commander-in-Chief was extremely anxious to lessen the severity of corporal
punishments, and if possible, to abolish them entirely ; and that, of late, and principally through
his means, they had been very rarely inflicted.   I
consented to withdraw my motion.

Clerks of assize and clerks of the peace to make returns of criminals.

At my instance, Mr. Hiley Addington (the under
Secretary of State) has brought a Bill into Parliament to compel clerks of assize and clerks of
the peace regularly to make returns to the Secretary of State, in order that they may be laid before
Parliament, of all criminals tried at the assizes and
quarter sessions, and of their crimes and sentences.
Being brought in by Government, the Bill has
passed the House of Commons, without any objection being made to it.*

Landing of Bonaparte in France.

10th, *Fri.*   As I was coming out of the Court of
Chancery to-day, I was told that intelligence had just
arrived that Bonaparte had landed in the south of
France, on the 1st or 2d of this month †, at the head
of about 1000 men, and was marching towards
Grenoble.   I gave no credit to the information, but
I find that it is but too true.   It is in every body's

* It afterwards passed into an Act, stat. 55 Geo. 3. c. 49.
† He landed on the 1st.

mouth, and has filled every one with consternation. The name of Bonaparte is one

"—— at which the world turns pale."

From all the accounts we have long heard, there can be no doubt that there is great attachment to him in the army, and great indifference for the Bourbons in every part of France; though in many parts of it an earnest desire to remain at peace, whoever may be their sovereign. The defection of the first troops that are called upon to act against Bonaparte will probably be a signal for the revolt of the whole military force of the kingdom.

12th, *Sun.* The news of to-day is, that Massena has declared against Bonaparte; and great hopes are entertained of his being crushed.

22d, *Wed.* After twelve days of most painful and increasing anxiety, though with fallacious hopes now and then held out that the great body of the French nation would remain faithful to the King, and that great military preparations were making to surround and overpower the troops which accompanied Bonaparte, we received this evening, and while I was in the House of Commons, the certain intelligence that the soldiers had every where refused to act against him; that the King, finding resistance impossible, had withdrawn himself from Paris; and that Bonaparte must before this time have entered that city *, without a single shot having been fired from the first moment of his landing in France. So sudden, complete, and bloodless a revolution more resembles

Louis XVIII. quits Paris.

* He entered it on the 20th at night.

fiction than history. Napoleon seems, as it were at his pleasure, and just at his own season, quietly to have resumed his empire. But what a dreadful prospect is thus suddenly opened to mankind! What dismay must not these tidings strike into the hearts of hundreds of thousands of human beings in every station of life, from the throne to the cottage! What a deluge of blood must be shed! How various and how terrible the calamities which are now impending over states and over individuals!

24th, *Fri.* Set out for Tanhurst, to pass the Easter holidays, and stayed there till Monday, April 3d. We had all our children with us but William. My sister and her daughter and Dumont were also of our party. The state of public affairs, Dumont's alarms as to the future fate of Geneva, and some anxiety which we felt for William, who is still there, threw much gloom over our society.

April 3d, *Mon.* Returned to town.

Difference between Lord Grey and Lord Grenville. 4th, *Tu.* A very unfortunate difference of opinion subsists between Lord Grenville and Lord Grey, on the course which it is the policy of this country to pursue in the present state of things. Lord Grenville thinks immediate war almost indispensable, while Lord Grey is for preserving peace as long as it is possible. Several letters have passed between them; and it seems probable that it will not be long before this difference of opinion will appear by open declaration in Parliament.

Bonaparte has commenced his new reign by extraordinary moderation, and a professed desire to maintain peace. He has declared, in a public paper, that he has renounced the idea of the grand empire, of which for fifteen years he had only been forming the basis ; and that from henceforth the happiness and the consolidation of the French empire would occupy all his thoughts.　He pretends to be about to give a free constitution to France ; he has declared that there shall be no restraint on the liberty of the press ; and he has abolished the slave trade.　These, it is said, are all insincere professions : probably they are ; but that he should make such professions, is not among the least wonderful of the extraordinary events which are passing in the world.

6th, *Th.*　The Prince Regent's message to both Houses of Parliament.　It is to be taken into consideration to-morrow.　I attended at night a meeting of the Opposition at Mr. Ponsonby's. Mr. Ponsonby stated his intention of concurring in the address to be moved on the message ; as it will not pledge the House to war, but merely to increase our armaments, and to preserve a concert with the Allies.　It was observed by Tierney that, although he should not propose an amendment, yet, if an amendment were moved, as possibly it might be, merely recommending the maintaining peace, he should find himself bound to support it. Ponsonby said that, if such an amendment were proposed, he thought that it ought to be rejected. Mackintosh maintained the same opinion ; and on this subject a great difference of opinion prevailed. For myself, I declared that, if such an amendment were proposed, I should think it necessary to vote for it.　The truth is, that Whitbread, who did not attend the meeting, means to propose such an amendment. The meeting broke up without coming to any determination.

7th, *Fri.* The address proposed. Whitbread moved his amendment, which was opposed by Ponsonby. I voted for it, and to my surprise thirty-eight other persons voted for it. I expected to have been in a minority of 16 or 17 only.[1]

9th, *Sun.* I called at Lord Grey's, and he showed me the correspondence which has taken place between himself and Lord Grenville. Lord Grey's are admirable letters, written with great moderation and good sense, and stating reasons for not hastily plunging into war, which certainly are not answered by Lord Grenville, and which appear to me to be quite unanswerable.

Scotch Jury Bill.

12th, *Wed.* Upon the House of Commons going into a committee on the Bill for extending the trial by jury in civil cases to Scotland[2], I spoke at some length in favour of the Bill. I knew that there was not to be any opposition to it, farther than to the clause which required juries to give unanimous verdicts; but, as the Bill has gone through its former stages without any mention of the benefits which the measure is calculated to confer on Scotland, I thought it right to observe upon them, and to contrast the expeditious, cheap, and satisfactory mode of a trial by those who themselves hear the oral testimony of the witnesses, with the present most expensive, dilatory, and imperfect mode of trying facts on written deposi-

---

1 The number against the amendment was 220. — ED.
2 55 Geo. 3. c. 42. — ED.

tions. I took occasion to observe that all these evils, which the present measure is to relieve Scotland from, exist even to a still greater extent in our English Ecclesiastical Courts; and that the remedy provided by this Bill, of sending all questions of fact to be tried in issues by juries, is just as applicable, and may indeed be applied with much greater facility to our Ecclesiastical Courts than to the Courts of Scotland. I observed, too, that the Bill suggests what would be a very great improvement in our Courts of Equity; namely, to enable the Courts to direct issues, as soon as it appears to them that there is a question of fact, on which the cause depends, in dispute between the parties, instead of waiting, as is now the practice, till the hearing of the cause, and, consequently, till the expense has been incurred of taking the written depositions of the witnesses, and then sending an issue to be tried by a jury, which might just as well be tried at a much earlier stage of the cause, and with a saving of all that expense. Many petitions had been presented from different parts of Scotland, objecting to that clause in the Bill which required unanimity in verdicts; and stating the repugnance of the petitioners to take the oath prescribed to jurors, which is, that they will decide according to the evidence, when the law afterwards compels some of them to decide according to the opinions of others. I took notice of these petitions, and observed that I could not but respect the scruples of those who had presented them: that, however long, usage may have reconciled us to this oath, and may induce us to understand it in

Ecclesiastical Courts.

Issues in Courts of Equity.

a sense different from that which the plain words of it import, it was not to be wondered that it appeared very highly objectionable to those on whom it was now for the first time to be imposed; for, although unanimous verdicts are at present required in Exchequer causes, they were not numerous, and were confined to Edinburgh : that respect for oaths cannot be too much encouraged; and that even unfounded scruples, though I could not consider these as such, should be listened to with indulgence and favour.   In the committee, a clause was added to the Bill, that if the jury, after having been enclosed for twelve hours, should not agree in their verdict, the Judge might discharge them, and cause a fresh jury to be summoned.   I had suggested that the juror's oath might be altered, and that he might merely swear conscientiously to discharge his duty as a juryman, instead of swearing that he would give a true verdict according to the evidence; or that a majority of the jury, as in criminal cases in Scotland, should give the verdict.   But the expedient of discharging the jury, if they did not agree, had been settled by the Chancellor and Adam, (who has been newly made a Baron of the Exchequer, and who is to be at the head of the Jury Court,) and was preferred.

Bigamy.   17th, *Mon.*   I moved in the House of Commons for a copy of the report of the Recorder of London to the Regent, of the case of Robert Lathrop Murray, tried in January last at the Old Bailey for bigamy.   I had before presented a petition from this man to the House, which had been received and ordered to lie on the table.   The offence had been committed under circumstances which made it, as appeared to me, one of no aggravation. The first marriage had taken place when the offender was very young, and with such irregularity as might well have raised doubt in his mind as to its legality. The second wife was fully apprized of the first marriage, before the second was solemnized. The offence had been committed thirteen years before the prosecution ; and the prosecutor was unconnected with the family of either of the wives, and was a total stranger, who, through revenge for some private wrong the prisoner had done him, instituted the prosecution. The prisoner, however, was a man of bad private character, and for that reason, (for no other could be suggested, though it was denied that his bad character was taken into consideration,) the Recorder sentenced him to seven years' transportation ; and his application to the Regent for mercy was rejected. I thought that so improper an exercise of the very large discretion which Judges possess with respect to the punishment of this offence was a fit subject of animadversion in Parliament. I stated that the great distinction to be taken in this offence, as to its enormity, was, whether the second wife was informed, or was kept in ignorance, at the time of her marriage, that the man who proposed himself to her had already a wife living : that the cases where she was kept in such ignorance could alone be considered as cases of great aggravation * : and I showed, from the returns made to the House

* See, in the third edition of my *Observations on Criminal Law*, the note relating to Bigamy.

of Commons, that, in eight years, from 1805 to
1812 inclusive, there had been convicted of bigamy
at the Old Bailey, and on the different English
circuits, 104 persons, who had been sentenced to
the following punishments : — 23 to be transported
for seven years, 13 to be imprisoned for two years,
29 to be imprisoned for one year, 35 to be imprisoned for six months, and 4 to be only fined.   It
was manifest, therefore, that in this man's case an
unusual degree of severity had been exercised,
which nothing in the circumstances of his case
called for or could justify.   The Attorney-General
and Hiley Addington opposed the motion ; and, of
course, it was lost.   The Attorney-General, though
he endeavoured in his way to aggravate the offence,
could state nothing material, but that the second
marriage was by licence obtained by the prisoner,
and consequently that he had falsely sworn that he
was a single man to obtain it.   He talked a great
deal about the inconvenience of the House of
Commons listening to complaints with respect to
the administration of justice, and extolled all the
Judges, and particularly the Recorder.

Punish-
ment of the
pillory.

21st, *Fri.*   On the second reading of a Bill
brought into Parliament by Michael Angelo Taylor to abolish the punishment of the pillory, no
person rose to give any opposition to it, as no one
had opposed the bringing it in.   It would have
passed in total silence ; but I thought it right to
mark the unanimity with which the Bill was received ; as I suppose that, though it may be allowed
to pass the Commons, it will probably be thrown
out by the Lords.[1]   I therefore said that the Bill

[1] See 5th July, 1815. — ED.

had my entire approbation, as it appeared to have that of every other Member of the House.

28th, *Fri.* Whitbread moved, in the House of Commons, that an address should be presented to the Regent, praying that his Royal Highness would not involve the country in war on the ground of the Government of France being in the hands of any particular individual, or to that effect; for I do not recollect the precise words of the motion. I voted for the motion, in a minority of 72 against 273. I had some thought of speaking, but every thing that had occurred to me was much better said by others than it could have been by me, and I contented myself with giving a silent vote.

Whitbread's motion against war.

The principal arguments of those who opposed the motion, and were for making war, were, — That experience had proved that there could be no security for this country as long as Bonaparte was at the head of the French Government: that his ambition was insatiable, and the destruction of this country the object nearest his heart : that no reliance could be placed on his present professions : that to conclude a peace with him was only to enable him at his leisure to make preparations to overwhelm us : that, as long as he was the ruler of France, it must be a military nation, and its relations with this country must be those of actual or suspended war, of open hostility or an armed truce : that an armed peace was a state little less mischievous to England than open war : that the expense of it would be most burdensome, if not ruinous to the country ; and that such a great military peace establishment, as must be kept on foot, was wholly

Arguments for war.

inconsistent with the spirit of our Constitution, and would justly excite alarms for the liberties of the nation : that, at the present moment, the Allies were all united, and were prepared for very great exertions in the common cause ; but what they might be at some future period, when, having for the present suffered ourselves to be deceived into an anxious security, we should at last awake unrefreshed from our haunted and disturbed repose to a sense of our real danger ; what views might have opened to their ambition in the interval, what jealousies might have arisen, what successful seductions might have been practised, what a state of incapacity to engage in immediate war any of the Allies might have fallen into, the most sagacious could not foresee : that, in these circumstances, our greatest safety seemed to be in war, and was unquestionably in co-operating with our Allies, whatever might be their determination.

Arguments
for peace.

To this it was answered, That it would readily be admitted that Bonaparte was not sincere in his professions of moderation : that if he had the power he would at present grasp at the same objects of unbounded ambition as he had done formerly ; but that in reality he was now deprived of all power : that he now, for the first time, felt the necessity of cultivating the favour of those who were friendly to the establishment of a free government : that without their concurrence, he could not raise such an army as would set him above the control of every domestic party, and make him an object of jealousy to foreign states : that the hostility of the Allies was what could alone relieve him from

these difficulties, and set him free from all restraint : that the threat of a hostile invasion, and
the preparations carrying on to execute it, would
make indispensable great levies of troops in France,
and must necessarily invest with the command
Bonaparte, as the military chief, in whose talents
the nation could best confide ; and that when once
he was placed at the head of a great military force
which he could lead to victory and conquest, he
would scorn all domestic parties : that the most
extraordinary expedient that ever was thought of
for preventing the French from becoming a military
nation, was to force them reluctantly into a war :
that in determining on the expediency of war, we
must consider our means and our resources ; and
that with the present exhausted state of our resources, the most sanguine could hardly hope that
we should be able to supply the expenditure necessary for carrying it on for a period of more than
two years : that if peace would afford France time
to recruit her strength, and put herself in a formidable state of military preparation, it should be
recollected that it would afford the same advantage to the Allies, who seemed to stand in still
greater need of it : that if the union of the Allies
was not to be depended on in time of peace, how
much less could any reliance be placed on it during
the various occurrences of war, which were continually opening new situations to work upon their
hopes or their fears, and to seduce them from their
alliance ?

May 9th, *Tu.* I stated in the House of Commons
my reasons for objecting to a Bill which Sergeant

Sergeant
Best's
Insolvent

Best has brought in to alter Lord Redesdale's Insolvent Debtors' Act. The objects of the Sergeant's Bill are two : — 1st, To compel debtors,
after they have been imprisoned a certain time in
execution, to deliver in, upon oath, an account of
all their property, and of all the debts they owe,
and to compel an assignment of all their property
for the benefit of their creditors, and to punish a
refusal to give in such an account, or the giving a
false account, with transportation for seven years
as a felony; and, 2dly, To extend the term of imprisonment of those who take the benefit of the
Act beyond three months (the period at which
they are now entitled to the benefit of it) to longer
periods, proportioned to the amount of the dividends their estate may pay. With respect to the
first of these objects, although I highly approved
of the compelling the application of a debtor's property against his will to the payment of his debts,
yet I greatly disapproved of the modes by which
this was to be accomplished. To begin by impri-
soning a man for three months; then to oblige him
to account upon oath for all his property; to hold
out to him temptations to commit perjury, and, if
he refuse to expose himself to such temptation, to
punish him with the same severity as thieves and
highway robbers, according to the mode in which
the criminal law is usually administered, are now
exposed to, appeared to me to be unjustifiable. I
thought it too as impolitic as it was unjustifiable.
The excessive severity of the law would prevent
the execution of it, as was already the case with
the Bankrupt Laws and with the Lords' Act, in

which there was a provision exactly to the same
effect as the one now proposed, but which had not
(except in some very rare instances) been carried
into execution. As to the second object of the
Bill, I could not understand on what principle the
length of a debtor's imprisonment was to be proportioned — not to his good or bad conduct, but
to his inability to pay his debts; so that the severity of his punishment should increase according
to the extent of his misfortunes. I took this opportunity of stating these objections; but at the
instance of Sergeant Best, the further consideration
of the Bill was postponed.*

13th, *Sat.* Went out of town with Anne and
my children, to pass the Whitsun holidays with
Mr. Nash, at Cumberland Lodge in Windsor Park.

18th, *Th.* Returned to town.

22d, *Mon.* I objected in the House of Commons to the new very heavy stamp duties proposed
to be laid on law proceedings in Scotland.

Taxes on law proceedings.

25th, *Th.* The Prince's message communicating
to the House of Commons the treaties he has
entered into with Russia, Austria, and Prussia, at
Vienna, on the 25th of March last, was taken into
consideration by the House to-day, and an address
voted approving of the treaties. Lord George
Cavendish moved an amendment, expressing disapprobation of the stipulation in the treaties, by
which the parties " engage not to lay down their
arms until Bonaparte shall have been rendered un-

Treaty with Austria, Russia, and Prussia against Bonaparte.

---

* The Bill was afterwards postponed from time to time; but was
never read a second time; and on the 7th June, Sergeant Best stated
that he should proceed no farther with it, but bring in another Bill in
the next Session.

able to create disturbance, and to renew his attempts for possessing himself of the supreme power in France." The amendment was rejected by a majority of 331 against 92. After Lord Castlereagh had opened the subject and moved the address, the whole debate was carried on by members of the Opposition ; Grattan, Plunket, Lord Milton, and Charles Williams Wynn having supported the address, and declared their entire approbation of the war. That Grattan and Plunket should state their reasons for differing from the great majority of those with whom they have concurred in opinion on all public matters for many years back cannot surprise one ; but that they should take extraordinary pains, and exert all their eloquence, to show how much their former friends are, in their opinion, in the wrong, is not very easy to be accounted for. In the House of Lords, two days ago, on the same question, Lord Grenville supported the Ministers. Erskine, who has lately accepted a green riband from the Regent, voted with the Ministers, but did not speak. One might have expected, however, that he would have explained how it happened that his opinions now were so different from those which he entertained during the last war, and which he published in a pamphlet that had great celebrity. This pamphlet I remember his carrying with him to Paris after the peace of Amiens, and giving to a number of persons there, telling every one of them that there had been still later editions than that which he gave them, and which was the twenty-sixth [1], or some other

Grattan and Plunket.

Lord Erskine.

---

[1] It appears from notes made by Sir S. Romilly at the time, that it

great number, for I do not recollect exactly which it was.

26th, *Fri*. On the question of subsidizing the Allies, I voted against it, and in a minority of only seventeen.[1] Most of the Opposition (I know not why) would not give themselves the trouble of attending.

The subsidies to the Allies.

A Bill has been brought into the House to enable the Crown to call out the militia. It has been brought in as a matter about which so little consideration was necessary, that the Bill was not even ordered to be printed, till I moved the printing of it. The Bill, as brought in, enacts, that it shall be lawful for His Majesty, under the present circumstances, at any time after the passing of the Act, and before a day to be named, to draw out and embody the whole or any part of the militia. If passed in this form, the Act must have left it entirely at the discretion of the Crown to keep the militia embodied as long as it should think proper ; for who could say when the present circumstances had so far altered that it could be affirmed that the occasion of calling out the militia had ceased ? I proposed therefore in the committee to insert, instead of the words " under the present circumstances," the following words : " in the present situation of the country, there being the prospect of an immediate war with France," and Lord Castlereagh adopted these words; so that they now stand in the Bill.

Bill to enable the King to embody the militia.

---

was the thirty-third edition, and that Lord Erskine stated that five editions had been published since. — ED.

[1] The number in favour of the motion was 160. — ED.

30th, *Tu.* Sir Henry Parnell moved for the appointment of a committee to take into consideration the claims of the Catholics of Ireland. The same question, moved two years ago by Mr. Grattan, was carried, but it was now lost; the numbers being, — against it 228, for it 147. This is to be accounted for in a great degree by the rash and intemperate conduct of the Catholic Board. I did not speak; but I voted for going into the committee. It appeared to me that the indiscreet manner in which a few individuals, who were desirous of distinguishing themselves, without regard to the interests of the great body of the Catholics, had insisted upon the claims of that large and deserving description of persons, could not alter the nature of these claims; and that it was both just and highly expedient that they should be allowed: that the securities for the Protestant Establishment which had formerly been talked of, and of which nothing was now said, either in the petition of the Catholics, or in the resolutions which Sir Henry Parnell stated that it was his intention to propose to the Committee, were by no means essential to the granting the Catholics' demands. The supposed dangers appeared to me to be chimerical: if they really existed, no guards that I have ever heard talked of would be an effectual security against them; and to me it seems that the best security is to be found in the common interest which the Catholics, when admitted to the enjoyment of the same rights as ourselves, would have in the prosperity of the country. To admit the Catholics to a participation in these advantages has always appeared to me wise and politic; and, in my opinion, it is most peculiarly so at the present moment, when we are just on the point of engaging in a war, the consequences and the duration of which the most sagacious cannot foresee. When we are entering upon a contest which will probably have the effect of uniting all parties against us in France, it is most important that we should take care not to perpetuate the causes of disunion and dissension amongst ourselves. The now granting freely to the Catholics what they demand, would render that part of the empire a source of strength and power to us, when we shall stand most in need of all our resources; instead of being, what, as long as the present exclusion and disqualification of so large a part of the population continues, it must ever be a cause of weakness, of anxiety, and of alarm. If the war continues long, all that is now demanded by the Catholics will infallibly be granted to them; but it will be granted, not as an act of justice and of kindness, but as a measure of necessity, and when it will be too late to derive from the concession those very beneficial consequences which now would flow from it.

June 2d, *Fri.* Mr. Gordon moved to-day for a committee to inquire into the conduct of General Ainslie, in Grenada and Dominica, while he was acting as governor of these islands, and I very strenuously supported the motion. Mr. Goulburn, the Under Secretary of State for the Colonial Department, undertook that an inquiry should be instituted by Government into the General's con-

Conduct of Governor Ainslie at Grenada and Dominica.

duct; and that he should not be sent out again to the West Indies till the result of that inquiry should be known, and he should have satisfactorily answered the charges against him; and on this undertaking, Mr. Gordon withdrew his motion. The principal charges against General Ainslie were, that, while acting as Governor of Grenada, he had published a proclamation, commanding all the free men of colour in the island to come in and take the oaths of allegiance before him within a week, under pain of being immediately carried out of the island: that a short time afterwards, he had gone attended by three soldiers into a private house, and had by force taken away a free man of colour of the name of Michel, and carried him to the market-place, and there by his sole authority had him publicly flogged, and then imprisoned and kept on bread and water for three days; although the man had actually taken the oaths in his own presence; and that, while Governor of Dominica, he published a proclamation, declaring " that the utmost rigour of military execution shall be put in force against all those runaway slaves that might be apprehended after three weeks from the date of the proclamation — neither age nor sex spared, all indiscriminately shall be put to the bayonet." To those who came in during the three weeks a pardon was offered. It did not appear that the island was in any such state as could justify the publishing such a proclamation, even if it were merely meant as a threat. Among the papers produced by General Ainslie in his defence, is one purporting to be a return of

Maroons executed, killed in the woods, and pardoned by him, Governor Ainslie. It is in these words: —" Hanged, 9 ; otherwise punished by banishment, working in chains for a short time, &c., 42 ; killed in action with the rangers, whose heads were afterwards stuck on poles for the sake of example, 12 ; restored to their owners, many of whom had been from ten to thirty-five years in the woods, 530 : since the above, there have been restored to their masters 85." It appears from this return, that 615 persons of colour, taken in the woods, have been delivered up to particular individuals as their own property, although some of them had been for thirty-five years in the enjoyment of their liberty. How it was proved that individuals so long *de facto* free were legally slaves did not appear. By the law, indeed, of this as of all the other West India islands, every man of colour is presumed to be a slave, and the burden lies on him of proving that he is free; and by another law, no man of colour can be heard to give evidence in a civil suit. With the assistance of these laws, to be sure, there could be no difficulty in establishing the fact of slavery ; for what man of colour would be able to find white persons living who could prove such facts as must have passed more than thirty years before, and as would tend to show that his condition then was that of a free man ? Still however it would remain to be proved, who these owners were to whom the different individuals were delivered up as being their property. For myself, I very much suspect that this expedition against the wild negroes, who have existed, I

believe, in the mountains ever since the island became part of the British possessions (which was at
the peace of 1763) was merely a pretext for extirpating (what certainly is a great inconvenience)
the haunts of these people, to which all runaway
negroes may resort as to an asylum ; and for getting a supply of fresh negroes for the plantations of
individuals, which cannot, since the abolition of
the slave trade, be procured by any regular means.
I think of moving for some further accounts on
this subject.

Proposed
registry of
slaves in
the colo-
nies.

3d, *Sat.* I attended this morning at the Duke
of Gloucester's, at a meeting of the Committee of
the African Institution, for the purpose of considering the expediency of attempting to pass a law
to compel the registry of all slaves in the colonies.   This measure has been long in the contemplation of the society; and they have lately published, as a report of their committee on that
subject, a very good pamphlet written by Stephen.
They have been prevented, however, taking any
step towards accomplishing the object, because
they have always supposed, and been given to understand from Ministers, that they would bring
forward such a measure themselves.   At last
Ministers have declared that they do not approve
of it, and will not support it.*   Still Wilberforce,
who is unwilling ever to act against the wishes of
Government, has doubted whether it will not be

* Stephen resigned his seat in Parliament in consequence of this
declaration.   He thought he could not conscientiously support the
measures of the Ministers, if they would not give their support to an
Act which he thought so important.   This conduct is certainly highly
honourable to him.

advisable farther to postpone doing any thing, in the hope that next year the Ministers may see the matter in a more favourable point of view. Every one else present, Lord Grenville, Lord Lansdowne, Stephen, Horner, William Smith, &c., thought that the measure ought not to be delayed any longer; and Wilberforce has undertaken immediately to move for leave to bring in a Bill to establish a registry of slaves in the colonies.

5th, *Mon.* News arrived of the capitulation of Naples to the Allies.*

(The Champ de Mai held at Paris June 1st, and the additional act of the Constitution accepted by the French nation.)

7th, *Wed.* On my motion, the House of Commons resolved to address the Regent to give directions that there be laid before the House an account of the 615 persons of colour stated in the return of Governor Ainslie to have been restored to their owners, and many of them to have been from ten to thirty-five years in the woods; distinguishing their sexes, ages, and names, and which of them were negroes and which were other persons of colour; and stating the names of the several persons to whom they, and each of them, have been restored; and in what manner such of them (if any) as have not been restored to their owners have been disposed of. †

Margin note: Account required of the 615 slaves stated by Governor Ainslie to have been restored to their owners.

---

* The capitulation was signed on the 20th of May, and the despatches announcing it arrived here on the 6th of June.

† This account was given in the following session of Parliament, and the name was stated of every person to whom his supposed slave was restored. That the negroes were delivered to these different individuals may be perfectly true, but that such individuals were the legitimate masters of such negroes remained to be proved.

Master of
the Rolls in
Ireland.

On the same day, I with others opposed an increase of the salary of the Master of the Rolls in Ireland.

Proposed
registry of
slaves in
the colonies.

13th, *Tu.* Wilberforce made his motion for leave to bring in a Bill for establishing a registry of slaves in the plantations. The motion was opposed by several persons who have an interest in West India property; by Anthony Browne, by Marryatt, and (though not very strenuously) by Barham. They affected to consider the measure as intended merely to prevent the illicit importation of negroes into the islands, and they denied that there had been any such illegal importation, and they insisted that a registry was therefore unnecessary. But beyond this, they said, that the attempt to carry such a measure was likely to produce very alarming consequences; that the British Parliament's right to legislate as to the internal concerns of the colonies was disputed, and such an Act as this could not but excite the greatest jealousy and alarm on their part; and they hinted that it might produce open resistance. Browne moved, as an amendment, that, instead of leave being given for bringing in the Bill, a committee should be appointed to inquire whether slaves had been smuggled into the islands since the abolition of the trade.* Lord Castlereagh said he should

* I opposed the appointing such a committee, and supported the original motion, on the ground that the registry was proposed, not merely as supplementary to the abolition, and as giving complete effect to that measure, by rendering the clandestine importation of negroes into the plantations impossible, but as a regulation indispensably necessary for the gradual improvement of the condition of the slaves, and as one step towards their final emancipation. If no persons of colour could be considered as slaves but those whose names were on the not object to bringing in the Bill, if it were merely to be printed and suffered to stand over to the next Session. The right of the British Parliament to pass such a law, he said, could not be disputed; but it was very inexpedient to do it, if the colonial legislatures could be prevailed on to pass such Acts themselves; and, in the hope that they would, he suggested the expediency of postponing the measure to another Session. This suggestion it was thought prudent to adopt; and Wilberforce said that, if permission were given to bring in the Bill, he should merely bring it in, have it printed, and take no further step upon it at present. Browne's amendment was withdrawn. A great deal has been gained by this debate. It is of great importance to put an end to the notion entertained, or at least professed, by the planters, that their colonial legislatures have the sole and exclusive right to make laws to regulate their own internal concerns.

21st, *Wed.* When the Mutiny Bill was brought into the House, Mr. Bennet was very desirous of moving to add a clause to it for restraining Courts Martial from inflicting by their sentence more than 100 lashes on any offender; and it was settled between us that he should move it instead of me.

Motion for leave to bring in a Bill to restrain the severity of military punishments.

Registry, there would be an end of that cruel presumption, which prevails in all the colonies, that every black man is a slave; which presumption he is to rebut as he can by legal evidence, and which is attended with the most fatal consequences. I insisted upon the right of the British Parliament to make such a law, and mentioned various instances of Acts passed to regulate the internal affairs of the islands; and I showed, by many instances, how little was to be expected for the protection of the slaves and amelioration of their condition from the colonial legislatures.

There was no opportunity, however, of doing this, (so late was the Bill brought in, and so necessary was it to hurry it through the House,) but at one o'clock in the morning, when the House was tired with long debates on other subjects. At my suggestion, therefore, he abandoned his intention, and gave notice of a motion for leave to bring in a Bill to limit the number of lashes which Courts Martial may by their sentences inflict ; and that motion he made on this day. The debate turned very much upon the expediency of retaining the punishment of flogging in the army, or of abolishing it altogether. I spoke and endeavoured to fix the attention of the House to the real question, which was, not whether such punishments should continue, nor whether the power of Courts Martial should be restrained to inflicting 100, or any other particular number of lashes, but whether there should be any limitation at all to such punishments. Courts Martial now might inflict 1000 lashes, or even a greater number ; and there have been instances, though not very recent ones, of as many as 1500 lashes being the sentence on an offender. Sentences were pronounced which it was known could not be executed, the offender not having by nature a capacity to endure all the punishment which he was doomed to undergo. Formerly, these punishments were inflicted at different times, as much, or nearly as much, as the sufferer could endure at one time, and the rest at a future period, when he was so far recovered as to have acquired a renewed capacity of being tortured to the utmost limit of human endurance. This practice has been

of late discontinued in England, but I doubt
whether it has in the remoter possessions of the
Crown ; and it is certain that the threat of executing the remainder of the sentence has been
held out to compel men to enter into regiments
serving abroad, and in unhealthy climates.   These
evils, it is said, have of late years been greatly
diminished, and the Commander-in-Chief, highly
to his credit, discountenances them as much as
possible; but there ought to be some more solid
security that they will not be revived, than the
disposition of the Commander-in-Chief.   His suc-
cessor may take a different view of the subject;
and, as it is admitted that excessive and unnecessary severities of this kind have existed, and
that not many years back, they may again exist, if
there be no legislative provision against them.
These were the principal topics I touched on ;
and I endeavoured strongly to impress upon the
House, that, by voting against the motion, they
were declaring that there should be no limit whatever to these severities.   The motion, however,
was lost, and without a division.   Manners Sutton
declared in the course of the debate, that, in his
opinion, when a criminal had been brought out and
had suffered some portion of the lashes to which
he was sentenced, it was illegal to inflict any more
of them on him at any future time; or, by the
threat of inflicting them, to compel him to enter
into any other regiment.   Such an explicit declaration from him may do much good.   Great
benefits already have been derived from the discussion of this subject in public.   It is to these

discussions, which have attracted the public attention to these punishments, that the recent mitiga-
tion of them, which is admitted to have taken
place, is principally to be ascribed.

News arrived late this evening of the great
victory obtained by the Duke of Wellington over
Bonaparte at Waterloo, on the 18th of June.
Hostilities commenced by the action between the
French and the Prussians on the 15th. The vic-
tory has been complete, but our loss immense.*

Transport-
ation of
felons and
imprison-
ment in the
hulks.

22d, *Th.* On the question of going into a
Committee on a Bill to continue the system of
transportation and of imprisonment on board the
hulks, generally and without limit, the former Acts
having been temporary and being about to expire,
Mr. Holford suggested many important improvements to be made in the management of the hulks ;
and he reprobated very strongly the present mode
of conducting them, and pointed out the great
evils which attended them. I declared that I
could not vote for making either the present system of transportation, or that of confining prisoners
in the hulks, perpetual ; that I thought there
were great defects in both, but particularly in the
hulks ; that, instead of reforming offenders, they
only made them more depraved and more dangerous to society. The Committee which sat in 1812
had reported this to be the effect of these punishments ; and yet we persevered in inflicting them,
and in sending very young persons to be tutored,
in these floating prisons, in every species of vice

* Bonaparte returned after his defeat hastily to Paris, and on the
22d of June he abdicated the throne.

and of villany. It appeared by the returns made to the House, that at the present moment, there is one boy in the hulks who is only 11 years old, two who are only 12, one who is only 13, and four who are only 14; and, altogether, no fewer than 112 who are under the age of 20. I mentioned the bad effects of our punishments and our police towards preventing crimes, and showed how, under our present system, the number of offenders in the metropolis had been gradually increasing; and I mentioned the number of persons committed for trial at the Old Bailey for eight years down to 1813, in proof of this.* To whatever cause such an increase of crimes, (the more remarkable as it happened during a time of war, in which the commission of offences generally is diminished,) to whatever cause it was to be ascribed, whether to our laws or to our police, it must be admitted that it was extremely reproachful to the country, and that it was our duty to inquire into it, and to supply a remedy if it were possible. It was too late in the Session to do this at present; but I said that I hoped that the House would merely pass a Bill to continue the present Acts as long as should enable the House, early in the next Session, fully to inquire into the subject. This suggestion was adopted, and the Bill was in the Committee made to continue only till the 1st of May next.

Increase of crimes in the metropolis.

* The numbers were as follows: —

In 1806	-	-	899	In 1811	-	-	1252
1807	-	-	1017	1812 -	-	-	1397
1808	-	-	1110	1813	-	-	1478
1809 -	-	-	1242	1814	-	-	1413
1810	-	-	1214				

24th, *Sat.* The Lord Chancellor, who has been long confined with the gout, sat to-day (in Lincoln's Inn Hall) for the first time since the sittings after Easter term. It was said, before a Vice-Chancellor was appointed, that a resource always in the Chancellor's power for clearing off the great arrear of business in his Court was to be ill and incapable of attending : — a year's illness of His Lordship, it was formerly observed, would enable the Master of the Rolls, who upon such occasions was always accustomed to supply the Chancellor's place, to get rid, with his ordinary despatch of business, of the whole arrear. But the Vice-Chancellor, who is even much slower in hearing causes than the Chancellor, though he has not the additional defect of never deciding what he slowly hears, has done scarcely any thing in the Chancellor's absence ; and the delay and impediments in the decision of causes have become a most grievous and intolerable evil to the suitors. Amongst the other obstructions to the prosecution of suits, has been the Chancellor's delay in the appointment of a Master in the place of Mr. Morris. That gentleman died on the [13th] of [April] last, and it was only yesterday that

Mr. Jekyl was appointed to succeed him. The Prince's favour has procured him that appointment. As soon as the vacancy happened, it was known that Jekyl was to be appointed. The Chancellor, however, has delayed all this time filling up the office, at very great inconvenience to the suitors, only, as it should seem, to show his sense of the impropriety of the appointment ; and a more improper one could hardly be made, for, with a thousand good and amiable qualities as a private man, and with very good talents, Jekyl is deficient in almost every qualification necessary to discharge properly the duties of a Master in Chancery.   If the Chancellor had meant to show with what deliberation he could make a bad appointment to a very important judicial office, and with how strong a sense of the impropriety of it he could surrender up to the Prince that patronage which it is a duty he owes to the Public to exercise himself, he could not have contrived matters better than he has done.   His conduct indeed had been nearly the same when he appointed Mr. Stephen a Master in Chancery ; that gentleman had never practised in that Court, and, though a man of very considerable talents, he had not the character of being a lawyer, and his services in Parliament were understood to be his only recommendation.   The Chancellor was said to disapprove of such a political appointment to so important a judicial office, but, after a very long delay, he most deliberately made it.

30th, *Fri.*   The Chancellor's illness has been the cause of suspending for a long time all proceedings in the House of Lords on my Bill for subjecting freehold estates to the payment of simple contract debts.   Lord Grenville, who had considered, and made himself quite master of the subject, would have brought it on some time ago ; but Lord Ellenborough desired that it might be deferred till the Chancellor could attend, who, he said, had many weighty objections to urge against the Bill.   Lord Grenville yielded to this, but said,

Bill to subject freehold estates to simple contract debts.

that he must in consequence of it give up taking
any part upon it as he was impatient to go out of
town. I then requested Lord Grey to bring the
Bill on, which he very kindly and very willingly
undertook, telling me that he highly approved it.
I furnished him, as I had done Lord Grenville, with
a written statement of all the objections to the
Bill worth noticing that I have ever heard of,
and which appear to me to be complete, and with
answers to them. The debate came on yesterday
(June 29th) on the question of going into a Committee. I was unable to attend, but I see by the
newspapers of to-day, that Lord Redesdale, the
Chancellor, and Lord Ellenborough, all spoke against
the Bill. If those reports are correct, (which, however, they very seldom are,) Lord Redesdale told the
Lords that the measure, if adopted, would bring
almost all the freehold estates in the kingdom into
the Court of Chancery, and would be the means
of annihilating, in a course of years, all small free-
holds. The Chancellor spoke with admiration of
that regard which our ancient law had always had
for landed property ; deplored the ruinous expense
of Chancery proceedings ; and said, that if every
simple contract creditor had not a security which
would affect land, it was his own fault, and " vigilan-
tibus non dormientibus," &c. : and Lord Ellenborough said, that such dangerous innovations tended
to destroy the law of primogeniture, and to reduce
all lands to Gavelkind tenure. Such nonsense could
not have been talked if there had been any lawyer
in the House to have answered it ; and, probably,
no such nonsense was talked, for there should be

better authority for it than that of the blundering and ignorant newspaper reporters, before it can be credited.   Those three Lords, however, all strenuously opposed the Bill, and it was of course rejected.   Lord Grey, who appears to have very well supported and defended the Bill, thought it most prudent not to divide the House.   My present intention is to bring the Bill on again in the next Session.

July 4th, *Tu.*   Sir Henry Parnell moved an address to the Regent, to appoint a commission to inquire into the nature and effects of the Orange Societies in Ireland.   I voted for the question, and, as is always the case in important questions of this kind relative to Ireland, in a very small minority.   We were only 20, the majority being upwards of 80.

Orange Societies in Ireland.

5th, *Wed.*   On the motion of Lord Ellenborough, the Bill for abolishing the punishment of the pillory was rejected by the House of Lords.   He admitted that it ought not to exist as a punishment in all the cases in which it may now be inflicted, but said that the subject required consideration and ought to be referred to the Judges * (observe that the Bill has been now more than two months depending in the House of Lords).   He talked about the antiquity of the punishment both in England and the rest of Europe, and said that it was mentioned by Fleta, and that its antiquity appeared from Ducange ; and, as usual, declaimed against

Punishment of the pillory.

* On the 10th of July, 1815, the House of Lords ordered the Judges to prepare and lay before the House a Bill for reducing into one Act all the laws now in force which impose the penalty of the pillory.

innovation.* This is the fifth Bill sent up by the Commons, in the course of the present Session, for making very material improvements in the law, which has been rejected at the instance of Lord Ellenborough and Lord Redesdale. The four others were: 1st, The Bill to render the remedy by habeas corpus more effectual, which was the same as one drawn in the latter end of the reign of Geo. II. by Mr. Justice Foster, and then approved by all the Judges. 2d, The Bill to prevent the binding poor children apprentices at a great distance from their parishes. 3d, The Bill to make Freehold Estates assets for the payment of simple contract debts. 4th, The Bill to prohibit British subjects embarking their capital in the foreign slave trade. Except this last, all these Bills passed the Commons without one dissentient voice.

Very beneficial Bills, which had passed the Commons unanimously, rejected by the Lords.

Thanks to the Duke of York.

Yesterday, *July* 4th, the thanks of the House of Commons were voted to the Duke of York, upon the motion of Sir J. Majoribanks, the Lord Provost of Edinburgh. The Duke has, I believe, great merit, but to vote thanks to a Commander-in-Chief, or any other person at the head of any ministerial department, merely because during his administration a great victory has been obtained, was never before heard of, and was a piece of gross adulation in the person who moved it. I waited with great inconvenience to myself, a long time to

---

* In the next year an Act was passed for abolishing the punishment of the pillory in all cases, except perjury and subornation of perjury. — See Stat. 56 Geo. III. c. 138.[1]

---

[1] The punishment of the pillory was finally abolished in all cases by 1 Vict. c. 23. — ED.

vote against it, but was at last obliged to go to the Rolls, before I had any opportunity of voting or speaking. I see by the newspapers, that Sergeant Best took that opportunity of pronouncing a high panegyric on the Regent.

6th, *Th.* Poor Whitbread this morning de- Whitbread. stroyed himself, as it should seem, in a sudden fit of insanity. His friends have, for some time past, felt great anxiety about him. His health has been manifestly declining, and though he spoke, only two days ago, in the House of Commons, against the vote of thanks to the Duke of York, he has, I understand, for some time past, occasionally discovered an unaccountable despondency. A greater loss the country could not at the present moment experience than it has suffered in poor Whitbread. He was the promoter of every liberal scheme for improving the condition of mankind, the warm and zealous advocate of the oppressed in every part of the world, and the undaunted opposer of every species of corruption and ill-administration. The only faults he had proceeded from an excess of his virtues. His anxious desire to do justice impartially to all men certainly made him, upon some occasions, unjust to his friends, and induced him to give credit and to bestow praises on his political enemies to which they were in no respect entitled.

(3d. Paris capitulated to the Duke of Wellington and Marshal Blucher.

8th. Louis XVIII. re-entered Paris.)

12th, *Wed.* Parliament prorogued.   Parliament prorogued.

Aug. 3d, *Th.* Bonaparte has now been a short   Bonaparte.

time in this country, but has not been permitted to land in it. After having delivered himself up, as he termed it, to the generosity of the English nation, he was brought by Captain Maitland, to whom he had surrendered himself, to Torbay. From thence he was removed to Plymouth, where he still is on board the Bellerophon, Captain Maitland's ship. It is the intention, it seems, of Government, to send him very shortly to the island of St. Helena. The newswriters are in the daily habit of loading him with the lowest and meanest abuse; while some individuals take a very strange interest in his fate. Sir Francis Burdett called upon me this morning, and told me that, if moving for a writ of habeas corpus would procure him his liberty, or in any way be useful to him, he would stand forward to do it. I told him that I thought that Bonaparte could not possibly derive any benefit from such a proceeding.

Sir Francis Burdett.

6th, *Sun.* I received a letter from General Savary (Duke of Rovigo), of which the following is a copy: he was to me a total stranger.

         " A bord du Bellorophon,
         " Plymout, le 1er Aout, 1815.

General Savary's letter from on board the Bellerophon.

  " Monsieur le Chevalier,

    " La reputation dont vous jouissez et le caractere personnel bien connu que vous y avez reuni m'ont donné la confiance de solliciter le secours de vos lumières, dans une circonstance où l'honneur du pavillon Britannique est autant compromis que ma sureté personnelle est menacé de l'etre, pour y avoir eu confiance. Je vais vous exposer ma situation, et vous prie de m'accorder vos conseils et votre assistance dans cette affaire, que je n'ai nul moyen de suivre dans un pays ou je suis tout a fait étranger.

" Mon nom seul vous expliquera comment j'ai eté amené dans ce pays à la suite de l'infortune la plus illustre dont l'histoire nous a rapporté la souvenire.*

" Je suivois l'Empereur Napoleon lors qu'un concours de circonstances l'ont determiné a venire chercher un azile sur les vaisseaux de votre nation, après s'etre assurré d'avance de l'inviolabilité de sa personne et avoire recu des paroles positives de

---

* The faults of spelling and grammar in this copy are all to be found in the orginal.[1]　In the same cover as contained the letter of Savary and the copies of the letters referred to in it, was enclosed a paper not in any manner mentioned or referred to in any of the letters ; it was entitled " *Considérations sur Napoléon Bonaparte et sa situation civile et politique en abordant en Angleterre ;*" and in the margin was written, " Tirer des extraits pour les papiers publics, et faire de ce document les bases d'un plaidoyer célèbre et digne du talent et de l'ame elevée d'un bon Anglois, et meriteroit la reconnoissance et le suffrage de tous les cœurs grands et généreux.　In this paper three questions are discussed.—1. Quels seroient les droits du gouvernement sur Napoléon s'il étoit prisonnier de guerre ?　2. Napoléon est-il prisonnier de guerre ? 3. Enfin l'ordre donné par le Gouvernement Anglois au Capitaine Maitland de le recevoir, lui et sa suite, pour le mener en Angleterre, s'il se presentoit, ne l'a-t-il pas admis de fait à la protection des lois du pays ?"　The most remarkable passage in this memorial is one, in which it is represented that Bonaparte, when he went on board the Bellerophon, might still, if he had remained in France, have been extremely formidable :—" Le General Clauzel " (it observes) " tenoit à Bordeaux à la tête d'une armée, et l'on sait que c'est un de ses plus chauds partisans.　Le General Lamarque tenoit à Nantes et lui est également devoué.　Les garnisons de Rochefort, de l'isle d'Aix, étoient tout à lui.　Le pavillon tricolore flottoit partout.　Davoust arrivoit sur la Loire, et pour tout dire en un mot, ce n'est qu'après l'appareillage du Bellerophon que le pavillon blanc à été arboré dans le pays. Il étoit donc le maitre de demeurer en France à la tête de corps considerables, et pouvoit au moins faire des conditions : contester ces faits c'est contester les dates, les époques de la soumission des troupes et du déployement du pavillon blanc."

---

[1] In a subsequent letter from Savary, no such faults are to be found. See *infrà*, p. 267. — ED.

protection de la part des loix Angloises qui etaient audessus de la volonté des Ministres.

" C'est dans cette confiance que nous montames à bord du Bellorophon dont le capitaine nous declara etre autorisé à nous recevoire : nous dumes donc nous considerer comme sous la protection des loix Angloises et des lois inviolable sans leur concours : depuis notre arrivée en le port, sous pretexe d'une coutume ou loi envers les estranges, nous y somme depuis huit jours soumis à un sequestre rigoureux jusqu'a ridicule, et que les politesses les plus observées ne sufficent pas pour rendre suportable.

" Hier un messager du Gouvernement est venu notifier à l'Empereur la resolution des Ministres du Roi qui l'oblige à aller à St. Helene : vous etes jurisconsulte, Monseiur le Chevalier, il est inutile que je traite avec vous cette matiere qui ne peut eschapper au burain de l'histoire.

" Dans cette notification un article expresse m'excepte nominativement ainsi que le General Lallemand du nombre des personnes par les quelles il est permis à l'Empereur de se faire accompagner.

" Si cette exception n'est que la consequence d'une opinion que le Gouvernement Anglois a de mon caractere particulier, il a prendre le droit de me separer de l'Empereur dans les meme loix dont il la atteint lui meme ; mais il me semble que cela ne peut compromettre en rien ma liberté individuelle qui est ma proprieté, et que je ne puis perdre que par le concour de l'action civile, puisque je n'ai point combattu, et que je ne me trouve sous le Pavillon Britannique, que par suite d'une transaction verbale entre le Capitaine du Bellorophon et moi.

" Le Gouvernement peut bien la désapprouver, l'annuller meme si il croit le pouvoire, mais il ne peut jamais en resulter la perte de ma liberté parcequ'en detruisant l'acte il en detruit les consequences.

" Je ne puis etre prisonnier puisque c'est comme demisionnaire qui je me suis rendu à bord.

" Mais un autre inquietude m'occupe d'avantage, Monsieur le Chevalier ; il vient de paroitre en France des listes de proscription qui sont des consequences naturelles des maux qui devorent ma malheureuse patrie ; les revolutions les amenent toujours, et si la sagesse ne preside pas au conseil, les vengeances, et les passions compriment la justice.

" La coincidence de l'inconcevable exception que le Gouvernement Anglois a fait de moi avec l'apparution de la proscription fait entrer dans mon esprit le soupçon que cette mesure pouvoit etre suivi de ma translation en France ; quelque odieuse que me soit cette pensée elle est en moi je vous l'avoue, et je viens Monsieur vous communiquer tout ce qu'elle ma suggeré d'ecrire à Monsieur l'Amiral Keit et au Lord Melleville premier Lord de l'Amirauté. J'y joins une copie de la lettre que le capitaine du Bellorophon lui a ecrit lui meme comme ayant son honneur compromis dans cette affaire.

" Je sollicite votre appuy Monsieur et vous prie d'evoquer de ma reclamation devant qui de droit, j'ai signifié à Monsieur le Capitaine du Belloro-

phon, que je ne sortirois point de son vaisseau,
autrement que pour passer sous la protection d'un
magistrat, et que si la violence etoit employé pour
m'obliger j'employerois mes armes pour me deffen-
dre me reservant de partire de cette declaration
pour poursuivre devant les tribunaux l'acte in-
tenté contre moi. Cecy posé Monsieur je vous
prie de me dire ceque je puis encourire, si j'ai le
malheur de tuer quelqu'un en me deffendant avant
d'avoire recu l'assurrance que ma sureté seroit re-
specté : si l'on se croit le droit de me faire prisonnier, je dois etre protegé par les loix de la guerre,
dans ce cas la translation seroit une honte ; si je
ne suis pas prisonnier j'invoque la loi commune et
la meme translation devient un crime personnel a
ceux qui l'auront signé et execute ; mon intention
est de laisser après moi dequoi les poursuivre.

" Quand je suis venu à bord du Bellorophon, je
connoissois la justice qui avoit ete faite du gouver-
neur de Gibraltar pour un cas semblable.

" Le Roi Louis 18., lui meme fit, il y a un an,
destituer un agent civile, dela ville de Paris qui
avoit osé dans la capitale meme et sur l'invitation
de l'ambassadeur d'Espagne y faire arretter un chef
d'insurgés Espagnole qui s'étoit armé contre le
retour des abus qui etoient rentrer en Espagne avec
Ferdinand 7.

" L'Angleterre a eu ses revolutions et la France
est peuplé de famille Angloises qui sont venu y
chercher azile, aucune n'a eté livré. Les peuples
d'Affrique respectent l'hospitalité ; l'Angleterre re-
fuseroit elle appuy à l'infortuné, et seroit elle re-
duite a lui tendre des pieges pour en abuser.

" Voici, Monseiur le Chevalier, ma situation, je vous demande votre secours pour l'ameliorer : je n'ai pu obtenire de l'amiral Keit de communiquer avec un homme de loi de cette ville comme vous verrez que je l'avois demandé. Ayez la bonté de devenire mon guide dans une affaire qui est commune au General Lallemand et à moi, et croyez Monsieur que quelque isçue quelle puisse avoire, elle ne diminuera en rien notre reconnissance pour une aussi genereuse obligeance.

"Je saisis cette occasion, Monsieur, de vous offrire l'assurrance de ma plus haute considération.

" LE DUC DE ROVIGO."

This letter enclosed copies of General Savary's letters to Lord Melville and to Lord Keith (which are not worth preserving), and of Captain Maitland's letter to Lord Melville, which was in these words : —

" H. M. S. Bellerophon, Plymouth Sound, 31st July, 1815.

" My Lord,

"I am induced to address your Lordship in consequence of having observed, in the intimation delivered to Napoleon Bonaparte, of the number of persons allowed to accompany him to the island of St. Helena, that the names of Savary and Lallemand are expressly excepted ; which, together with their being proscribed in the French papers, has created in them a belief that it is the intention of His Majesty's Government to deliver them up to the King of France. Far be it from me to assume such an idea ; but I hope your Lordship will make allowance for the feelings of an officer, who has

Captain Maitland's letter to Lord Melville.

nothing so dear to him as his honour, and who could not bear that a stain should be affixed to a name he has ever endeavoured to bear unblemished.

"These two men, Savary and Lallemand (what their character or conduct towards their own country may be I know not) threw themselves under the protection of the British flag ; that protection was granted them with the sanction of my name : 'tis true no conditions were stipulated for ; but I acted in the full confidence that their lives would be held sacred, or they never should have put foot in the ship I command, without being made acquainted that it was for the purpose of delivering them over to the laws of their country.

"I again beg leave to repeat to your Lordship, that I am far from supposing it to be the intention of His Majesty's Government to deliver these men over to the laws of their country ; but as they are strongly impressed with that belief themselves, and I look upon myself as the cause of their being in their present situation, I most earnestly beg your Lordship's influence may be exerted that two men may not be brought to a scaffold, who claimed and obtained at my hands the protection of the British flag.   I have the honour to be, with much respect, your Lordship's most obedient humble servant,

"(Signed)

"FREDERICK L. MAITLAND — Captain.

" To the Right Honourable Viscount Melville, &c."

Interview with the Lord Chancellor.

7th, *Mon.* Having desired to see the Lord Chancellor this morning, before he went into court,

I apprized him of the letter I had received. I told him that Savary was an entire stranger to me, but that I thought myself bound, as he had no friends here, to do what I could for him; and that the only thing useful which it appeared to me that I could do, was, to make a representation to the Chancellor of what I had learned from him. I then stated to the Lord Chancellor the General's apprehensions that it was intended to deliver him up to the French Government; and that, when he went on board the Bellerophon, Captain Maitland had declared to him that he was authorized to receive him; and that he and those who accompanied him considered themselves as coming under the protection of the English laws; and that this indeed was expressly stated to them; and I here read to the Lord Chancellor that part of Savary's letter in which this is affirmed. I told him that Savary had signified to Captain Maitland that nothing but force should remove him from his ship, unless it were to pass under the protection of a magistrate; and this, too, I stated to the Lord Chancellor in Savary's own words. I also told him that when Savary entered on board the Bellerophon, he recollected that our Ministers had themselves condemned the conduct of the Governor of Gibraltar with respect to the Spanish refugees; and I then showed the Chancellor the copies of Captain Maitland's letter to Lord Melville, and of Savary's letters to Lord Keith and to Lord Melville. The Chancellor heard me with great attention. He then said, that Captain Maitland's letter he had seen before, but the two other letters

were new to him : that he believed there was no
intention in Government to deliver up Savary or
Lallemand to the French Government; but that
he mentioned this to me in confidence ; and that
it was not yet determined what was to be done with
them. He said that Captain Maitland had been
directed to state exactly what had passed between
him and Bonaparte and his Generals, before he received them on board his ship ; but that his statement in compliance with this requisition had not
yet been, and could not have been, received. I
said that I wished to answer Savary's letter, merely
to tell him that I could render him no other service
than to make the statement which I had done to the
Lord Chancellor, and that I purposed sending my
letter under a cover, addressed to Captain Maitland.
The Lord Chancellor then told me that he believed
the Bellerophon was no longer at Plymouth : that
orders had been sent for her to sail from that port ;
and that the Northumberland was to meet her at
sea, when Bonaparte was to be removed to that
latter ship, and to proceed immediately to St.
Helena. How strange that all this should have
been determined on and carried into execution
before Ministers knew with certainty and exactness
what passed between Captain Maitland and Bonaparte, and in what manner Bonaparte understood
that he was received on board a British ship ! The
Chancellor asked if I had any objection to his
mentioning to Lord Melville what had passed between us, to which I answered certainly not.   He
then said, that a council was to meet again to-
morrow, on the subject of these Generals of Bona-

parte, for that nothing was yet determined respecting them.

8th. The Lord Chancellor sent for me into his room at Lincoln's Inn Hall, and said that he wished, before he went to the council, that I would refresh his memory with what I had stated yesterday. I did so, and wrote and delivered to him a copy of that part of Savary's letter, which states under what circumstances he, together with Bonaparte and Lallemand, were received on board the ship.*

I wrote to Savary, merely to inform him that I had stated his case to the Lord Chancellor, as being the only step which I thought I could take usefully for him. I told him, too, that if, in resisting force to remove him from the Bellerophon, any person should be killed, I thought that it would be deemed murder by our tribunals; and I enclosed my letter to Captain Maitland, desiring him to deliver it.

20th, *Sun.* I set out upon a journey to Geneva, to see my son William. My dear Anne, my daughter, and my son John accompanied me. I was desirous of avoiding a disagreeable journey through France, overrun as it is at the present moment with foreign troops. We determined therefore to pass through Flanders, and, travelling along the banks of the Rhine, to get by Schaffhausen or Basle into Switzerland. Tour on the Continent.

Our journey was a very delightful one, and performed in the finest weather imaginable. We crossed the sea at Dover, and passed through St.

* Savary and Lallemand were afterwards sent by our Government to Malta.

Omer, Lisle, and Tournay, to Brussels. We were very much struck with the excellent cultivation of the country we passed through, and with the appearance of prosperity and of an abundant population, which every where presented itself to our view, notwithstanding the long and destructive war in which France has been for so many years engaged. In almost all the towns we passed through, we saw the remains of the public rejoicings and illuminations, which had recently taken place for the restoration of the King to the throne of France. Brussels was crowded with English, great numbers of whom had crossed the sea from Margate and Ramsgate, and other watering places, that they might gratify their curiosity in gazing on the field where the battle of Waterloo was recently fought. Our road lay across it; for we were advised to take Namur in our way to Liege, and on the high road to Namur was the field of battle. The battered walls of a farm-house pierced with bullets and cannon-balls, and the remains of a villa consumed by fire, were the only vestiges of the late devastation which remained visible. At the little village of Genappe, where we slept, the shutters and the walls of the room we supped in were pierced with musket-balls; and at Namur, the next day, we saw everywhere the marks of the sanguinary battle which had been fought upon the bridge over the Sambre in the centre of the town. From Namur we passed, on the banks of the Meuse, which we crossed at Huy, to Liege. Nothing can exceed the beauty and variety of the scenery on both banks of the river. From Liege

we passed on to Aix-la-Chapelle, and so on to
Bonn, Cologne, Coblentz, and, by the magnificent
road which Bonaparte has made on the left bank
of the Rhine, to Bingen, and from thence to
Mentz.   We then proceeded to Frankfort on the
Main, and from thence to Darmstadt, and to
Heidelberg, most beautifully situated on the Neckar.
We then visited Carlsruhe, and passed through
Rastadt to Offenburgh ; and from thence through
the valleys of Kinzig and Guttark to Hornberg,
the most beautiful and picturesque town I ever
beheld ; and then, passing through Donauschingen,
we arrived at Schaffhausen.   After visiting the fall
of the Rhine, about two miles out of the town,
we proceeded to Constance, and from thence to
Zurich, Berne, Lausanne, and Geneva.   At Geneva I met my excellent friend Dumont, and
formed an acquaintance with Sismondi, the his-
torian, with M. Bonstetten, and with the Professors
Prevost and Pictet, or, I should rather say, renewed my acquaintance with the latter.   The peo-   Geneva.
ple of Geneva have more reason to rejoice, and do
in truth feel more unmixed joy at the events which
have lately taken place, than the inhabitants of
any other part of Europe.   Those events have
secured to them that liberty and independence
which they had recently recovered, and have delivered them from the greatest danger that any
state was threatened with.   The society of Geneva I own a little disappointed me ; they have
a great deal of literature and of science, but still
their conversation seems rather too much confined
to the trifling topics which generally occupy the

attention of a provincial town; and cards for the old, and dancing for the young, are the never-failing substitutes for conversation.

Sept. 14th, *Th.* We set out with Dumont and William on a little tour to the glaciers of Savoy. But after the first day we had bad weather; and the Mont Blanc, which, from Morges and Geneva, had appeared to us in all its magnificence, without a cloud to intercept for an instant the beams of the setting sun with which it was illuminated, was, upon this our nearer approach to it, enveloped in clouds, and to us invisible. We saw and passed over the Glacier des Bossons; but the weather was too bad to admit of our ascending Mont-anvert, or visiting the Mer de Glace. The Glacier des Bossons is rapidly extending itself; and, if it continues to advance in future as it has done during the last three years, in five years more it will have passed across the road, and in twenty years will have extended itself across the whole valley.

17th, *Sun.* We returned to Geneva in the evening; but time enough to be present at a national festival celebrated on the lake, in honour of what they call *Le Roi de la Navigation.*

Tour in a very small part of Italy.

20th, *Wed.* Dumont and William accompanied us on a little excursion into a part of Italy. Our project was to pass the Alps over the Simplon, to see Milan, Genoa, and Turin, and return over Mont Cenis; and we accomplished it very successfully, and got back to Geneva on the 7th of October. We passed through Thonon and Evian in Savoy, and over the fine road which Bonaparte has lately constructed at a very great expense, on the south bank of the Lake of Geneva, under the rocks of Meillerie. Even in this sequestered and romantic spot we found the remains of the ravages of war. The shattered walls of the cottages and houses of Meillerie bore testimony of the action which, only a few months ago, took place there between a part of the French and Austrian armies. The Valais did not appear to me, from the little *The Valais.* I could learn and observe in rapidly passing through it, to be that seat of happiness and innocence which Rousseau and other writers have represented it. The Government is severe and tyrannical, and the people ignorant in the extreme. In the whole state there is not a single bookseller, not even at Sion, the capital. A person of that trade, not long ago, set up a shop there, but was soon obliged to give it up for want of customers. The road over the Simplon, made with such im- *Road* mense labour, and at so enormous a cost, (one of *across the Simplon.* the most wonderful productions of human art and perseverance, and formed amidst some of the wildest and most dreary scenes in nature,) and which seemed alone sufficient to transmit the name of Bonaparte to the most remote generations, is rapidly falling into decay, for want of a comparatively trifling expense at which it might be maintained : and, as if time and accident were too slow in their progress, many individuals have, in different places, occupied themselves in hastening this work of destruction. At Milan, almost every *Milan.* thing that is grand and splendid in the external appearance of the city is connected with the name of Bonaparte. The amphitheatre, the unfinished triumphal arch, the Brera collection of pictures, and the cathedral (so long in building, but so rapidly advanced and nearly completed within the few last years), are all his works.   It is much less, however, in public edifices and monuments than in the manners and character of the inhabitants, that the French dominion appears to have had a very beneficial influence in Italy. Several instances were mentioned to me; but the most striking was the diminution of the number of assassinations. They had almost ceased under the French government; but since the restoration of the ancient order of things, accompanied with the facilities for refuge which small neighbouring states and the asylums of the Church afford, they have become as frequent as ever.   Sismondi mentioned to me that, in the town of Pescia, with which he was particularly acquainted, the assassinations, both before it belonged to France, and now again that it has been delivered from French dominion, were, and still are, on an average one in every week; though while the town was dependent on France, scarcely any assassinations had been committed. Dreadful, indeed, are the evils which Bonaparte has brought on the human race; but he must be strangely prejudiced who can deny that, in Italy at least, against those evils are to be set some very considerable benefits of which he is the author.

Assassinations.

Genoa.

I was enchanted with the beauty of Genoa. Its port, its lighthouse, its palaces and churches, and public edifices, the adjoining hills studded with villas, and the fine mountains of the Apennines behind them, form altogether a scene more striking and beautiful than any that I had ever before beheld. It is impossible however to see this magnificent city, filled as it is with the monuments of its ancient prosperity and renown, and to behold the fine race of inhabitants that crowd its streets, without feeling the most lively indignation against the base and unprincipled policy of England and the other great powers of Europe, who have lately taken on themselves to deliver over this whole state, with all its territory, into the hands of a narrow-minded and bigoted Prince, a stranger to them, disliked and despised by them, and who never had any pretensions to aspire to dominion over them.

The King and Queen of Sardinia were lately here, King of Sardinia. and endeavoured by their courtesy and affability to ingratiate themselves with their new subjects. The only public acts, however, which they did, were that the King, finding that an ancient monastery had been converted into a cotton manufactory, turned out all its active and industrious inhabitants, men, women, and children, to reinstate a dozen Capuchins, all that could be found of its former inmates; and that the Queen assisted with great pomp at the ceremony of a young woman taking the veil. The first acts of the King's government at Turin have been in the same spirit. He has sent away every French family in the town, and has expelled all the Jews who had established themselves there. Prince Koslofsky, the Russian Ambassador at Turin, told me that he represented to the Minister that, if he wished to show what the true nature of this measure was, he ought to have prefixed some such preamble as this to the edict, — " Whereas His Ma-

jesty finds in the metropolis a mass of population
and of capital, which he considers as burthensome,
and is therefore desirous of seeing dispersed and
distributed amongst other states, it is ordered,"
&c.   They tell a story at Turin, which has perhaps
been only invented to throw ridicule on the proceedings of the Court.   When the King returned
to that city (to Turin), he brought back with him
an old gardener, who had accompanied him to
Sardinia.   That faithful servant, when he first re-
visited the royal garden, and found in it a number
of new and curious plants from New South Wales
and other remote parts of the globe, with which
the French had enriched it, manifested his loyalty
by tearing them up by the roots, and trampling
them under foot as Jacobin innovations.

We stayed but a few days at Geneva on our return, and then proceeded by the road of Macon,
Autun, and Auxerre to Paris.

At Paris I renewed my acquaintance with several persons whom I had formerly known there,
particularly Lafayette, the Duke de la Roche-
foucauld (formerly Liancourt), my excellent friend
Gallois, and Delessert, and with MM. Morellet,
Suard, &c.

Removal
of the mo-
numents of
art from the
gallery of
the Louvre.

We arrived at Paris just after all the pictures
and most of the statues claimed by foreign states
had been removed from the gallery of the Louvre.
The rest were carried off while we were there.   It
was by English soldiers that this was done: on the
English all the odium of the measure has fallen;
and it is astonishing how great that odium is.   Till
this event happened, the English, whose recent

good conduct had been contrasted with the rapa-
city and brutality of the Prussians, were very popular; but that popularity has been suddenly succeeded by the most bitter hatred.   It is hardly to
be conceived by any one who had not been an eye-
witness of it, what a degree of importance the
French, or at least the inhabitants of Paris of all
ranks and descriptions, attached to this national
gallery.   A woman of very mean condition, who
was lamenting over its loss, was asked by a friend
of mine why she took such an interest in the matter, and what she knew of statues and pictures.
Her answer was,—I understand nothing about
them; but I know that they have attracted
strangers here from all parts of Europe; that they
have excited the admiration and the envy of other
nations, and that they were purchased with the
blood of our sons and our brothers.   This seems
to be the general feeling of the people.* As if the
act itself were not sufficiently odious, those who
undertook to execute it seem to have studied how
they could most mortify the nation, and strike deep
into their hearts the stings of hatred and resentment.   The spoliation of the gallery lasted for
many weeks; it was carried on principally in the
middle of the day, when the streets were most
peopled; and, as the statues were removed singly,
it was day after day, and hour after hour, that the
crowds that thronged the streets had to make way
for the ostentatious carrying off, by British soldiers

* A print was published at this time at Paris, which was a portrait
of the Duke of Wellington, with an inscription under it of " Blucher :"
a double satire, the meaning of it being, that Wellington was the most
barbarous of conquerors.

with fixed bayonets, of some fresh trophy over their humiliation and disgrace.

Paris presented, while I was there, a very extraordinary spectacle — a metropolis in a state of peace, but yet given up to a foreign army ; the King appearing to be possessed of no authority, but remaining a quiet and indifferent spectator ; while foreign commanders affected to inflict punishment on the nation, and, according to the language of the Duke of Wellington, in his letter of justification, to make them an example to after times. Legislative assemblies pretending to debate, while the streets were filled with troops, and while loaded cannon were stationed on the neighbouring quays, and soldiers ready with lighted matches, that not a moment might be lost, at the first appearance of danger, in taking a signal vengeance on the inhabitants ; and during all this time a treaty of peace is negotiating — a peace, it must unquestionably be, just such as the conqueror chooses to exact from the conquered. That a peace of long duration can arise out of this seems hardly possible ; and yet the victory of Waterloo and all the successes of the war could to us be a subject of real joy, only as they enabled us to lay the foundations of a solid and permanent peace.

The unhappy King, to whom nothing but the basest adulation can have given the name of the "long desired," seems so little to have been wished for by his subjects, that he has been obliged to come among them in the train of an insolent invading army ; and that it is by those invaders that he is at this moment maintained upon his throne. Never, surely, was humiliation greater than that which must be suffered by this ill-fated prince, condemned from the very windows of his palace to see, with shame, foreign armies giving the law to what his predecessors used to call their good city of Paris.

The French bitterly complain of the perfidy of the allied powers. They approached Paris professing hostility only to Bonaparte and those who were armed in his support; and when with these professions they had lulled the country into a fatal security, when they had succeeded in numbing the feelings of the people, when they had gained possession of Paris by a convention in which safety was promised to all who had acted under the usurper, and when they had induced the army which was on the banks of the Loire to disband, then, and not till then, — not till by artifice they had made all resistance impossible, did they begin to talk about inflicting punishment on the nation, and requiring from it securities, and exacting indemnities and contributions.

Alleged perfidy of the allied powers.

The more reason the nation imagines it has to complain of the allied princes, and the more bitter its hatred against its invaders, the more unpopular must the present Government be; for it is impossible for the people to forget that it is to their King that they owe all the calamities of the last invasion, and that the contributions, and the severe terms which they fear will be imposed on them by the treaty, are the price they are to pay for the King's restoration.

Instability of the present French Government.

From all I observed during my short stay at Paris, I cannot think that, when the foreign armies shall be withdrawn from the country, the present Government can maintain itself. If it does, it will certainly be from the difficulty of knowing what to substitute in its place, and not from the attachment of the people.

We returned to England the end of October.

Oct. 28th.   Arrived at Tanhurst.

30th.   London.

Nov. 20th. The treaty of peace with France signed.

Dec. 16th.   On this day died the Duke of Norfolk, after an illness of several months. Though an old man, he might have lived many years longer but for his indiscretion.

25th.   I pass these Christmas holidays in town.

1816.

Jan. 10th.   I went with Anne and some of our children to Cumberland Lodge, where I stayed till Saturday, January 13th.

Feb. 1st.   Parliament met, this day being the day to which it had been prorogued.

I do not recollect any instance of a prorogation to so late a period.   Parliament, it is true, has sometimes met for the despatch of business after the Christmas recess as late and even later than this.   It did so indeed in the three last years ; but then on each of those occasions it had sat before Christmas, and its proceedings had been interrupted, not as now by a prorogation by the Crown, but, by the adjournment of the two Houses : there has, however, been no period of our history in which more important events have passed, and upon which the counsels of Parliament (if they be of any utility) were more to be required than have passed during this long prorogation.

To the address upon the Regent's speech an amendment was moved by Mr. Brand, and seconded by Lord John Russell.   The objects of it were, to censure the Ministers for not having called Parliament together sooner, and to pledge the House immediately to take into consideration the state of the country.   The most considerable Members of the Opposition thought it not advisable to divide

Parliament met after an unusually late prorogation.

Amendment moved to the address.

the House ; for it was known that a great many of
our friends were absent, and that, of those who attended, the persons who adhered to the politics of
Lord Grenville would not concur in any alteration
of the address. Sir Gilbert Heathcote, however,
a country gentleman, insisted, after a great number
of Members on both sides had gone away, upon
having a division. Though the House had been
very full, and the division took place as early as
half after nine o'clock, the numbers were only 23
for the amendment, and 90 against it, exclusive of
the tellers on both sides. It was thought expedient by most of the Opposition to avoid touching,
upon this occasion, on foreign politics, that we
might delay a little longer the public expression of
that difference of opinion which prevails amongst
us. This did not at all agree with my inclination.
I did not, however, enter into any argument on
these matters ; but I thought it necessary, on this
the first day on which Parliament met, after the
Government had openly avowed and acted towards
France on principles which they before had always disclaimed and protested against, to express
my strong disapprobation of their conduct. I
mentioned the manner in which the French nation
had been deluded, by the professions made by the
Allies of not interfering with the internal affairs of
the state, farther than to remove Bonaparte, to
forbear making a resistance which they might, and,
but for that delusion, certainly would, have made ;
and I stated my opinion, that the peace was not
likely to be durable.

Ponsonby, who has been called the leader of the

Opposition, was absent, being detained in Ireland, by the private concerns of his family. Whitbread's loss to the public will now be most severely felt.

7th, *Wed.* I moved and obtained leave to bring into Parliament a Bill to subject the freehold estates of persons who die indebted to the payment of their simple contract debts. I took occasion, in moving for it, to mention all the objections to the Bill which were stated last Session in the House of Lords by the Chancellor, Lord Ellenborough, and Lord Redesdale, and to show the futility of those objections. No Member said a word in support of any of them ; and the motion passed unanimously.*

Fri. 9th. Leach has vacated his seat in Parliament, by accepting the Chiltern Hundreds. This is preparatory to his taking the office of Chancellor of the Duchy of Cornwall, to which he is to be immediately appointed. Personal attachment to the Prince, who, he says, has always shown great kindness to him, is the excuse he alleges for accepting a favour from the Regent, to whose Government he has been constantly in opposition. The office, he says, is given to him on an express declaration that it is not at all to affect his political conduct; but yet he does not think that it would be proper, while holding such an office, to appear in active opposition to the Regent's Ministers. He therefore retires ; and the man he is to bring in

Bill to subject freehold estates to the payment of simple contract debts.

Mr. Leach.

---

* This Bill passed the House of Commons without a word being said in opposition to it in any of its stages.[1]

---

[1] It was again rejected by the Lords. See *infrà* June 19th, 1816. — Ed.

as representative of Seaford, of which he has the
command, is Sir Charles Cockerell, who will invariably vote with Ministers.   The plain meaning
of all this is, that he has gone over to Government; but, to avoid the ridicule and the reproach
which commonly attends an immediate and sudden desertion of former friends, he wishes to interpose some decent interval between his past and
his future politics.   His loss is not very great.
His attendance on Parliament was not very constant.; and, though he always voted, he never once
spoke, on the side of the Opposition.   Unless I
am much mistaken, in the course of the eight or
nine years that he has been in Parliament, he has
only made four speeches, of which two were on
matters which personally regarded the Regent, the
third was in defence of the Duke of York, and the
fourth was against the project of creating a Vice-
Chancellor.   He aspires undoubtedly to the highest offices, and is flattered with the expectation
of succeeding Lord Eldon as Chancellor.   His
talents are certainly very considerable.   He has
great facility of apprehension, considerable powers
of argumentation, and remarkably clear and perspicuous elocution : but with all this, he is, of
all the persons almost that I have known in the
profession, the worst qualified for any judicial situation.   He is extremely deficient in knowledge as
a lawyer.   All that he knows he has acquired, not
by any previous study which would have enabled
him to understand the general system of our law,
and the grounds and reasons of its particular provisions, but by his daily practice.   This has thrown

in his way a great deal of desultory information, which a good memory has enabled him to retain. In judgment he is more deficient than any man possessed of so clear an understanding that I ever met with. If ever he should be raised to any great situation, his want of judgment and his extraordinary confidence in himself will, I make no doubt, soon involve him in some serious difficulty. This short sketch of his character would be incomplete, if I did not mention the ambition he has of being thought to unite the character of a fine gentleman to that of a great lawyer. Constant attendance at the opera and at the gayest assemblies appears, in his opinion, to be as necessary to the support of his reputation, as his presence in Westminster Hall; and he prides himself upon hastening every night from the dull atmosphere of the Rolls and Lincoln's Inn, to the brilliant circles of high birth and fashion.

14th, *Wed.* It has long been the practice of grand juries in Ireland to find bills of indictment without examining any witnesses. They merely read the examinations taken before the magistrates who have committed the prisoners, which examinations are always returned to them; and on these alone they find or reject the bills. This appears to have been almost the universal course of proceeding, except in cases of rapes, and in these cases witnesses are often examined. This strange practice, which in effect takes away from the people of Ireland the benefit of grand juries, has, it seems, the sanction of the Irish judges. The fact of bills being found on this evidence, *Irish grand juries.*

appeared by a report made last Session by a committee appointed to inquire into the proceedings of grand juries in Ireland; and Horner, who was a member of that committee, gave notice that he should, early in this Session, bring in a Bill to declare the law upon this subject. He accordingly moved to-day for leave to bring in a declaratory Bill on the subject. Peel (the Irish Secretary) did not oppose the motion, but yet contended that the practice observed hitherto in Ireland was legal, and that, if a Bill were to be passed, it should not be a declaratory, but an enacting Bill; insisting that it would be very dangerous to give the countenance of Parliament to a notion that such important proceedings, which had taken place for such a length of time, had all been illegal. Sir John Stuart, formerly Attorney-General for Ireland, maintained the same opinion. He admitted that the common law of Ireland was the same as the common law of England; and yet contended that by law grand juries were not bound to require any other evidence to warrant their finding bills of indictment, than the mere written and unauthenticated examinations returned by the magistrates. I combated this doctrine, and insisted that grand juries were bound themselves to examine the witnesses upon whose evidence the charge was preferred. I observed how great a security to the lives and liberties of men the institution of grand juries had always been considered; and how different in the estimation of the world was the reputation of a man against whom the grand jury had refused to find a bill, from that of a prisoner acquitted by a petty jury; and that all the benefits of this institution were, by the practice adopted by the grand juries of Ireland, lost to that nation.

On the same day, the Chancellor of the Exchequer moved for the appointment of a committee to consider and report to the House where a court could be built for the Vice-Chancellor (this was the object, though these were not the terms of his motion). As the building of a new court proceeded on the assumption that the Vice-Chancellorship was to continue a permanent office, I took this opportunity of observing that my opinion respecting the expediency of this measure was not at all altered, but, on the contrary, very much confirmed by the experience which we had now had of it for nearly three years: that all the evils which I had imagined would result from the measure had been experienced, and to a much greater degree than I could have supposed would, in so short a time, have been possible. That the Lord Chancellor, since the Vice-Chancellor had been appointed, had heard no original causes (two or three in the first year, but since that time he never even appointed days for hearing them); and that the appeals to the Lord Chancellor had increased from about twenty-four to upwards of seventy.

Office of Vice-Chancellor.

16th, *Fri.* I obtained leave to bring in a Bill to repeal the Act of King William which punishes the crime of privately stealing in shops, to the amount of five shillings, with death. I prefaced my motion with an answer to all the objections which, when the same Bill was last Session

Bill to repeal the Shoplifting Act.

rejected by the House of Lords, were urged against it by Lord Ellenborough and the Chancellor; and I endeavoured to disprove (and, I think, succeeded in doing so) the assertion that the repeal of the Act of Elizabeth had been the cause of an increase in the number of pickpockets. I adverted to the increase of crimes of all descriptions in the metropolis, and to the bad state of the police. Nothing was said in opposition to my motion.

Police of the metropolis.

19th, *Mon.* The debate on the late treaties of peace was commenced to-day in the House of Commons, and, having been continued to a late hour, was adjourned to the next day,—

The late treaties of peace.

20th, *Tu.*, When I took occasion to express my sentiments on them. The topics on which I principally dwelt had not been touched upon by any speaker who had preceded me; but most of them were afterwards very eloquently enforced in an admirable speech made by Horner.

I reminded the House of the frequent assurances which the Ministers had given, that they had no other object in view than to dispossess Bonaparte of his authority; and how frequently, and how earnestly, they had disclaimed any intention of forcing upon the French nation any form of government, or any individual as their sovereign: that it was as late as in the last year that those assurances had been most solemnly renewed, and that the Ministers had treated the design of restoring the Bourbons to the throne as a most unjust and calumnious imputation on them. I observed that, by giving credit to these representations, the nation had been induced to make the greatest sacrifices to persevere in the war ; and that, in the end, the Ministers had just done what it was always suspected that they intended, but which they had so repeatedly disavowed, — established, by a military force, Louis XVIII. on the throne : that the faith of Government had been pledged, on this point, to France, as well as to England ; and that the most solemn assurances had been given the French that we would not interfere with their government, till, in a great degree, by means of those assurances, we had reduced them to a situation in which it was impossible for them to resist our interference. I read Lord Castlereagh's declaration on the exchange of the ratifications of the treaty of the 25th of March, between England and the allied powers, in which he declared that the treaty was not to be understood as binding His Britannic Majesty to prosecute the war with a view of imposing on France any particular government ; and the letter of Lord Clancarty, written from Vienna on the 6th of May, 1815, on the occasion of Bonaparte's overture for peace, in which he says that the allied powers "do not desire to interfere with any legitimate right of the French people. They have no design to oppose the claim of that nation to choose their own form of government, or intention to trench in any respect upon their independence as a great and free people. But they do think they have a right, and that of the highest nature, to contend against the re-establishment of an individual as the head of the French Government, whose past conduct has invariably

Lord Clancarty's letter.

demonstrated that, in such a situation, he will not
suffer other nations to be at peace." I had mentioned these papers shortly on the first day of the
Session; and Lord Castlereagh, yesterday, observed
that I had selected particular passages, and omitted
the guards and correctives with which they were
accompanied. As I read them, therefore, to-day,
I (as he intimated his wish that I should do) read
the parts which he thought material. He called
on me particularly to read, in his own declaration,
the words following: "However solicitous the
Prince Regent must be to see His Most Christian
Majesty restored to the throne, and however
anxious he is to contribute, in conjunction with his
Allies, to so auspicious an event, he nevertheless
deems himself called upon to make this declaration
on the exchange of the ratifications; as well in
consideration of what is due to His Most Christian
Majesty's interests in France, as in conformity to
the principles upon which the British Government
has invariably regulated its conduct." With respect
to this passage, I said I knew not what the meaning
of it was, or what mental reservation it indicated;
but I could hardly understand it in so odious a sense
as that the interests of Louis XVIII. would be
best consulted by lulling the people into a fatal
security, that the pretensions of the Allies to seat
him on the throne were not to be openly avowed,
till all resistance to them should have become
impossible. That the French nation might be induced the more implicitly to rely on these assurances, Lord Clancarty appealed to the conduct of
the Allies last year in these words: "It should

seem that the glorious forbearance observed by the
Allies, when masters of the French capital in the
early part of the last year, ought to prove to the
French that this is not a war against their freedom
and independence." I stated that this system of
delusion of the French had been carried on quite
to the moment of the convention of St. Cloud, by
which Paris had been surrendered to the Allies.
I mentioned that when, after the battle of Waterloo, plenipotentiaries had been sent by the provisional French government to treat with Marshal
Blucher and the Duke of Wellington for an Plenipo-
armistice, though both those Generals had evaded tentiaries
from the
treating with them, the Duke had had frequent French pro-
conversations with them, from their first obtaining govern-
an audience of him till his near approach to Paris, ment to
they attending him during his march; and that in lington.
the course of these conversations he had distinctly
told them that the Allies were making war, not for
Louis XVIII., but solely against Bonaparte : that
the French were at liberty to choose what King
they pleased ; but that if they chose any other than
Louis XVIII., securities must be required for the
allied powers, which, with him, were unnecessary ;
his personal virtues and his known character being
considered by them as the best guarantee for
peace that France at that time could offer; and
he proceeded even to name to the plenipotentiaries
individuals, and particularly one of the family of
Bourbon, whom, if they thought proper, they
might raise to the throne, but whom the Allies
must consider as an usurper, though of illustrious
birth, and with whom therefore they must insist

on securities.* I had shortly mentioned these facts on the first day of the Session, but neither then nor now did Lord Castlereagh take any notice of them. I then observed, that it was not till after the French, relying on these assurances, had omitted to exert the powerful means of resistance which they still possessed, and after we had thus become the masters of the country, that we fixed the King upon the throne without regard to the people's wishes: that to me it appeared that the peace was a most insecure one, and would last only as long as all means of resistance and revenge were withheld from the nation: that the nation was exasperated by the deceit which had been practised, and the severe terms which had been imposed upon them; and that all descriptions of persons, even the Royalists as well as the rest,

* I was informed of these facts last autumn at Paris by Lafayette and Gallois, in different conversations I had with them; and Gallois made a short statement of them in writing, which, to be more correct, he showed to one of the plenipotentiaries, and had his confirmation of the accuracy of it before he delivered it to me. The five plenipotentiaries were Boissy D'Anglas, Valence, Andreossy, Flaugergue, and La Bernardière. A part of this statement was in these words: — " Dans l'une de ses conversations, le Duc de Wellington dit, que les vertus personnelles, que le caractère connu du Roi Louis XVIII. étaient regardés par toutes les puissances comme la meilleure garantie que la France pouvait leur offrir en ce moment. ' Si les Français,' ajoutat-il, ' voulaient un autre roi, le Duc d'Orleans, par exemple, ce serait un usurpateur, bien né sans doute, mais enfin ce serait toujours un usurpateur, alors la France aurait besoin de plus grandes garanties. Si l'on voulait le petit Napoléon, mais (dit-il, en s'interrompant et comme rejettant loin de lui cette idée) cela est impossible, mais enfin si l'on voulait le petit Napoléon alors il faudrait de bien plus grandes garanties encore, peut-être une grande partie des territoires de la France.' Il revint encore à l'idée que Louis XVIII. était le roi qui convenait le mieux à la France, en même tems qu'à l'Europe. Il rejetta fort loin la prétension de la part des Français de proposer au roi aucune condition, et dit qu'il fallait s'en rapporter uniquement à lui, à ses bonnes intentions et à ses principes éprouvés."[1]

[1] The remainder of this paper will be found at the end of this volume. —Ed.

were eager to redeem their honour. To Lord Castlereagh's assertion that the treaty of peace had met
with the general approbation of the French nation,
I opposed the addresses of the legislative assemblies upon it to the Crown, and the answer of the
King, in which his Majesty declared that, at the
head of any other nation, he under such circumstances must abandon all hope ; but that a French
king, at the head of the French nation, never
would despair. Though I knew it to be a very
unpopular subject, and one on which my opinion
differed from that of almost every other Member in the House, I censured the removal of the
statues and pictures from the Museum. Whatever
might be the justice of it, I said that on the
impolicy of it I could have no doubt. It had,
more than any other measure, stamped on the
hearts of the French people a sentiment of hatred
against the English. I also said that I was by no
means satisfied of the justice of that proceeding.
It was not true that those objects of the fine arts
had been all carried away as the spoils of war ;
many, and the most valuable of them, had become
the property of France by the express stipulation
of treaties ; and it was no answer to say that those
treaties had been made necessary by unjust ag-
gressions and unprincipled wars ; because there
would be an end to all faith between nations, if
treaties were to be held not to be binding because the wars out of which they arose were unjust, especially as there could be no judge to decide
upon the justice of the war but the nation itself.
By whom, too, was it that this supposed act of jus-

tice had been done; and this moral lesson, as it was called, had been read? By the very powers who had at different times abetted and supported Removal of the monuments of art from the gallery of the Louvre. France in these her unjust wars. I mentioned that among other articles carried from Paris, under pretence of restoring them to their rightful owners, were the Corinthian horses which had been brought from Venice; but how strange an act of justice was this, to give them back their statues, but not to restore to them those far more valuable possessions, their territory and their republic, which were at the same time wrested from the Venetians. But the reason of this was obvious; the city and the territory of Venice had been transferred to Austria by the treaty of Campo Formio, but the horses had remained the trophy of France; and Austria, while she was thus hypocritically reading this moral lesson to nations, not only quietly retained the rich and unjust spoil she had got, but restored these splendid works of art, not to the Venice which had been despoiled of them, the ancient, independent, republican Venice, but to Austrian Venice,—to that country, which, in defiance of all the principles she pretended to be acting on, she still retained as part of her own dominions. That the peace, however, was not to be condemned merely on account of its being insecure, of its having sown the seeds of future war, and having been concluded under circumstances which had been brought about by a violation of good faith, pledged both to England and to France, but on account of the most alarming example which it had set, and which threatened the liberties of this country and of all Europe.

We are now united with the sovereigns of the most despotic governments of Europe, and with that King of France whom we have made, to establish and to maintain in that country a form of government and a royal family which we represent as best calculated to insure their happiness and our tranquillity. Who can assure us that the time will not come when the sovereigns of the same states, including that of France, will be united with an English king, to force by their confederated armies a new form of government on this country? The example which we have set of making war upon the nation, with its king for our ally, may be followed in after times against ourselves: and an English king, in alliance with the enemies of the nation, may levy war upon his people. The same law of nations which we now invoke may be cited hereafter against ourselves; and it may be declared by Russia, Austria, Prussia, and France, that the turbulence of English liberty is incompatible with the peace and security of the continent of Europe. As we now hear it alleged that all the evils which in late times have desolated Europe are to be traced to the wild notions of liberty which, in the beginning of the revolution, were entertained in France; we, or our children after us, may be told by the sagacious statesmen of those times, with the pretension of a still deeper insight into political causes, that the French revolution itself, with all the calamities and horrors which have followed in its train, arose out of exaggerated and distorted notions of English liberty; and that nothing will give such stability to the governments of Europe

as extirpating altogether that well balanced constitution, those salutary checks on the exercise of
royal authority, that security for personal liberty,
that freedom and publicity of our debates, and
those lofty privileges with which the English by
their seducing example mislead the well-affected,
and encourage and inflame the ill-disposed and
the seditious in other countries. The liberty of
the press alone, it perhaps will be said, as it is
exercised in England, is incompatible with the
security of the thrones of Europe; that press
which sets at nought the sacredness of foreign
princes, and audaciously drags them from the
sanctuary of their palaces, and from amidst the
armed multitudes which surround and guard them,
and arraigns them like the meanest culprit at the
bar of public opinion. The noble Lord (Lord
Castlereagh) has already given us some very signi-
ficant hints on this subject. He has censured in
strong terms the freedom with which the conduct
of foreign monarchs has been canvassed in this
House; and he has told us that our liberties are in
no danger, but from the intemperate use we are
making of them. His Lordship is preparing us
for the time, when, to extirpate the contagious
spirit of licentiousness and sedition, which will be
represented as issuing from this island, and spread-
ing its baneful influence over every part of the
civilized world, will be deemed by the jealous des-
pots, who will have dominion in Europe, an object
sufficiently important to call forth the utmost efforts of their confederated arms. On what resources this country, in a season of such untried

dangers, will have to rely, no man can now pronounce. On a British army, indeed ; but not perhaps on an army which will have encountered dangers, and shed its blood, in defence of the rights of this or of any other people ; but which may have long known no other military service than that of maintaining a foreign King upon his throne against the will of his people ; and of enforcing the severe and cruel mandates by which alone such an authority can be long maintained.

Though my speech was not a good one, yet, as I consider this as the most important occasion that I ever spoke on, I have been desirous of preserving the memory of some of the things I said.[1]

Tu. 27th. The Ministers have proposed to keep on foot an army of 149,000 men, including those which are to be stationed in France. They persevere, too, in their intention of renewing the property tax, though they consent to diminish its amount. Numerous petitions to Parliament have come up, and are coming from all parts of the country, against this tax, and against the immense and unexampled military establishment which is to be maintained in this season of peace. I presented such a petition to-day from my constituents at Arundel. The objects petitioned against have been the subjects of debate on many of these petitions ; and I took occasion to-day, in one of these debates, to express my opinion on them, and at the same time to contradict what Lord Castlereagh had a short time ago asserted in the House,

Great military peace establishment.

[1] The numbers, on the division were, for the amendment 77, against it 240 ; majority for Ministers 163. — Ed.

that there was little foundation for the pretended persecution of the Protestants in the south of France; and that the officious interposition of people here on that subject had been deprecated by the Protestants. Vansittart, who spoke just before me, had objected to putting off the consideration of the tax, as had been desired, to a more distant day than that which had been appointed, because the tax was so soon to expire, namely, on the 5th of April next. I observed that, if there remained so little time for considering a matter of so much importance, and in which the public took so lively an interest, it should be recollected, that it was because the Ministers had thought proper to advise the Regent to prorogue the Parliament to a

Property tax.

later period than that at which, for a great many years past, it had been usual for it to meet: that the question of renewing the property tax appeared to me to be one of the greatest importance, not merely on account of its being in itself a most unequal, unjust, and oppressive tax, and of the odious means necessary to be resorted to to make it productive, and because the renewal of it was a violation of the solemn pledge given to the public, when it was imposed, that it should be continued during the war and *no longer;* but much more on account of the other alarming measures with which this was inseparably connected; the maintaining a great standing army in time of peace, and the forcing upon the French people a government which was not of their choice : that the tax was necessary because so great a military force was to be kept on foot, and that force was requisite because we had guaranteed the throne of France to the house of Bourbon: that it ought to be well understood, that, if we were to be subjected to all the hardships and vexations of this tax, it was not for any national objects of our own, but in order that we might be able to preserve in France the present government, — a government which had destroyed the liberty of the press, abolished all the guards and protections of personal security, grossly violated in the nomination of the present Chamber of Deputies the freedom of election, and acquiesced in a cruel persecution of its Protestant subjects.   I said that, when I made this last assertion, I ought to explain what I meant by it; and, from information which I had received, and of the authenticity of which I had no doubt, it appeared that, although the Government had not persecuted the Protestants themselves, they had taken no step whatever to bring to justice any of the numerous individuals who had been their most savage persecutors: that, although in the department of the Gard more than 200 persons had been murdered; more than 2000 robbed by the populace, exacting contributions from them by force; and more than 250 houses burned or destroyed, and thirty women of good education and respectable connexions stripped naked in the streets and scourged with such cruelty that eight had died of the treatment they received, — not a single individual had been punished or even prosecuted.*

Persecution of Protestants in France.

---

* I received intelligence of these facts from different quarters: the most important of my intelligence came from M. de Végobre of Geneva, who has near relations living at Nismes, and whose information is the more to be relied on, because, though Protestants, they are most zealously attached to Louis XVIII. and his family.

The prefect and the mayor of Nismes, under whose administration these unpunished outrages were committed, had not been either recalled or removed. I reminded the House of the conduct which our Government had observed in 1780 when the Catholics were persecuted, but not in the same barbarous manner, by a misguided populace; of the severe measures which had been resorted to, the many lives which the justice of the country had exacted, and the prosecution instituted against the Lord Mayor, merely because he had been prevented by his timidity from doing his duty. As a proof of the criminal connivance of the prefect, I mentioned that, when General La Garde was wounded by one of the fanatical mob, though the man was well known (being one Boisset, a sergeant of the Royal Volunteers, and having been described as such in a proclamation in a neighbouring department by the prefect of Avignon), the prefect of Nismes affected not to know by whom the crime had been committed, and offered a reward to discover the author of it.   I said that, though the Duke of Wellington had declared that the French Government had done every thing they could to prevent these enormities, the fact was that they had done nothing but make professions. I also said that I believed that the interposition of persons in this country, so far from being prejudicial to the Protestants in France, had been of essential service to them; and that it was to that interposition that they owed the comparative tranquillity they now enjoyed.   I called it only comparative tranquillity, and I mentioned vexations to which they were still exposed.

Lord Castlereagh unfortunately was not in the House, and no one controverted my statement.

March 14th, *Wed*. Lockhart moved for leave to bring in a Bill to suspend the operation of the Insolvent Debtors' Act*, and which is in substance to repeal it.   The Act has been grossly abused; numerous frauds have been committed under it; and, from the ignorance of the magistrates who have executed the Act in the country, nothing has been more easy than to practise such frauds. A great many petitions for the repeal of the Act have been presented from London, Westminster, Bristol, and many other towns, and I have no doubt that the Bill will be repealed.   I have endeavoured, however, to make the experience which the operation of this Bill has afforded useful, with a view to some future insolvent debtors' Act, if any such shall be attempted.   With this object I suggested the propriety of appointing a committee to inquire into the effects which had been produced by the Act.   This suggestion met the approbation of the House, and such a committee was appointed.[1]

Insolvent Debtors' Act.

This day a message was brought down to the two Houses of Parliament, announcing the intended marriage of the Princess Charlotte of Wales with the Prince of Saxe Cobourg.

15th, *Fri*.   The Bill to repeal the shoplifting Act of King William was read a third time and passed.   It would have passed, as it had done in all its former stages, without a word being said

Shoplifting Act.

* Vi. *infrà*, June 13th, 1816.

---

[1] By a majority of 11 : 82 for the motion, and 71 against it. — Ed.

upon it, but I took this occasion to mention that while the Bill had been in its progress through the House, a boy of the name of George Barrett, who was only ten years of age, had been convicted at the Old Bailey, under the Act, and was then lying in Newgate under sentence of death. I said that I should not have taken notice of the case of this miserable child, if I had not observed that it was stated a little more than a year ago *, in the newspapers, that the Recorder of London had declared, from the Bench at the Old Bailey, that " it was the determination of the Prince Regent, in consequence of the number of boys who have been lately detected in committing felonies, to make an example of the next offender of this description who should be convicted, in order to give an effectual check to these numerous instances of youthful depravity." I said that I hoped that this was only a threat never meant to be carried into execution, and that the inhuman intention had never been really entertained of executing against children who were without education, or friends, or means of support, and who had so much to urge in extenuation of their guilt, a law of such excessive severity that there was not, for a great many years, a single instance of its being enforced against men of mature age.†

A boy only ten years old capitally convicted under it.

---

* September, 1814.

† A few months after this, a boy of the name of Blunder, who was only in his 16th year, and who had been convicted of a highway robbery, was ordered for execution. The execution was to have taken place on the 14th of June; but, by a very great exertion made by Bennet, a respite was procured for him the night before he was to have been executed. Lord Sidmouth told Bennet, he understood that the boy was 17; but Bennet produced the register of his baptism, by which it

The Attorney-General said he doubted whether the Recorder had ever used the expressions imputed to him; and certainly no intention of executing the law against children could possibly be entertained. Of the Bill he did not say a word, not even that he disapproved of it. He pronounced a panegyric on his excellent friend, as he called him, the Recorder. I said nothing, but I recollected, as must have done many others of those who heard him, the savage conduct of this Recorder, in the late case of Eliza Fenning.[1]

appeared that he was not quite 16 when he was convicted; and Bennet, who saw him in Newgate, said, that he had the appearance of being a much younger boy.

[1] The following is an extract from one of Sir S. Romilly's MSS., entitled "Case of Eliza Fenning."—ED.

"The case of Eliza Fenning is that of a servant girl who, in the month of April, 1815, was tried at the Old Bailey, before the Recorder of London, for the crime of administering poison to her master and mistress, and her master's father, which, by an act of Parliament, commonly called Lord Ellenborough's Act, has been made a capital felony The only evidence to affect the prisoner was circumstantial. The poison was contained in dumplings made by her; but then she had eaten of them herself, — had been as ill as any of the persons whom she was supposed to have intended to poison; and her eating of them could not be ascribed to art, or to an attempt to conceal her crime; for she had made no effort whatever to remove the strongest evidence of guilt — if guilt there was. She had left the dish unwashed; and the proof that arsenic was mixed in it was furnished, by its being found in the kitchen, on the following day, exactly in the state in which it had been brought from table. No motive, besides, could be discovered for an act so atrocious. Her mistress had, indeed, reproved her about three weeks before for some indiscretion of conduct, and had given her warning, but had afterwards consented to continue her in her service. This was the only provocation for murdering not her mistress only, but her master also, and the father of her master. A crime of such enormity, produced by so very slight a cause, has probably never occurred in the history of human depravity.

"The Recorder, however, appeared to have conceived a strong prejudice against the prisoner. In summing up the evidence, he made some very unjust and unfounded observations to her disadvantage, and she was convicted. The singularity of the trial attracted the notice of many persons to her case. They interested themselves in her favour. They applied

The property tax rejected.

18th, *Mon.* The resolution proposed by the Chancellor of the Exchequer, for continuing the property tax for two years longer, was rejected by a majority of 37 ; there being for the resolution 201, against it 238. It was generally supposed that the resolution would have been carried, and the most sanguine only hoped that the Ministers would have a majority of not more than five or six.

Increased salary of Secretary to the Admiralty.

20th, *Wed.* A motion of disapprobation of the increase which has lately been made of the salary of Secretary to the Admiralty, in time of peace, from 3000*l.* to 4000*l.* a year, was rejected by a majority of 29 ; there being for the motion 130, and against it 159. In the course of the

Brougham's attack upon the Regent.

debate upon it, Brougham, who supported the motion, made a violent attack upon the Regent, whom he described as devoted, in the recesses of his palace, to the most vicious pleasures, and callous to the distresses and sufferings of others, in terms which would not have been too strong to have described the latter days of Tiberius. Several persons who would have voted for the motion were so disgusted that they went away without voting ; and more, who wished for some tolerable pretext for not voting against Ministers, and who on this occasion could not vote with them, availed them-

---

to the Crown for mercy. The master of the girl was requested to sign a petition in her behalf ; but, at the instance of the Recorder, he refused to sign it. An offer was made to prove that there was in the house when the transaction took place, a person who had laboured a short time before under mental derangement ; and in that state had declared his fears that he should at some time destroy himself and his family : but all this was unavailing : the sentence was executed, and the girl died apparently under a strong sense of the truths of religion, but solemnly protesting to the last moment that she was innocent."

selves of this excuse and went away too ; and it is generally believed that, but for this speech of Brougham's, the Ministers would have been again in a minority. If this had happened, many persons believe or profess to believe that the Ministers would have been turned out. Poor Brougham is loaded with the reproaches of his friends ; and many of them who are most impatient to get into office look upon him as the only cause that they are still destined to labour on in an unprofitable opposition. I have no doubt that, whatever had been the division, the Ministers would still have continued in office. But it is not the less true that Brougham's speech was very injudicious as well as very unjust ; for, with all the Prince's faults, and they are great enough, it is absurd to speak of him as if he were one of the most sensual and unfeeling tyrants that ever disgraced a throne. Brougham is a man of the most splendid talents Brougham. and the most extensive acquirements, and he has used the ample means which he possesses most usefully for mankind. It would be difficult to overrate the services which he has rendered the cause of the slaves in the West Indies, or that of the friends to the extension of knowledge and education among the poor, or to praise too highly his endeavours to serve the oppressed inhabitants of Poland. How much is it to be lamented that his want of judgment and of prudence should prevent his great talents, and such good intentions, from being as great a blessing to mankind as they ought to be.

26th, *Tu.* Lord Stanhope, whom I saw to-day

Lord
Stanhope's
objection
to the
Shop-
lifting Bill.

in the House of Lords, told me that he was against both my Bills. His arguments against the Freehold Estates Bill are not worth repeating; but of the Shoplifting Bill he said, "it was a Bill to screen the greatest villains upon the face of the earth, men who were much worse than murderers." I stared with astonishment, as well I might; and my astonishment was not much diminished when he proceeded to explain his meaning. There are, he says, in London, a great number of young children who are thieves by trade. They are educated, he says, to this trade by men; such men are the greatest of villains. Shoplifting is sometimes, nay frequently, committed by these boys, and when the boys are capitally convicted, the men who put them on committing these crimes are accessories before the fact, and might be capitally convicted too; and by this means one might bring to the gallows these worse than murderers.

April 2d, *Tu.* Brougham made a motion in the House of Commons of censure on the Lords of the Treasury, for remitting the penalties which had been incurred by one Gibbs for frauds upon the Excise laws, in consideration of his zeal and active services in support of Government and their measures. It appeared to me, upon the minutes of the Treasury, the memorial of the party, and the testimonial in his favour, to have been a gross case of partiality, and consequently a corrupt exercise of the prerogative of mercy entrusted to the Treasury; and I therefore spoke in support of the motion.[1]

---

[1] The motion was lost by a majority of 76; the numbers being, in favour of it 48, against it 124. — ED.

3d, *Wed.* Bennet, at my instance, moved to-day for the appointment of a committee to inquire into the present state of the metropolis. The Ministers were at first disposed to resist the appointing the committee; but finally they agreed to it, and I am upon it. I expect very important information to be derived from this measure. Bennet's zeal and activity in promoting every thing useful to the public is well suited to such an inquiry, and I rejoice that I have prevailed upon him to undertake it.

Police of the metropolis.

5th, *Fri.* I went this evening to Tanhurst, where Anne and my children are, and stayed till *Monday, April* 8th.

10th, *Wed.* I presented to the House of Commons four petitions from the prisoners confined for debt in the jails of Durham, Exeter, and Bristol, and the Fleet Prison, against Lockhart's Bill to repeal the Insolvent Debtors' Act.

11th, *Th.* I went out of town to Tanhurst, and passed the Easter holidays with my dear Anne and all my children. I did not return to town till *Monday, April* 22d.

24th, *Wed.* The House of Commons met, this being the day to which it had adjourned.

May 1st, *Wed.* Lord Castlereagh has brought into the House of Commons a Bill to establish regulations respecting aliens coming into, or resident in the kingdom, which he is pleased to call a Peace Alien Bill; as if it were now settled that the ancient policy of this country, which was to encourage foreigners to establish themselves amongst us, had been entirely departed from, and

Alien Bill.

there was always to be a system of restraint maintained with respect to foreigners, even in time of peace. The Bill seems to be exactly the same as that which was passed two years ago. It gives the King power under his sign manual to send any foreigner out of the country; and for the purposes of the Act, it presumes every man within the realm to be an alien, and throws upon him the burthen of proving that he is a natural subject. The danger to this country supposed to exist when the first Alien Bill was passed in 1793, it is universally admitted has long ceased. No person now believes that we can have anything to fear from any attempt to bring about a revolution, by means of foreigners propagating amongst us extravagant notions of liberty. But the new system which has been established in Europe, the alliance which England has entered into with the most despotic princes, to maintain in France a particular form of government and the present reigning family, points out very obviously a use which Ministers may make of the extraordinary powers with which this Bill is to arm them, very different from that which was originally given to them. They may be used against those foreigners who shall endeavour to obtain an asylum here from the political persecutions to which they may be exposed in their own country; and the mere circumstance of the Bill being now brought in by the Secretary for the Foreign Department, and not (as was always before done) by the Home Secretary, adds strength to that apprehension. From some facts which have been stated to me, I believe that these powers have been already exercised at the instance of foreign Ministers. To have that fact ascertained, I moved to-day in the House for an account of the number of foreigners who have been sent out of the country under any of the Acts relating to aliens, upon the application of any foreign minister, distinguishing the numbers in each year. Lord Castlereagh opposed the motion, on the ground that it would be very improper to disclose any communication which might have taken place between foreign Ministers and the Secretary of State on the subject of any aliens; though, in truth, the motion did not require that the communications should be disclosed. Hiley Addington asserted that no foreigner had ever, as far as he could learn, been sent away upon the application of any foreign Minister. Mr. Baring, however, mentioned a very remarkable instance of the kind which came within his own knowledge. The motion was lost by a considerable majority.[1]

10th, *Fri.* The Alien Bill was read a second time.[2] I opposed it, as did Brougham, Horner, and Mackintosh. Tolerably accurate accounts of my speech appeared the next day in several of the newspapers, particularly in the *Morning Chronicle.* Alien Bill.

20th, *Mon.* Upon the report of the Alien Bill, I again spoke against it; and I moved as an amendment that the Bill should continue in force only for one year. The amendment of course was rejected.[3]

---

[1] A majority of 51; the numbers being, for the motion 31, against it 82. — ED.

[2] For the second reading 141, against it 47; majority 94. — ED.

[3] For the amendment 44, against it 124. — ED.

22d, *Wed*. Lord Holland moved in the House of Lords, the second reading of my Bill to take away the punishment of death for the crime of shoplifting. There was little said upon it; the Bill was rejected, and there was no division. Lord Holland wrote me a note a little time back, to say that he thought little impression would just now be made on the public by any debate upon the Bill; but that a record of the opinion of those who approved the Bill on the Journals might give some effect to the measure at a future time; and he therefore requested me to draw up a protest which he might sign. I accordingly wrote and sent him one. In the course of the little that was said upon the Bill, Lord Ellenborough again asserted that the repeal of the Act of Elizabeth which punished the crime of picking pockets with death, had *caused* a great increase of that offence. There is no ground for this assertion.

Persecu-
tion of the
Protestants
in the
south of
France.

23d, *Th*. The Committee for the relief of the French Protestants a little time ago applied to me to bring the condition of those unhappy persons under the notice of Parliament. Before I undertook to do this, I requested them to put into my hands the report which has been recently made to them by Mr. Perrot, whom they sent to make inquiries and procure information on the spot, and the other papers in their possession, that I might be master of the whole case. I accordingly carefully read these papers, and compared them with the information I had received from Gallois, and through the means of De Végobre. No doubt can be entertained that the Protestants in the department of the Gard and its immediate neighbourhood have been the objects of a most cruel persecution by the populace; and that those who were in authority in the department have rather encouraged than repressed those acts of violence. Political animosity and revenge have been the pretext, but only the pretext for these atrocities. The imputation on the Protestants that, while they had the ascendancy, they committed similar crimes is wholly without foundation; and in proof that those who have been exposed to this cruel treatment have *not* really suffered for their political conduct, not one of them had distinguished himself by his zeal for Bonaparte or his enmity to the Bourbons. The Protestants indeed had enjoyed so much more security under Napoleon than under Louis, that it was natural to suppose that they must be in their hearts attached to Bonaparte; and thence Protestant and Bonapartist are, by the Catholics of the Gard, considered as synonymous; and therefore all Protestants are deemed enemies of the established government. If political opinions had been the cause of this persecution, we should not have seen, as we have, the churches attacked and demolished; the Ministers particularly the objects of the rage of the people; and the late mayor, who had always particularly distinguished himself by his zeal for the Bourbons, compelled to quit his office. For some months past, the acts of open violence against the Protestants have ceased; but they are harassed with groundless accusations, and at every moment threatened with a renewal of the oppression they have suffered.

For all the murders, and robberies, and plunder, and house burnings, which have been committed, not a single individual has been brought to justice; and in the meantime the prisons are filled with Protestants, to whom are only imputed seditious expressions. Such of them as are brought to trial are convicted by the Prevotal Courts, upon the slightest and most suspicious evidence, and are punished with the utmost severity. I this day brought the subject before the House of Commons, by merely moving, " that there should be laid before the House copies or extracts of all communications which have passed between His Majesty's Government and the Government of France relative to the Protestants in the southern departments of that kingdom." I introduced my motion by a detailed statement of what had passed at Nismes and in its neighbourhood. I took care to exaggerate nothing, but rather to understate the case.* I relied very much on the proclamations of the prefect M. D'Arbaud Joucques, and of the Mayor, M. de Vallonques, which, upon the whole, were more calculated to excite than to restrain the violence of the people, notwithstanding the vague terms of censure they contained. Lord Castlereagh opposed the motion. He contended that, whatever

* I have since seen a printed report concerning the "sufferings of the Protestants in the south of France, presented to a meeting of the inhabitants of Edinburgh, held on the 24th June, 1816, by the committee appointed at a former meeting," in which it is said of me, — that I asserted in the House of Commons, that I was certain I should be within the number in stating that 200 women had been murdered, and nearly 2000 men ; and for this a newspaper report of my speech is quoted. I certainly never made any such assertion ; I stated the whole number murdered to be at least 200, and I believe that I greatly understated it.

might have passed in France with respect to the
Protestants, it could not justify the interference of
the British Government; and yet in the same speech
he said that the Government had already actually
interfered.   He read, in the course of his speech,
a written statement of facts collected by a person
whom the Ministers had sent for the purpose to
Nismes, which corroborated every thing that I had
asserted, and made the murders that had been
committed much more numerous than I had stated
them.   His Lordship represented my motion as
likely to be very mischievous to the Protestants,
and my speech as having a tendency to revive religious animosities which had long been lulled to
rest.

Nothing would have given me more pain than
the reflection that anything I said could have such
a tendency.   But no person could have really
thought that it could ; and the man who made the
observation is the same Lord Castlereagh who, in
1807, had availed himself of the cry of " No
Popery," and in defiance of all his former professions, had joined with those who had endeavoured
to excite the populace to a religious persecution, as
a favourable means of getting into office.

I did not divide the House, as I thought it might
be injurious to the Protestants if there were but a
small division upon such a question.

29th.   The newspapers which are in the interest
of Government, particularly the *Courier*, have made
a violent attack upon me for the part I have taken
respecting the French Protestants.   The following
epigram, which has appeared in that paper, will

Attacks on
me in the
news-
papers.

give a just idea of the nature and liberality of their attack.

> " Pray, tell us why, without his fees,
> He thus defends the refugees,
> And lauds the outcasts of society?
> Good man! he's moved by filial piety."

The Committee sent me a resolution of thanks as follows: —

"Williams's Library, May 28. 1816.

Thanks of the Committee for the relief of the French Protestants. "At a meeting of the Committee for inquiry, superintendence, and distribution of funds contributed for the relief of the persecuted French Protestants, resolved unanimously, that Sir Samuel Romilly be respectfully requested to accept the best thanks of this Committee for the distinguished ability and eloquence with which he vindicated the cause of the persecuted French Protestants in the House of Commons on Thursday the 23d of May, 1816.

" THOMAS MORGAN, Secretary."

I acknowledged the receipt of the copy of this resolution in the following letter, addressed to Mr. Morgan.

" Sir,

" I have had the honour to receive the resolution of the Committee for inquiry, superintendence, and distribution of funds contributed for the relief of the persecuted French Protestants, giving me their thanks for the exertions I have made on behalf of those unhappy persons. It is highly gratifying to me to have met with the approbation of gentlemen for whom I have such high respect as I have for the Committee. In the endeavours which I have made to interest the British Parliament in the fate of the Protestants of France, I have only discharged what I consider as an important public duty ; and I shall be ready at all future times, when it shall appear that I can do it with any prospect of success, to contribute to the best of my power my humble efforts towards procuring for that much-injured class of men security in the exercise of their religious worship, and redress for the cruel wrongs which have been done them."

Lord Holland has entered a protest on the rejection of the Shoplifting Bill, which has been signed by the Dukes of Sussex and Gloucester, and by Lord Lansdowne, as well as himself. It is in these words : —

Protest upon the Shoplifting Bill.

"*Dissentient.*—1st, Because the statute proposed to be repealed appears to us unreasonably severe, inasmuch as it punishes with death the offence of stealing property to a very inconsiderable amount, without violence, or any other aggravation. 2dly, Because, to assign the same punishment for heinous crimes and slight offences tends to confound the notions of right and wrong, to diminish the horror atrocious guilt ought always to inspire, and to weaken the reverence in which it is desirable that the laws of the country should be held. 3dly, Because, severe laws are, in our judgment, more likely to produce a deviation from the strict execution of justice than to deter individuals from the commission of crimes ; and our apprehension that such may be the effect is confirmed, in this instance, by

the reflection that the offence in question is become
more frequent, and the punishment, probably on
account of its rigour, is seldom or never inflicted.
4thly, Because the value of money has decreased
since the reign of King William, and the statute
is, consequently, become a law of much greater
severity than the Legislature which passed it ever
intended to enact.

"WILLIAM FREDERICK. AUGUSTUS FREDERICK.
"VASSALL HOLLAND.   LANSDOWNE."

The protest which I had written and sent to
Lord Holland contained all the same principles,
but was rather differently expressed.   It was in
these words : —

"*Dissentient.*— 1st, Because the statute proposed to be repealed, which appoints the punishment of death for the offence of stealing, without
violence or any circumstance of aggravation, property of a very small amount, is a law of excessive
severity, is ill-suited to the character of the nation,
and is repugnant to the spirit of our holy religion.
2dly, Because to ordain the same punishment for
crimes of the greatest atrocity and for offences
which are low in the scale of moral guilt tends to
confound all notions of justice, and to diminish the
horror which crimes of the deepest dye ought to inspire.   3dly, Because the excessive severity of laws
prevents the execution of them, and, by affording
in many instances complete impunity to offenders,
has a tendency to increase instead of preventing
crimes.   4thly, Because, by the alteration which
has taken place in the value of money since the

statute of King William passed, it has become a
law of much greater severity than ever was intended by the Legislature which passed it."

30th, *Th.* I supported a motion of William
Smith's in the House of Commons, for the appointment of a committee to inquire respecting
abuses committed in suing out the Crown process
of extents in aid. I suggested that an effectual
remedy of the abuses which existed would be to
provide that an extent in aid should never issue,
but on an affidavit; that the debt due to the
Crown would be endangered unless such an extent
issued. The Attorney and Solicitor-General both
opposed the motion; and it was lost, but only by a
majority of nine.

Abuses of the Crown process of extents in aid.

31st, *Fri.* On the third reading of the Alien
Bill, Lord Milton proposed to add a clause to exempt from the operation of the Bill the alien wives
of British subjects. I supported this clause; but,
as it was opposed by Lord Castlereagh, it was
rejected by a great majority.[1] I again moved to
limit the duration of the Act to one year, and this
motion too was rejected.[2]

Alien Bill.

June 2d.   Whitsunday.

I spent the Whitsun holidays at Cumberland
Lodge with Mr. Nash. Mr. West, the painter,
passed two days there with us. Our time was
spent very delightfully. Anne and four of my
children were with me. The weather was very
fine, and seemed the finer for the long dreary

Whitsun holidays.

[1] The numbers were, for the clause 31, against it 91. — ED.
[2] By a majority of 50; the numbers being, in favour of the amendment 29, against it 79. — ED.

winter which we have but just got through. I enjoyed the fine knolls and groves of beeches which form the enchanting scenery of this part of **Windsor Park.** Windsor Park the more, on account of the close application which I have lately been obliged to give to business.* West, though very reserved in large companies, talks a good deal and very freely in the intimacy of private society. He speaks, **West the painter.** indeed, so deliberately and in so low a tone of voice, that it is something of an effort to listen to him; but his conversation is very interesting, particularly when he talks (as he does very willingly) of the fine arts, and of the incidents of his own life. Galt's account of West's early life and studies has just been published, or at least printed; and, having read it, I was able to lead him to speak of the most interesting periods of his life. Though he is now seventy-eight, the vigour of his mind and the strength of his memory are not at all impaired. His long life must have been a very happy one, for he told me that he would not have wished it to have been in any part of it different from what it has been. On the Tuesday, we went **Stoke.** together to Stoke, and visited the monument which

* On one of the days while we were at Cumberland Lodge, the Regent came to see the new cottage which Nash has been building for him, at immense expense, in Windsor Park. Nash attended him. In the course of conversation, the Prince asked him if he had any company with him at the Lodge. Nash answered that he had, and mentioned me; and I became for some time the subject of the Prince's observations. He spoke of me (according to Nash) in very friendly terms, but lamented my politics; and said it was my own fault that my juniors and my inferiors were passing me in the honours of the profession. To whom he alluded I cannot guess; unless it be to Leach, who is indeed my junior, and to Plumer, who is, however, senior to me by several years. But how little does the Prince know me, if he imagines that the promotions which have taken place, or any of those which may follow, have excited, or are likely to excite in my mind any feeling of regret!

Mr. Penn has erected to Gray, and the church-
yard in which he is buried, and which is the scene
of his elegy.

6th, *Th.*   Returned to town.

11th, *Tu.*   I moved in the House of Commons
for copies or extracts of all despatches received by
the Secretary of State from the Governor of the
Mauritius, which in any manner relate to the case
of Peter Damas Perrot. This man, who was a
planter in the island, was taken by the Governor's
order from his house and family as a prisoner, and
was sent to this country, without any charge whatever against him as a justification of his imprisonment, and without any allegation that, whatever
his crime was, he could not have been tried in the
island. As soon as he arrived here, he presented a
memorial to Lord Bathurst, and only received for
answer that Government had provided a passage
for him if he chose to go back to the Mauritius and
take his trial, and that he should be allowed 5*s.*
a day till the vessel sailed, but not for a day longer.

The motion was rejected by a great majority,
but in a thin House.[1]

I knew nothing of the man, but that, having
heard of my name, he had applied to me and stated
his case to me.

12th, *Wed.*   I was examined as a witness before the committee of the House of Commons appointed to make inquiries respecting the education of the lower orders of the metropolis. I
was examined as to the manner and expense of

Case of
Peter D.
Perrot of
the Mauri-
tius.

---

[1] For the motion 19, against it 51.—Ed.

proceeding in Courts of Equity, touching charitable trusts.

Lotteries.

On a motion of Mr. Lyttelton on lotteries, I, as strongly as I could, endeavoured to impress on the House all the mischievous effects of that pernicious measure of finance.[1]

Insolvent Debtors' Act.

13th, *Th.* I attended the committee of the House of Commons on the Insolvent Debtors' Act; and I persuade myself that I contributed very much to prevent the committee from reporting it as their opinion, that all further proceedings on the Act should be suspended till an amended Act can be brought in. Such a suspension would, in truth, have been a repeal of the Act; and, if it were repealed, it is quite certain that no other insolvent debtors' Act, however free from the defects of the present Act, or however perfect, would have any chance of being passed.

Geo. Wilson's death.

14th, *Fri.* I received the melancholy news of the death of my most excellent friend George Wilson.[2] He was found lifeless in his bed last Tuesday morning, at his house at Edinburgh.

Bill to subject freehold estates to the payment of simple contract debts.

19th, *Wed.* Lord Grey, in the House of Lords, moved the second reading of my Bill to subject freehold estates to the payment of the simple contract debts of a deceased debtor. He supported the Bill by a very excellent speech, in which he answered all the objections which on former occasions had been insisted on by the Chancellor and Lord Ellenborough. Both those Lords were pre-

---

[1] Mr. Lyttelton's motion, which was for a resolution of the House condemning the establishment of state lotteries, was lost by a majority of 26; 21 having voted for, and 47 against it.—ED.

[2] See *suprà*, Vol. I. p. 433.—ED.

sent, and remained silent.   Lord Redesdale alone spoke against the Bill.   Lord Grey did not divide the House, but entered a protest, on its being rejected[1], which I drew up for him in these words: —

" *Dissentient.*— Because it is highly inexpedient and unjust that persons who have contracted debts and have the means of paying them should be allowed at their deaths to transmit to their heirs, or their devisees, the secure enjoyment of their property ; while, by the non-performance of their engagements, their unsatisfied creditors may be reduced to bankruptcy and ruin ; and this injustice is the more flagrant in the case of a trustee, who, having employed the money entrusted to him in the purchase of real estates, may transmit to his representatives the fruits of his violated trust, whilst the orphans or others, whom his conduct may have reduced to indigence, are left without remedy or resource." *Protest.*

On the same day, a long debate took place in the House of Commons, on the projected Bill for the registry of slaves, on the late insurrection in Barbadoes, and on the present state of the West Indies. *Registry of slaves.* *Insurrection at Barbadoes.*

The Registry Bill, ordered last year to be printed, excited great discontent and bitter complaints in the West Indies.   Violent resolutions were come to at Jamaica, Barbadoes, and other of the islands, and angry pamphlets were published here, and circulated with very great industry, insisting that the rights of the West Indians were about to be vio-

[1] The freehold and copyhold estates of a deceased debtor have since been made subject to the payment of his simple contract debts, by stat. 3 & 4 Will. 4. c. 104. — ED.

lated; that the English Parliament, in which they were not represented, could not, according to the principles of the British Constitution, make laws to regulate their internal concerns; and that an interposition by the British Parliament between master and slave would be an encouragement to rebellion; and asserting that the pretended philanthropists (so they called Wilberforce and his friends) had now openly in their speeches avowed that emancipation was their object.

That the late insurrection at Barbadoes was at all connected with the Registry Bill has not been satisfactorily shown; but those who pretend that that Bill was the cause of it, themselves allege that the Bill was misunderstood by the slaves, who supposed that it was immediately to make them free. Such a misconception, if it exists, has, it is evident, originated with the West Indians. They have themselves, by their exaggerations, connected the notions of a registry and of emancipation; and they have most unintentionally, by foolishly foretelling, really caused this calamity. They pretend that our newspapers are read and explained to the negroes, and that therefore the mere discussion of these matters here produces the worst effects in the islands; and yet they publish their own exaggerations in their Colonial Gazettes: and in this very debate, in the course of a speech full of violence and asperity, made by Mr. Barham, he did not hesitate to declare that, if an insurrection of the slaves were to break out in Jamaica, it must be successful, and the island must be irrecoverably lost.

I had intended to have gone fully into the subject of the debate, but it being extremely late (one o'clock in the morning) before I had an opportunity of speaking, I said very little. I rose, indeed, principally to answer the apology which Canning had made for the law, passed in 1805, by the Barbadoes legislature, to punish the murder of a slave. When Lord Seaforth was Governor of that island, he was very much shocked to find that the murder of a slave was only punishable with a fine of about 11*l.* sterling. He endeavoured to procure an alteration of the law ; and his zeal was the more excited, because several instances of very cruel murders of slaves occurred while he was resident in the island. He acordingly sent a message to the assembly, proposing that they should pass a law to punish the murderer of a slave with death. This message gave great offence to the assembly ; the proposition was rejected ; and one of the members, after expatiating on the danger of an European Governor's interference between the white inhabitants and their slaves, moved that a committee should be appointed to prepare an answer to the message ; " an answer, moderate and respectful, but calculated to repel insult, and evince that the House understood its interests and asserted its rights." This was in 1801.* Four years afterwards, however, the assembly was represented to have passed a law to punish with death the murder of a slave ; and they had credit for this act of justice and humanity, till the laws passed in the

Barbadoes' law against the murder of slaves.

* See the House of Commons' papers relative to the slave trade, printed in June, 1804.

West Indies for the protection of slaves came in the present Session to be printed; when it turns out that the terms of this act of assembly, passed in 1805, are, that if any man shall wantonly and without provocation murder a slave, he shall suffer death. Brougham had pointed out very forcibly that this law must be altogether nugatory. Canning attempted to defend it; but it is very manifest that the law was passed merely for the purpose of delusion. Any provocation, however slight, though only in words, or in a silent disobedience of the most frivolous order, would be a provocation, and consequently an excuse for the most cruel murder; and the taking away a human life in mere wantonness or sport, has scarcely ever happened but by those who had derangement of mind to urge in their excuse. The debate ended by an address, moved by Mr. Palmer, an agent for some of the West India islands, calculated to remove the false impressions which are said to have been made on the minds of the negroes, being carried unanimously. Much was not said in the course of the debate on the question of the right of the British Parliament to legislate with respect to the treatment of the slaves in the islands. Something was said on it by Brougham, and something by myself, but very little by any other Member. But, though I did not think it expedient to enlarge upon it, I own that I feel a great deal of indignation when I hear the colonists endeavouring to revive the political controversy which preceded the American war. Can it be possible that the men who, on this occasion, maintain

West Indians' claim to the benefits of the British constitution.

that they are not to be bound by any laws but such
as have been made by themselves or their representatives, and who so loudly claim the benefits of
the British constitution, can have reflected in what
it is that the spirit and genius of that constitution
really consist ?   Do they recollect that liberty and
an equal protection by law of men of all ranks
and descriptions are its most essential character-
istics ?   Do they recollect that, where a British
constitution really exists, there can be no slavery,
either political or domestic — that the moment a
slave has come within its genial influence, he loses
his servile character and becomes as free as ourselves ?   In truth, the greatest calamity which, in
the present state of ignorance and barbarism of
the slaves, could befall both them and their masters, would be to proclaim in the West India
islands that British constitution in all its purity
which the colonists so rashly and inconsiderately
invoke ; since it must be attended with the sudden
and unprepared emancipation of all who are now
in bondage. The real purpose, however, for which
these noble doctrines of the British constitution
are appealed to by the West Indians, is to render
domestic slavery more absolute and more intolerable, under the auspices of English liberty, than it
has ever been even under the yoke of the most un-
controlled despotism. The arbitrary governments
of France and Spain did not leave the slaves in
their dominions to the legislative mercy of their
masters. They took them under their own protection, and, by the humane provisions of the Code

Noir * and of the Spanish Cedula, enforced upon
their owners an obedience to the dictates of justice,
and restrained the excesses of private tyranny. But
the spirit of English liberty, it is pretended, for-
bids any such interposition, and compels us to abandon these most helpless of our fellow creatures
to whatever fate their masters may ordain.

Alien Bill
a virtual
repeal of an
important
provision
in the
Scotch Act
to prevent
wrongous
imprison-
ment.

While the debates on the Alien Bill were going
on in the House of Lords, where Lord Ellenborough asserted, in his strong and intemperate
way, that the King had, by his prerogative, in
peace as well as in war, a right to order any
foreigners to quit the kingdom (in support of
which opinion he most absurdly cited the authority
of Vattel) ; I happened to recollect the Scotch
Act of King William to prevent wrongous imprisonment, passed in 1701. That Act, the great
Habeas Corpus Act of Scotland (as it has been
often called), which was meant to secure to the
inhabitants of that part of the island the same personal liberty as they enjoy in England, declares,
that no person shall be transported forth of the
kingdom except with his own consent given before
a judge, or by legal sentence. If it should be
contended that the words "no person" mean no
natural born subject, the answer is, that the contrary has been expressly decided by the Court of
Session, in the case of Jos. Knight, a native of
Africa, bought in Jamaica as a slave, and brought
by his master into Scotland. The Court inhibited

---

* In the Code Noir, the King of France calls the slaves *his*, as denot-
ing that they were entitled to his protection. "*Nos* esclaves" is the
expression. In the British dominions, though the slaves of their masters, they are the subjects of the King.

the master from taking him out of the kingdom, holding (*inter alia*), that he was entitled to the benefit of this Act.* I mentioned this to Lord Holland, and hoped he would have noticed it in the Lords on the last debate on the Alien Bill; but he omitted to do it. I should afterwards have mentioned it in the House of Commons, on agreeing to the amendments made in the Bill by the Lords, but I could not attend at the time. It is curious that the repeal of so important a clause in the Act of wrongous imprisonment should have been made by this and by all the former alien Acts, and never should have been noticed in any of the debates.

25th, *Tu.* The Recorder of London having been lately examined as a witness before the Committee of the House of Commons appointed to inquire into the state of the police of the metropolis, and having asserted, in his evidence, not merely as matter of opinion, but as a certain fact, that a cause of the increase of felonies in the metropolis was the taking away the capital punishment for picking pockets; I availed myself of this opportunity of exposing the fallacy of that statement, which has been so often made by the Lord Chancellor and Lord Ellenborough; and I accordingly attended the committee to-day as a witness, and stated the facts which appear to me entirely to disprove that assertion. My statement will of course be printed with the rest of the evidence which the committee intend to report to the House.

The Recorder and I examined as witnesses before the Police Committee.

* This case occurred in January, 1778, and is mentioned in a note in Howell's *State Trial*, vol. xx. p. 2.

Facility
with which
capital
punish-
ments are
enacted.

Yesterday was read a third time in the House of Commons and passed, a Bill to make the destroying, or beginning to destroy, by persons riotously assembled, any of the machinery employed in collieries, a capital felony. The Bill was brought into the House by Mr. Lambton, a considerable owner of collieries; but neither on moving for leave to bring in the Bill, nor in any stage of it, was the attention of the House in any manner called to this penal enactment. The offence is already by a former statute a felony, punishable with transportation. That this severity has not been sufficiently efficacious; that the crime is in any degree increasing; that any remarkable instance of it has of late occurred, was not stated by any one. But, as if the life of man was of so little account with us, that any one might at his pleasure add to the long list of capital crimes which disgrace our Statute Books, the Bill passed through all its stages as matter of course, without a single statement or inquiry, or remark being made by any one. As soon as I knew of the Bill, I watched it through its last stages; but, after consuming many hours in the House to my great inconvenience in a fruitless attendance, I was never able to be present when the Bill came on. To-day, on occasion of the third reading of a Bill requiring the clerks of assize and of the peace in Ireland to make returns to Government of the criminals tried at the different assizes and quarter sessions, I spoke of this penal Bill which had passed yesterday; animadverted upon the facility with which such Bills were passed; and expressed a hope that in the Lords, in which such great difficulties were made whenever it was proposed to abolish any one capital offence, some more attention and consideration would be given to this Bill for adding to such offences, than had been done in the Commons. I made these observations in the confident expectation that they would appear in the newspapers of the next day, and be read by some of the peers; but, to my mortification, I did not observe that any notice was taken in any of the papers of what I had said.

27th, *Th.* I mentioned this Bill to Lord Lauderdale, Lord Holland, and Lord Shaftesbury, and they all said they would attend to it. The real reason, I believe, for making this new capital felony, is, that the principal object of the Bill is to give the owners of collieries, whose property is injured by any such outrages as the act contemplates, an action against the hundred; and there is not, that I know of, any instance of such an action being given, but in the case of a capital felony. It is not from any desire to hang the poor wretches who may be convicted on this law that it is passed, but because, without exposing them to be hanged, the proprietors of collieries do not know how to decide that they may have a remedy against the hundred.

July 2d, *Tu.* Parliament was prorogued.

13th, *Sat.* On the invitation of the family of Richard Brinsley Sheridan, I this day attended his funeral.* I understood that it was to be very

Sheridan's funeral.

---

* He died on Sunday, the 7th of July.

private, and that he was to be followed to the grave
only by a few of his friends, and of those who had
been particularly connected with him in politics.
When I arrived at Peter Moore's house in George
Street, to which the body had been removed, as
being near to Westminster Abbey, where it was to
be buried, I was astonished at the number and the
description of persons who were assembled there * ;
the Duke of York, Lord Sidmouth, Lord Mul-
grave, Lord Anglesea, Lord Lynedoch, Wellesley
Pole, and many others, whose politics have been
generally opposite to Sheridan's, and who could
grace the funeral with their presence, only to pay
a tribute to his extraordinary talents. How strange
a contrast! For some weeks before his death, he
was nearly destitute of the means of subsistence.
Executions for debt were in his house; and he passed
his last days in the custody of sheriffs' officers,
who abstained from conveying him to prison merely
because they were assured that to remove him
would cause his immediate death; and now, when
dead, a crowd of persons the first in rank, and
station, and opulence, were eager to attend him to
his grave. I believe that many, and I am sure that
some, of the mourners were self-invited. Such
certainly were three of the Prince's friends, Lord
Yarmouth, Bloomfield, and Leach. They sent a
letter from Carlton House the day before the funeral, expressing a desire to attend, and their offer
was not refused. The Prince, about ten days be-

* Among his old friends who attended were the Duke of Bedford,
Lord George Cavendish, Lord Robert Spencer, Lords Holland, Erskine, and Lauderdale.

fore Sheridan's death, when he was in great distress, and after some of the newspapers had observed upon the strange inattention he met with, had sent him a present of 200*l.* ; but Mrs. Sheridan had the spirit to refuse it, and when she communicated to her husband what she had done, he approved her conduct. The immediate cause of his death was reported to be an abscess; but the truth is, that his constitution was nearly worn out, and that his death was rapidly accelerated by grief, disappointment, and a deep sense of the neglect he experienced.

30th, *Tu.* My dear Anne, with all our children, except William, who is in Shropshire, and John, who is at school, set off this day for Cheltenham, and I remain in town till the Chancellor's sittings shall terminate.

Aug. 30th, *Fri.* I set out (after coming out of Court, for the Chancellor's sittings have lasted till this morning) for Cheltenham.

31st. Through Oxford to Cheltenham.

Sept. 1. 2. & 3. Remained at Cheltenham. Met there M. de Bourke the Danish Minister, Mr. Pattison the American, Matthias, &c.

4th. Set out with Anne and the children, passed through Gloucester, Newnham, by the banks of the Severn to Chepstow, and from thence through Cardiff to Cowbridge.

5th, *Th.* Looked over my estate at Barry and Porthkerry, and in the evening returned from Cowbridge to Cardiff, where we slept.

6th, *Fri.* By the banks of the Taaffe, a beautiful drive to Merthyr Tydvil, from thence to

Brecon, Hay, and Cabalva, Mr. Davies's; remained at Cabalva, where William met us, till

21st, *Sat.* When we went to J. Whittaker's at the Grove, not far from Presteign. Stayed there till we removed to Knill, on Wednesday, *Sept.* 25.

Oct. 8th, *Tu.* Set out for Tanhurst, passed through Hereford and Ledbury, slept at Upton.

9th, *Wed.* Through Oxford, slept at Henley.

10th, *Th.* Arrived at Tanhurst.

Wetness of the season. The weather has been uncommonly wet throughout the summer, and during the whole of this last journey through Herefordshire, Worcestershire, Oxfordshire, Berkshire, and Surrey, we saw the greatest part of the harvest on the ground, drenched with the heavy rains which have lately fallen, in an extremely bad state, and great part of it likely to be lost. In the neighbourhood of the Thames, and in many other places, the country was flooded to a very great extent. In other places, the crops were still standing; and often in the adjoining fields, the new wheat was rising and very high on the ground. **Prospect of scarcity.** In Radnorshire and the part of Herefordshire we have been staying in, the prospect is extremely alarming. There must be a very great scarcity of wheat and barley. The potatoes, too, which form so large a part of the food of the poor, have greatly failed; and, to add to their distress, the long continuance of rain has prevented them from getting peat from the moors, and laying in their usual stock of winter fuel.

Oct. We left Tanhurst and returned to town.

The Lord Mayor's dinner. *Nov.* 9th, *Sat.* I dined at Guildhall at the Lord Mayor's dinner. Though always invited, I never dined there before. Wood, the Lord Mayor of the last year, with whom I am personally acquainted, was re-elected for the present year. His conduct during his mayoralty has been highly meritorious; particularly in detecting an atrocious conspiracy of thief-takers to get innocent men convicted of coining, that they might share the rewards given on such occasions. It is usual for the Ministers to dine with the Lord Mayor; but as the present Ministers do not approve of Mr. Wood's politics, they all absented themselves. They had done the same last year.

Dec. 2d, *Mon.* A meeting was held to-day of a great multitude of persons in the Spa Fields near Islington, pursuant to an adjournment of a former meeting which had been held in the same place about a fortnight ago. The ostensible object of that former meeting was, to petition the Regent on the subject of the public distresses; and that of the present, to learn in what manner the petition had been received, and what further steps were to be taken. Hunt, formerly candidate at Bristol, took the lead upon both these occasions, and made violent speeches against all public men, except Sir Francis Burdett, Cobbett, and Lord Cochrane. It was determined at this meeting, that a petition should be presented to the House of Commons, and that Lord Cochrane, and I believe Sir Francis Burdett, should present it. These proceedings would be hardly worth mentioning, had it not been that a party, headed by one Watson, issued forth from the meeting, and, proceeding into the city, broke into the gunsmiths' shops, armed themselves

Meeting in Spa Fields.

and committed many violent outrages, till they were dispersed, and some of the ringleaders secured by the courage and good conduct of the Lord Mayor.

26th. I left town for Tanhurst, and remained there with my dear Anne and all my children except William, who is still with Mr. Otter, till the 10th of *January*. Mine has been a happy life, but I know not any fortnight in it which I have passed more happily than this.

1817.

Jan. 10th.   On my return this day from Tanhurst, I found a letter which had come by some
private hand.   It was from General Savary, and
was dated at Smyrna, 4th of July, 1816.   It be-
gins in these words : — Letter received from
General Sa-
vary, Duke
de Rovigo.

"Ce n'est que depuis le recouvrement de ma
liberté que je puis vous remercier de la réponse
que vous avez eu la bonté de faire à la lettre que
j'ai eu l'honneur de vous écrire il y a environ un
an, lorsque je me suis cru en danger à bord du
Bellerophon dans la rade de Plymouth.   Tout ce
qui m'est arrivé depuis cette époque m'a convaincu
que je ne dois qu'à votre intérêt généreux de
n'avoir pas été victime d'une translation en France,
qui étoit alors vivement demandée par le gouvernement de ce pays.*   Pendant ma longue détention
je vous ai voué une bien sincère reconnoissance."
He then proceeds to the objects of his letter,
which are, to inquire how he should proceed to
obtain redress against persons who, he says, have
libelled him in publications in England, imputing
to him the murder of Captain Wright, and other
atrocities to which he was an entire stranger ; and
to communicate to me a narrative (which was
enclosed) of the transactions which preceded

* I do not believe that it was ever intended by the Ministers to
deliver him up to the French Government.

Bonaparte's going on board the Bellerophon, in
order that, if I thought proper, I might publish it,
or make what use of it I might think fit.   " Vous
vous rappellerez," he says, " que j'étois du nombre
des personnes qui avoient suivi la mauvaise fortune
de l'Empereur, et que, par suite d'une disposition
ministérielle, j'ai été conduit à Malte, et enfermé
au secret le plus rigoureux pendant sept mois,
ainsi que sept autres officiers qui étoient au même
cas que moi.   C'est en vain que l'on a cherché
des prétextes pour justifier une mesure aussi
étrange.   Le véritable motif de cette sévérité étoit
la crainte que je ne parlasse, ainsi que mes com-
pagnons, de toutes les circonstances qui ont pré-
cédé et suivi l'arrivée de l'Empereur à bord du
vaisseau de Bellerophon.   J'ignore les raisons que
l'on a eu de craindre des divulgations ; mais quelques soient les considérations qui aient déterminé à
agir comme on l'a fait, je ne m'en crois pas moins
obligé à tenir la parole que j'ai donnée à l'Empereur
en recevant son dernier adieu ; il m'a fait pro-

Bona-
parte's
request to
Savary.

mettre, Monsieur, de vous adresser tout ce qui
étoit relatif à cette partie de son histoire, et je
m'y suis engagé.   Il connoissoit votre nom et
votre caractère ; cela étoit suffisant pour entraîner
sa confiance ; et c'est avec le même respect que je
recevois ses ordres dans sa plus haute prospérité,
que j'exécute les dernières volontés qu'il m'a ma-
nifestées dans son infortune.   Je n'ai aucun but
agitateur en vous transmettant cette narration,
mais, si l'usage qu'il vous conviendra d'en faire en
rendoit la publication nécessaire avec l'attache de
mon nom, je suis homme d'honneur, Monsieur le

Chevalier, et, quelque danger qu'il pût en résulter pour moi, je vous prie d'en agir comme il vous plaira sans avoir égard à moi ; dût-il m'en coûter la vie, je mettrai de la gloire à convenir que c'est moi qui vous l'ai adressée." The narrative enclosed, and thus referred to, consisted of seventeen quarto pages, closely written, and in a small hand.* The most important part of it is that which relates the interview which took place between himself (Savary) and Captain Maitland, before Bonaparte ventured on board the Bellerophon. Bonaparte, according to this account, having arrived at Rochfort, and not having received the passport which Fouché had undertaken to apply to the Duke of Wellington for, to enable him to go to America, sent Savary and Las Cases on board the Bellerophon, to inquire whether Captain Maitland had received it. Captain Maitland had heard nothing of any passport, and was even ignorant of Bonaparte's abdication. In the course of the conversation which took place, Savary and Las Cases asked Captain Maitland how he would act if Bonaparte sailed for Rochefort in a French vessel, and how, if he were to take his passage in a neutral ship ; after answering that, in the first case, he should capture the vessel and make Bonaparte a prisoner, and that, in the latter, he should detain him till he had received directions from his admiral how he was to act, he added, according to the narrative : " L'Empereur fait fort bien de demander des passeports Anglois pour éviter des

---

* It is entitled " *Note sur les Evènements qui ont suivi le Départ de l'Empereur de l'Ile d'Elbe jusqu'à son transport à Ste. Hélène.*"

désagrémens qui seroient chaque jour renouvelés
à la mer, mais je ne crois pas que notre gouvernement le laisse aller en Amérique. Alors, Messieurs
Savary et Las Cases lui ayant reparti, 'Où donc
lui proposeroit-on d'aller?' Monsr. de Maitland
répondit, je ne le devine pas, mais je suis presque
certain de ce que je vous dis. Mais quelle répug-
nance auroit-il à venir en Angleterre? De cette
manière il trancheroit toutes les difficultés. M. de
Las Cases repartit, qu'il n'avoit pas mission de
traiter cette question, mais que lui personellement,
il croyoit que l'Empereur ne s'étoit pas arrêté à
cette pensée, parcequ'il craignoit peut-être les effets
d'un ressentiment qui seroit la conséquence naturelle
d'une longue mésintelligence entre lui et le gouvernement Anglois ; que d'un autre côté, il aimoit
les climats doux, et surtout les charmes de la conversation ; et qu'en Amérique il pouvoit trouver
l'une et l'autre, sans craindre aucun mauvais traite-
ment de qui que ce soit. Monsr. de Maitland ré-
pliqua, que c'étoit une erreur de croire que le climat
d'Angleterre fut mauvais et humide ; qu'il y avoit
des comtés, où le climat étoit aussi doux qu'en
France, dans celui de Kent par exemple ; et que
les agrémens de la vie sociale y étoient incompara-
blement supérieurs à tout ce que l'Empereur pouvoit rencontrer en Amérique ; que quant aux res-
sentimens qu'il pourroit craindre de la part des
Anglois, c'étoit le moyen de les éteindre tous que
de venir vivre au milieu d'eux sous la protection
de leur lois ; que là il étoit à l'abri de tout, et
rendoit les efforts de ses ennemis impuissans ; que,
quand même les Ministres voudroient le tracasser,

ce qu'il ne croyoit pas, ils ne le pourroient pas, parceque (ajouta-t-il), chez nous le gouvernement n'est pas arbitraire, il est soumis aux lois. Je crois bien, continua-t-il, que le gouvernement prendra, vis-à-vis de lui, des mesures également propres à assurer sa tranquillité et celle du pays où il résidera, telles que celles qui furent prises à l'égard de son frère Lucien (par exemple) ; mais je ne concevrois pas que cela pût être étendu au-delà, parceque, je vous le répète, les Ministres n'en ont pas le droit, et la nation ne le souffriroit pas.   Monsr. de Las Cases observa de nouveau à Monsr. de Maitland, qu'il n'avoit pas mission de traiter ces objets, mais qu'il avoit bien retenu sa conversation, qu'il la rap- porteroit à l'Empereur, et que, s'il se décidoit à aller en Angleterre, il lui en feroit part ; et il lui fit cette question, ' Dans le cas où l'Empereur adop- teroit cette idée d'aller en Angleterre, et je con- tribuerai de tous mes moyens à l'y décider, pourra- t-il compter sur un transport à bord de votre vais- seau, tant pour lui que pour les personnes qui l'ac- compagnent ? ' Monsr. de Maitland a répondu qu'il n'avoit pas d'ordre pour cela, mais qu'il alloit en faire le sujet d'une question à son Amiral, et que, si l'Empereur lui demandoit passage sur son bord avant qu'il en eût une réponse, il com- menceroit d'abord par le recevoir." This convers- ation was immediately reported to Bonaparte, and two days afterwards, on the 14th * * *, he sent the General Lallemand and Las Cases again to Captain Maitland, on board the Bellerophon, " comme parlementaires. Il y eut entre ces Mes- sieurs et le Capitaine Maitland des explications sur la conversation qu'il avoit eu l'avant veille avec Messieurs Savary et Las Cases. Il avoit depuis lors été rejoint par une autre corvette appelée Le Henry, commandée par un Capitaine qui se nommoit Sertorius. Le Général Lallemand revint le même jour rapporter à l'Empereur le détail de tout ce qui s'étoit passé à bord du Bellerophon. Monsr. de Las Cases étoit resté à bord de ce vaisseau, d'où il écrivit à l'Empereur que le Capitaine Maitland l'avoit chargé de le prévenir que, s'il se décidoit à venir en Angleterre, il étoit autorisé à le recevoir, et qu'il mettoit son vaisseau à sa disposition." It was not till after all this had taken place, that, according to this narrative, Bonaparte went on board the Bellerophon. Besides this narrative, there was enclosed in the letter to me one addressed to the Lord Chancellor, requesting him to grant Savary a passport to come into this country. This letter I delivered to the Chancellor : he said that the granting passports was wholly in Lord Sidmouth's department; but that he would speak to his Lordship on the subject. About three weeks afterwards, he told me that he had accordingly applied to Lord Sidmouth, and that, without assigning any reason, he declined to grant it.

I had no doubt that the publication of Savary's narrative would be of no service either to Bonaparte or to himself, and that it would gain no credit in England; but yet, as it merely contained a statement of alleged facts, and as the parties concerned had not the means themselves of making what they state to be their case known, I had some scruple whether it was not almost a duty in me to publish it. I consulted Lord Holland on the subject, and showed the memorial to him, and to him only. Lord Holland strongly dissuaded the publication. In consequence of this I wrote to Savary[1] in these words:—

" Sir,

" Your letter, dated the 4th of July last, was not delivered to me till the 10th of this month. As soon as I received it, I waited on the Lord Chancellor." I then stated the result of my interview, and gave him my opinion as to prosecuting the persons he complained of. " The paper you have been pleased to transmit to me I have read with very great attention and interest. I understand it to have been submitted entirely to my judgment, as to the use which should be made of it; and, so understanding, my opinion is very decided that it would not be, by any means, expedient at the present moment to publish it. Whenever published, it must be with your name; for the whole importance of the paper depends upon its being known by whom the statements in it are made. I shall preserve the paper till I hear from you how you wish it to be disposed of."

Answer to General Savary.

28th. Parliament met. It was opened by the Regent in person. On his Royal Highness's return from the House of Lords, he was very grossly insulted by the populace. Stones were thrown at his carriage, and one of the glasses broken. Lord

Parliament met.

[1] Vide *suprà*, p. 199. — ED.

James Murray, who was in the carriage, was examined in each House of Parliament; and, from his deposition, it should seem that bullets were fired at the carriage, as he imagined, from an air gun*, no report having been heard. The Houses immediately voted addresses to the Prince Regent on the occasion; and the further consideration of the Speech was, in each House, adjourned to another day.

29th. Some petitions for a reform of Parliament, presented by Lord Cochrane, were objected to by several Members, on account of supposed disrespectful language in which they were couched. I spoke for the reception of them, thinking that, under the present circumstances, it was very unwise to seek out pretences for rejecting the people's petitions : they were, however, rejected.

An amendment was moved to the address by Ponsonby, and a division took place.

31st. Petitions for reform presented by Sir Francis Burdett, and again objected to. I urged the receiving them.

Feb. 4. Sealed up papers were, by order of the Regent, laid before each House of Parliament, and referred to a Select Committee. This is preparatory to some restraint intended to be imposed on the liberty of the people, on the ground of some dangerous conspiracies said to be in existence. Among the Committee of the House of Commons were Mr. Ponsonby, Sir Arthur Piggott, and Lord Milton.

---

* It seems since to have been fully ascertained that there was no ground for this supposition.

8th or 9th. The Privy Council granted warrants for seizing several persons charged with treasonable practices, and, after examination, they were committed.

Persons committed for high treason.

10th, *Mon.* Another meeting was held by adjournment in Spa Fields. A great crowd assembled, and Hunt appeared amongst them and harangued them. No outrage or riot, however, took place. The persons seized and committed for treason were obscure and indigent men, but who had acted a conspicuous part in the former meetings, and had signed the notices for convoking them.

12th, *Wed.* I moved in the House of Commons for leave to bring in a Bill to repeal an Act passed in the last Session, which added greatly to the severity of the Game Laws. It had passed quite at the close of the Session ; had stood in its different stages as an order of the day amongst forty or fifty other orders ; had passed without a single word being said upon it ; and received the Royal Assent the day before the Parliament was prorogued. The Act* professed in the preamble to be made against persons who went armed by night, and committed acts of violence and murders ; but, in its enacting part, it punished, with transportation for seven years, any person who should be found by night in any open ground, having in his possession any net or engine for the purpose of taking or destroying any hare, rabbit, or other game ; and, to add to the cruel absurdity of this law, it fixed the limits of night for the purposes of the Act to be between the hours of eight o'clock at night and seven in the

Game laws.

* This Act is 56 Geo. 3. c. 130.

morning, from the 1st of October to the 1st of
March (that is, three quarters of an hour after sun-
rise, and one hour and a half after broad daylight);
and between the hours of ten at night and four in
the morning, from the 1st of March to the 1st of
October. So that, according to this law, even a
qualified person (for there is no distinction made)
who should go out before seven in the morning, in
the beginning of October, to shoot game, is liable
to be transported as a felon. Leave was given to
bring in the Bill.

Report of Select Committee. 19th. The Select Committee to whom the
sealed papers had been referred made their unani-
mous report, stating that a conspiracy had been
formed to excite a general insurrection, and that
dangerous secret societies existed; and they concluded by saying, that they submitted to the most
serious attention of the House the dangers which
existed, and which the utmost vigilance of Government under the existing laws had been found in-
adequate to prevent. This last sentence was very
lightly inserted in the report. Sir Arthur Piggott
(a member of the committee) told me that he did
not know that it was there; and the truth was that
no evidence was laid before the Committee of any
vigilance exerted by Government to execute the
existing laws.

Bill for the suspension of the Habeas Corpus Act. 21st. A Bill was brought into the House of
Lords to empower his Majesty to secure and detain
such persons as his Majesty shall suspect are con-
spiring against his person and government; a Bill
which is generally called " A Bill for the Suspension of the Habeas Corpus Act."

In the House of Commons I presented a petition, signed by a great number of the inhabitants of the Tower Hamlet division, complaining of misconduct in the magistrates for that division, in granting and refusing licences to public-houses. I availed myself of this opportunity to animadvert on some of the matters which appear in the report of the Police Committee of last Session, particularly the great number of low public houses, the notorious receptacles of thieves; the great increase of crimes, particularly by children; and the mischiefs arising from rewards given upon convictions.

Abuses by Middlesex magistrates in licensing public houses.

24th. The report of the Secret Committee was taken into consideration in the House of Commons, and Lord Castlereagh stated all the measures which the Ministers intended to propose; which were, to suspend the Habeas Corpus Act; to revive the Act of 1795 for preventing seditious meetings; to revive the Act lately expired which punished with death the seduction from their allegiance of soldiers and sailors; and to pass an Act for making the same attempts on the life or person of the Regent high treason, as are now treason when made on the King. I spoke on this, and, in the course of my speech, observed that, before we made new laws, it was necessary that we should know what had been done to enforce those which already exist. The Attorney-General admitted that, till within a few days, he had not instituted a single prosecution.

Report of the Secret Committee.

27th. On the second reading, in the House of Commons, of the Bill for suspending the Habeas Corpus Act, I opposed it to the best of my ability,

Bill for suspending the Habeas Corpus.

in a speech of some length. I did not deny the existence of considerable danger; but I endeavoured to show, as I most sincerely think, that the proposed remedy is not at all adapted to the evil.

Habeas Corpus Suspension Bill, as it affects Scotland.

28th, *Fri.* The Bill was read a third time in the House of Commons, and passed. Before the business came on, a petition against the Bill from the Livery of London was presented to the House. I took this occasion to call the attention of the House to the situation in which the Bill would place the people of Scotland, who could not, from the remoteness of their situation, prefer their complaints, and express their alarms to the House, as the Livery of London could; although they would be placed in a much worse condition than the people of England. With respect to the English, the benefits of the Habeas Corpus Act were taken away only from persons committed for treason or suspicion of treason, under a warrant signed by a Secretary of State or six Privy Counsellors; but with respect to the inhabitants of Scotland, the benefits of the act against wrongous imprisonment were taken away from persons committed for treason or misprision of treason by any inferior magistrate, any Sheriff-substitute, or Justice of the Peace; and, when once committed, there was, according to the provisions of the Bill, no power of bringing them to trial but under an order signed by six Privy Counsellors, which there was no probability that obscure manufacturers or artisans would ever have interest enough to procure. This statement made a considerable impression on the House; and the Lord Advocate (M'Conochie),

who at first declined giving any explanation on the
subject, being afterwards, in the debate which took
place on the third reading of the Bill, called upon
to state, whether my representation of the effect of
the Bill was correct; very confidently asserted that
it was incorrect; and that, although the clause respecting Scotland expressly declared, "that no
judge, justice of peace, or other officer of the law,
should liberate, try, or admit to bail, any person or
persons that was or were or should be in prison for
such causes as aforesaid, without order signed by
six of the Privy Council," this must be construed
with reference to the former clause relative to England, and therefore must be understood, "any person committed by warrant signed by a Secretary of
State, or six Privy Counsellors:" and he was im-
prudent enough to say, that he was the more confident that this must be the construction of the law,
because a similar clause was contained in former
acts of the same kind, particularly those of 1794
and 1798; and he thought it quite impossible that
the persons who framed those acts could intend to
place the people of Scotland in so unhappy a condition as they would be in if my construction of
the Act were to prevail. I observed upon this, that,
as such was the opinion of the Lord Advocate,
there could be no objection on the part of Ministers to inserting a very few words in the Bill to
make that which was stated to be the intention of
the authors clear; and I therefore moved to insert
after the words " that the act for preventing wrongous imprisonment should be suspended," the words,
" with respect to persons so committed as afore-

Amend-
ments made
in it in the
House of
Commons.

said;" and after the words before cited, "any persons that were or should be in prison in Scotland," the words "under a warrant or warrants so signed as aforesaid." The Lord Advocate and the Ministers acceded to this, and these amendments were adopted.

The minority upon the division on the third reading was 103; on the second reading it had been 98. The majority were considerably more than two to one on both occasions.[1]

Lord Chancellor.

March 2d, *Sun.* I hear that the Chancellor is extremely angry at the amendments made to the Bill in the Commons, and says that the Act will be useless for Scotland: that the Lord Advocate has not known what he was about; and that it will be impossible for the Lords to agree to the amendments.

Amendments agreed to by the Lords.

3d, *Mon.* The amendments were taken into consideration by the Lords, and underwent some discussion. The Lord Chancellor said that they had made the Bill much worse than it was before, but yet he should propose to agree to them; and accordingly they were agreed to. The truth is, that the Chancellor and his colleagues are unwilling to have any further debates take place on the subject.

Panegyrics on Horner.

On the same day, a writ was moved for in the House of Commons to elect a Member for St. Mawes, in the room of Horner, who died lately at Pisa. He had gone thither last autumn, in the

---

[1] On the second reading, ayes 273; noes 98. On the third reading, ayes 265; noes 103. — ED.

vain hope of recovering his health. The motion was made by Lord Morpeth; and he took that occasion to pronounce very just encomiums on Horner's private and public virtues. Canning followed him, and joined in these praises, but he spoke of Horner only as a person who was rising into great eminence as a politician. Charles Williams Wynn dwelt also for some time on his many estimable qualities. All these gentlemen were little more than the acquaintance of Horner; but I had had a long and intimate friendship with him; and I thought myself called upon to mention those merits for which I most highly valued him; and to say that, which, if he could witness what is now passing amongst us, I thought he would most wish should be said. I noticed particularly his independence of mind, and observed that, while he was taking a most conspicuous part in our debates, and was commanding the admiration of the House, he never relaxed in the most laborious application to his profession (though without any success in it at all proportioned to his merit), because he thought it essential to maintaining his independence that he should look to his profession alone for the honours and emoluments to which his talents gave him so just a claim. I spoke, too, of his eloquence, as being not merely calculated to excite admiration and vulgar applause, but as ennobled and sanctified by the great and virtuous ends to which it was uniformly directed, the protection of the oppressed, the enfranchisement of the enslaved, the advancing the best interests of the country, and enlarging the sphere of human happinesss.* Considering his knowledge, his talents, his excellent judgment, his patriotic intentions, and the prospect of years which he had before him, I consider his death as a great public calamity.

Seditious
Meetings
Bill.

10th, *Mon.* In a Committee of the whole House on the Bill to prevent seditious meetings, I opposed, and divided the Committee on the clause, which empowers magistrates to order the taking into custody of persons who utter words which to them appear intended to excite the people to contempt of the Government and constitution; and if they are resisted, to declare the meeting an unlawful assembly, and command persons to disperse on pain of death. It was a very thin House; the numbers were 42 for the clause, and 16 against it.

14th, *Fri.* On the third reading of the Seditious Meetings Bill, I spoke against it at some length. The division produced only 44 votes against the Bill, and 179 for it.

Welsh
judges.

18th, *Tu.* On a writ being moved for in the House of Commons to return a Member for Bridport, in the place of Sergeant Best, who has been appointed to the office of a Welsh judge, I drew the attention of the House to the nature of the office, and stated how incompatible it was, in my opinion, with a seat in Parliament. Ponsonby said that, after the Easter recess, he would move for

---

* The speeches delivered on this occasion were published by Lord Holland in a pamphlet, which was translated into Italian by Ugo Foscolo. Most of the speeches so published were corrected by the speakers. It is intended to erect a monument to Horner by subscription in Westminster Abbey. [1]

---

[1] This has since been done. — ED.

leave to bring a Bill into Parliament to disqualify Welsh judges from sitting in the House of Commons.*

On the same day, Mr. Lyttelton moved several resolutions expressing the sense of the House on the mischievous effects of lotteries, and declaring that they should be abolished. I spoke in support of the resolutions. We both of us endeavoured to make the moral and pious Chancellor of the Exchequer sensible of the wickedness of this measure of finance, which he annually with such complacency resorts to.[1]

Lotteries.

21st, *Fri.* The Bill I have brought in to repeal the Game Act of last Session stood for a second reading to-day. Bankes, who is desirous that it should not pass before the next quarter sessions, if at all, moved to put off the second reading for ten days, on the ground that all the persons who are now in custody under the Act would otherwise be discharged and escape all punishment. They certainly would; but surely this is better, though some guilty persons would go with impunity, than exposing those who may have committed no greater crime than trying to snare a hare or a rabbit to the risk of being transported for seven years. The House, however, thought other-

Game laws.

---

* He never made this promised motion; but instead of it, at the suggestion of some of the Members for Wales, he moved for the appointment of a committee to inquire into the Welsh judicatures. The committee was appointed, but did not make its report till near the end of the Session.

---

[1] The motion was rejected by a majority of 46; the numbers being, for it 26, against it 72. Lotteries were subsequently abolished in 1823, by 4 Geo. 4. c. 60.; and in 1837, the advertising foreign or other lotteries was declared illegal by 6 & 7 Will. 4. c. 66. —ED.

wise, and put off the second reading. In the course of what I said on this occasion, I took notice of the pernicious effects of our present system of game laws; and particularly observed upon that spirit of inhumanity and ferocity which it seemed to excite in all orders of persons, on whom it could be thought to produce any effect. It was not only in poachers, but in the preservers of game, that a savage disposition was every day becoming more manifest. The poachers went out armed, prepared for acts of most desperate violence; while, on the other hand, the practice was becoming every day more frequent of placing spring guns and other engines of death or of mutilation in enclosed grounds and woods, by which the most dreadful calamities were brought often on persons who were perfectly innocent. I stated such expedients to be clearly illegal, and that if the death of a man produced by such means were not murder (as I supposed it was not), yet it was certainly a very aggravated manslaughter in those who placed, and in those who gave directions for placing, the engine where it was found. This practice, to our disgrace, is quite peculiar, I believe, to England. I have never heard or read of such means being resorted to in any other countries, even in those in which the most severe laws were made and enforced for the preservation of game.

Spring guns, &c.

Southey's application to the Court of Chancery for an in-

A matter which lately came before the Court of Chancery has been so much misrepresented in some of the newspapers, that it seems desirable to preserve some account of it, such as it really was.

Southey, the Poet Laureate, some time in 1793 or 1794, when he was a very young man, wrote a dramatic piece, which he entitled " Wat Tyler." It abounded with invectives against kings, and nobles, and governments, and boldly asserted the claims of the people to a perfect equality of rights and a division of property. The bookseller, to whom it was given soon after it was written, would not venture to publish it; and it remained disregarded and unknown, till Southey, by the violence of his censures on all those who maintained any popular opinions, provoked his enemies to bring this poem to light, that it might be seen to what extremes, on contrary sides, he at different times had gone. Southey, as the author, and having the copyright of the work, applied on the last seal, the 18th of March, for an injunction to restrain the booksellers from publishing it. I was counsel for the booksellers; and, to oppose the injunction, I was furnished with an affidavit, sworn by Mr. Winterbotham, a dissenting clergyman, who had been prosecuted, in 1794, for some sermons preached by him at Plymouth; and who stated that, while he was confined in Newgate, in consequence of that prosecution, Southey, together with a bookseller of the name of Eaton, came to him in prison; that Southey there produced the play of Wat Tyler, and said he was desirous that it should be published, but that he did not wish to derive any profit from it, and that it was the pure offering of his heart in the cause of freedom. Winterbotham also swore that he had at the time dissuaded the publication, thinking it extremely dan-

junction to stay the publication of Wat Tyler.

gerous ; and that he was an entire stranger to the present publication, and was not in any manner, either directly or indirectly, concerned in it. This affidavit, though sworn, had, by the negligence of the attorney, been omitted to be filed ; and, upon this objection being made, it became impossible for me to use it. Not being able, therefore, to show that Southey had relinquished his claim to any copyright, and had abandoned the work to the public, I could only submit to the Court, that the work was of such a nature that a Court of justice could not interpose on behalf of the author of it. The Lord Chancellor was clearly of that opinion, on reading the poem. He thought it (as it unquestionably was) of a most dangerous tendency, and refused to grant an injunction.

Some of the newspapers represented me as contrasting Southey's former with his present opinions, and as describing him giving a fraternal embrace to the person to whom he delivered the poem. Of this there was not a word of truth ; but nothing is more common, with some of the newspaper reporters of what passes in courts of justice, than to state speeches and strokes of humour as coming from the counsel, which are the pure invention of themselves, the reporters.

26th, *Wed*. I was prevented to-day, by a very bad cold attended with fever, from going into court.

I continued confined for several days.

Letter from inhabitants of Edinburgh on the suspension of the

29th, *Sat*. I received, a few days since, a letter from Edinburgh, signed by eighty-nine gentlemen resident there. It began in these words :— " As inhabitants of this city, we beg leave respectfully, but sincerely, to express the gratitude we feel for the important favours you have conferred on us, and the whole people of Scotland, by procuring an amendment to be inserted in the Bill for suspending the Wrongous Imprisonment Act. Your patriotic exertions have delivered us from a degrading distinction, and lessened the risk of our being exposed to the capricious and wanton tyranny of inferior magistrates." The letter then proceeds in terms of very high commendation of my conduct in Parliament, on this and on other occasions. This letter was enclosed in one from Mr. M'Culloch, in which he stated that it would have been more agreeable to himself, and to the rest of those who had subscribed the letter, to have voted an address to me at a public meeting; but that he need hardly explain the difficulties in the way of such a proceeding, and that no rotten borough in the kingdom was as rotten as Edinburgh; that the mass of the citizens seemed to have lost all sense of the value of freedom; and that an apprehension of appearing singular, and of drawing on themselves the hatred of power prevented many, really impressed with liberal sentiments, from venturing to express them; but that better times seemed to be approaching. He likewise mentioned that it was wished, if I saw no objection to it, that the letter of thanks to me should be published. I returned an answer in these words :—

" Sir,   March 29th, 1817.

" I have received the honour of your letter of the 22d instant, enclosing one signed by many gentlemen residing at Edinburgh, in which they are pleased to convey to me their thanks for the alteration which I procured to be made in the Act of Parliament recently passed, for suspending the Scotch Act to prevent wrongous imprisonment; and to express their approbation of my general conduct as a Member of Parliament. It has been extremely gratifying to me to find my conduct approved and applauded by gentlemen who are themselves so highly respectable; and I beg that you would have the kindness to express my sincere acknowledgments to them. I have to thank you, too, Sir, for the kind manner in which you have made this communication to me. You observe that it is the wish of the gentlemen who have signed the letter, to make it public, if I see no objection to it. There is but one objection, and that is a very serious one: it is, that the gentlemen who have subscribed it have expressed their opinion of me in terms a great deal too flattering, and have gone much beyond any praise that I can aspire to. If it were not for this objection, I should have thought it extremely desirable that the letter should be published. It appears to me to be of great importance that there should be some declaration of public opinion, on the subject of the law which the Ministers fully intended should have been passed for Scotland. It is generally supposed that before the present Act expires, a new Bill will be brought in for continuing it; and the declaration made by the Lord Chancellor, when the amendments of the House of Commons were taken into consideration by the Lords, can leave little doubt that, if a new Bill is brought in, it will be in the terms in which the present law was originally framed*; and how such an evil is to be averted I know not, if it shall appear that the people of Scotland are really indifferent about it.

" I have the honour to be," &c. †

April 4th. I still continued unwell, and to-day (Good Friday) being the first day that I was sufficiently recovered, I removed to Tanhurst. We had the comfort of having William and all our other children with us. We stayed till Tuesday, 15th April, when I returned nearly, if not quite, well.

14th, *Mon.* The House of Commons stood adjourned to this day; but, the Speaker being ill, it was farther adjourned to Thursday, April 24th. On that day it met.

House of Commons adjourned on account of the Speaker's illness.

26th, *Sat.* Met to-day, at dinner at G. Philips's, the Bishop of Norwich (Dr. Bathurst). It is the first time that I have seen him. He appears to be a most delightful old man, and the exact pattern of what a Christian Bishop ought to be.

28th, *Mon.* On presenting a petition to the House of Commons from some inhabitants of Gloucestershire, complaining of the expense and delay which attends the recovery of small debts, I

Writs of error and other contrivances to harass and delay creditors.

---

* The new Bill which was afterwards brought in was not in the terms of the Bill as originally brought in, but adopted the alterations made by the Commons.

† A few days afterwards, without any further communication with me, the original letter to me, together with this answer of mine, were published in a Scotch newspaper called *The Scotsman.*

took occasion to mention the great abuses which exist in the Common Law courts in bringing writs of error. The extent of these abuses came to my knowledge by mere accident. I, some time ago, franked a letter for some person who was a stranger to me, addressed to the debtors in the gaol of Liverpool. The letter was overweight, and, as none of the prisoners would pay the postage of it, it was returned to me from the post-office as to the person who had franked it. Seeing that it was a very thick letter, and not knowing but that it might contain money, I opened it, in order that I might send the contents of it under different covers. It did in fact contain a letter of recommendation of a person in the Temple to act as agent of insolvent debtors; a number of his cards to be distributed amongst the prisoners ; and a paper of advice to debtors, which the writer recommended should be preserved for the benefit of the future, as well as the present, inhabitants of the prison. This paper pointed out to debtors the modes by which they could most effectually annoy and harass their creditors, delay their proceedings, and weary them out for expense. The best modes of pleading sham pleas, bringing writs of˙error, and filing injunction bills were pointed out ; and various modes by which, according to the calculations in the paper, a debtor might, at the expense of five guineas to himself, put his creditor to the expense of 100*l.* ; and for 24*l.* and a fraction, oblige him to pay in fees and expenses above 300*l.* I stated the facts contained in this paper in the House of Commons ; but, on account of the mode in which I had learned its contents, I omitted to mention the name of the writer.

May 7th, *Wed.*   A clergyman of the name of Thirlwall, who was also a magistrate for Middlesex, was brought to-day to the bar of the House of Commons for a breach of privilege, in an attack made by him in print on the Committee appointed to inquire into the police of the metropolis. I had taken no part, but I was present in the House on a former night, when he was ordered to attend; and in consequence of something which passed to-night on the subject, I explained why I had silently concurred in the resolution. It was not that I had at all altered my opinion on the subject of privilege; but the publication in the present case consisted of charges of partiality and misconduct in the Committee, whose labours were unfinished, who had merely reported evidence, but had not yet come to any conclusion, or reported their opinion ; and it was published manifestly to influence their proceedings, and the future proceedings of the House. After making an apology, and expressing his contrition, Mr. Thirlwall was dismissed without any further proceeding.

9th, *Fri.*   Mr. Grattan moved in the House of Commons for a Committee on the state of the Catholics. The question was lost after a long debate, by a majority of 24 ; 245 against the question, and 221 for it. Canning and Lord Castlereagh both spoke in support of the motion ; Lord Castlereagh well, Canning extremely ill, and very little like one who was in earnest. They were probably neither surprized nor concerned at being

Margin notes:

Privilege of Parliament.

Catholic emancipation.

left in a minority. After being outvoted in the
Cabinet, it is not wonderful that they are outvoted
in the House of Commons. They still continue
in office; though they admit this measure, which
they are thus prevented from carrying, to be one
of the most important that can at the present moment engage the attention of Government. All
the Prince's personal friends voted against the
Catholics.

15th. Three days ago I received from my excellent friend Dr. Parr a letter, in which he tells
me that, in the two last wills which he has made,
he has left me a large quantity of plate; that it is
an article in which he is very rich, it being known,
he says, that, among many other peculiarities, he
is a man "cui stupet insanis acies fulgoribus;"
and that, in consequence of his fondness for masses
of gorgeous plate, he might well be called Philargyrus. That he had bought much, and much had
been given him by his friends and his pupils; that,
being grown old, he had lost the enjoyment of these
things, and that he had come to a determination to
convert his legacy into a gift, and to send it me in
his lifetime : and he adds, that previously to his
late marriage, he had apprized his wife of the promises he had made, and the legacies he had given;
and had told her, that nothing should ever induce
him to violate the one or to revoke the other. The
letter is full of kindness to me, and expresses warm
approbation of my principles and conduct; and
concludes with a request, that I would at some
distant time let my children read that his unfeigned testimony to what he is pleased to call the

moral and intellectual merits of their father. This
letter [1] has not a little embarrassed me. I have so

[1] The following is the letter referred to. — ED.

" Dear Sir Samuel Romilly,

" Though neither to you nor Mr. Fox did I ever utter one
syllable upon clerical preferment, yet I had a sincere and deep conviction that he, if he had continued Minister, would have given me a place
on the Bench of Bishops, and that you, if you had been Chancellor,
would have seated me in some lucrative and honourable prebendal stall,
and perhaps thrown in a living as a kind of " *mantissa*."

" My judgment and my feelings lead me to assign to the anticipated
will all the merit of the actual deed. I had long been accustomed to
look with reverence on the talents of those two worthies, with affection
upon their virtues, with triumph on their sympathies with my own
political sentiments ; and strange it were if the genial (or I should rather
say the holy) warmth of gratitude had not strengthened my confidence
and heightened my joy! I seldom dissemble what I really think ; I never
profess what I *do not* really feel ; and therefore, after noting these preliminary declarations, I shall proceed to business. You may have heard
that, among other peculiarities, I am a man

' Cui stupet insanis acies fulgoribus.'

So strong, indeed, and so inveterate is my saving habit, that, in consequence of my fondness, not for bags of hoarded money, but for masses
of gorgeous plate, I may justly be called Philargyrus.

" Remembering the danger of alliance between poverty and pride, I
never expended upon plate more money than, consistently with my
own views of a moderate and decent competency, I could well spare ;
and so it is that many of my pupils, and many of my friends, knowing my
love of finery in this one way, have decorated my table with many valuable presents. But our gratifications vary with our changes in years.
' Thy servant,' said Barzillai to David, ' is this day threescore and ten
years old ; and can I hear any more the voice of singing men or of singing women ? Can I taste what I eat, or what I drink ?' This, dear
Sir, is the language of uncorrupted nature, and thus, in the spirit of
old Barzillai, having passed my seventieth year, I shall cease to have
the same pleasure in gazing upon my silver. I recollect with satisfaction the joy which it has so long given me. I do not want it for my
own use — I do not desire it, and I wish to distribute it among those
whom I love and respect, as a memorial of my friendship ; and I will
not wait for death as a signal for me to part with that which I could
not either employ, or even behold in the grave. Under such impressions, I have this year given away plate to the value of near a thousand
pounds. Some I have sent away ; other articles I have secured to the
owners by having their names inscribed, and, with their permission, I
retain them for my occasional use, subject, however, to the peremptory
demands of the several claimants. Thus I have the exquisite satisfaction of knowing that my friends see and feel the sincerity of my
regard. Before marriage, I, with my wonted plain dealing, told
Mrs. Parr that I had given certain promises, and made certain
bequests ; and I added explicitly, that no earthly consideration should
induce me to violate one promise, or to revoke one bequest. Though

long known Dr. Parr, and have received so many proofs of his attachment to me, that I should be extremely sorry to give him any offence, and yet I by no means wish to receive his present. I have accordingly written to him to induce him to retain his plate as long as he lives, and to let it come to me only if I should happen to survive him.

Residence of the clergy.

16th, *Fri.* On the Bill respecting the residence of the clergy, upon which the House went to-day into a committee, much was said about the means best calculated to enforce residence. I did not take any part in the debate; but the most

---

the chief produce of the harvest be carried to other barns, the gleanings are quite sufficient for all purposes of real convenience, or reasonable vanity, in the widow of a country parson. And now, dear Sir, we come to the application of these garrulities as it may concern Sir Samuel Romilly. In my two last wills, I have left you the following particulars:— 'Forty-eight silver plates, four silver covers, which, being divided, will occasionally make eight dishes; two large silver dishes, a gorgeous silver tureen and stand, a silver waiter, which, from its bulkiness and exquisite workmanship, is not unfit for the sideboard of a Lord Chancellor, when he entertains the Cabinet, or the whole Bench of Judges, with the Attorney and Solicitor General at the bottom of the table.' Last summer, I determined to offer these things to you before I died. I determined to send them to you. That determination cannot be shaken. Pardon, dear Sir, my honest pride, when I express my hope that, like my other friends, you will on each article put a little memorandum of my name; and, casting away all superfluous and spurious delicacy, tell me how Dr. Parr can, with more propriety, bequeath these precious decorations of his table, than by presenting them to a man who, for so many years, and on so many accounts, has been entitled to his regard, his reverence, and his confidence, as Sir Samuel Romilly!

" In the course of the year we will make arrangements for the conveyance. I shall put the whole into a strong box or two. I shall send my trusty servant to Russell Square; and you, if it be your pleasure, shall pay his travelling expenses to and from London. Thus, I have unburthened my soul. Give my best compliments and best wishes to Lady Romilly; and, at some distant time, let your son [a] read this my unfeigned testimony to the moral and intellectual merits of his excellent father. I am, dear Sir, your most sincere friend, and faithful obedient servant,

" SAMUEL PARR.

" Hatton, May 10th, 1817."

---

[a] See Appendix. — ED.

effectual mode of enforcing residence, would certainly be to make non-residence a defence to a suit for tithes; and I mentioned this to Sir William Scott, to Lord Ebrington, and to Mr. Babington, who had spoken in the debate.

20th, *Tu.* Sir Francis Burdett moved for a committee to inquire into the state of the representation. I spoke and voted for the motion. It was lost by a very great majority — there being only 77 who voted for it.[1]

Parliamentary reform.

21st, *Wed.* Mr. Peel moved, and obtained leave to bring in a Bill to continue the Irish Insurrection Act. I intended to have opposed it; but, knowing that Sir Henry Parnell meant to oppose it too, I waited for him to rise first, as he meant to do. But the question having been put very hastily, it was declared by the Speaker to be carried, before he had risen; and it has, therefore, passed without opposition.

Irish Insurrection Act.

22d, *Th.* A petition was presented to the House of Commons, signed by many bank directors, and by all the principal bankers in London, complaining of the abuses which exist under the present mode of executing the Bankrupt Laws. I took this opportunity to state my opinion of the present system of Bankrupt Law, which I did at some length. Amongst other things, I observed, that the excessive severity of the law, which punishes capitally the offence of a bankrupt not appearing to his commission, and that of his withholding property from his creditors to the amount of 20*l.*

Bankrupt laws

[1] 265 voted against it; making a majority of 188 against the motion. — ED.

defeated the object of the law altogether. Though the crime was extremely common, and though the law had been in force now for more than eighty years, there had not been altogether more than five or six convictions under it. Men chose rather to submit patiently to the gross frauds which were practised on them, than to become parties to the execution of such cruel and sanguinary laws.

Irish Insurrection Act.

23d, *Fri.* I opposed, on the second reading, the further progress of the Bill for continuing the Irish Insurrection Act, on the ground that a measure of such extraordinary severity ought not to be continued but in case of absolute necessity; and that that necessity could not be apparent without an inquiry into the state of Ireland. That it was quite unjustifiable to persevere in such a system upon no better grounds than the mere statements of the Irish Secretary. None of the Members for Ireland supported me in this opposition, except Sir Henry Parnell and General Matthew.

25th & 26th. Whitsunday and Monday spent at Holland House. Brougham there.

Resignation of Mr. Abbot, and choice of a new Speaker.

30th, *Fri.* Mr. Abbot, the Speaker, resigned the chair.

June 2d, *Mon.* Mr. Charles Manners Sutton (the Judge-Advocate, and son of the Archbishop of Canterbury) was chosen Speaker, he being supported by the Ministry. The numbers were, 312 for him, 152 [1] against him. The other Member who was proposed was Mr. Charles Williams Wynn, a man far more eminently qualified for the chair than Mr. Sutton, and who has, by long attention to the subject, made himself completely master

[1] Tellers included. — ED.

of the law of Parliament, and the forms of Parliamentary proceeding.

6th, *Fri.* A Bill brought into the House of Commons to enable the clergy to grant leases for ten years of their tithes, with the consent of the patron and ordinary, which shall be binding on their successors, went through a committee of the whole House. In the course of the debate which took place on it, I mentioned the great evils that arise from the length of time which it is necessary to go back to establish any custom in bar of a demand for tithes, namely, to the time of Richard I.; though, with respect to all other property, sixty years is sufficient.

Tithes.

13th, *Fri.* On a motion for going into a committee on the Irish Insurrection Bill, I again resisted the further progress of it, and supported a motion of Sir Henry Parnell for an inquiry into the facts which were stated as the grounds of proposing the measure. General Matthew and Sir William Burroughs were the only other Members who opposed the Bill now; as they were the only Members who had, together with myself and Sir Henry Parnell, opposed the second reading.

Irish Insurrection Act.

17th, *Tu.* Watson, who was tried for high treason at the bar of the Court of King's Bench, was yesterday acquitted. The trial had commenced on the Monday preceding, and, consequently, had lasted seven days; the Court adjourning every evening, and the jury being kept by themselves at a tavern in Palace Yard. The prisoner was indicted together with three other persons, Thistlewood, Preston, and Hooper; but, as the prisoners severed in their challenges of jurymen, it was

Watson tried for high treason and acquitted.

necessary to try them separately. Watson being acquitted, the Crown lawyers did not think proper to proceed with the other trials; but, this day, on the prisoners being brought to the bar, declined to produce evidence against them, and they were all acquitted. The facts charged as constituting high treason in Watson, were, the disturbances and acts of violence which took place in the metropolis on the 2d of December last, in consequence of the meeting in Spa Fields, and which were represented to be the result of a previous conspiracy of the prisoners to overturn the Government. Ministers, whose object it has been to give an extraordinary degree of importance to every appearance of disaffection or tumult which has manifested itself in any part of the kingdom, thought proper to commit the prisoners to the Tower, to try them at the bar of the King's Bench, and to arraign them of high treason. If they had been committed to Newgate, tried at the Old Bailey, and indicted merely for a very aggravated riot, they would, without doubt, have been convicted. Instead of this, they are declared innocent, and they escape all punishment, except, indeed, a long and close imprisonment previous to trial, which, as they have been finally acquitted, has the appearance of a great injustice done to them.

Lord Folke-
stone's
motion re-
specting the

18th, *Wed*. I took part in the debate on Lord Folkestone's motion [1], for the purpose of reprobating the illegal and unconstitutional doctrine contended

[1] Lord Folkestone's motion was for copies of all instructions sent by the Secretary of State to all gaolers, magistrates, or other persons, respecting the custody and treatment of persons confined in consequence of the suspension of the Habeas Corpus Act.

for by the Attorney and Solicitor General, that *prisoners in*
the Crown, by committing men to prison charged *Reading*
with treason, or on suspicion of treason, might pre- *gaol.*
vent any magistrates having access to them; notwithstanding that, by the statute 31 Geo. III.,
magistrates are expressly authorized to visit gaols,
for the purpose of detecting and reporting to the
Sessions abuses which they may discover.[1]

19th, *Th.*   Dr. Parr would not listen to my re- *Dr. Parr.*
presentations; and this day his servant arrived by a
stage coach from Hatton, with the plate destined
for me packed up in two boxes.   It is much more
splendid and valuable than I had imagined; so
valuable that I feel very great regret at his having
sent it, notwithstanding that it is so flattering a testimonial of his good opinion of me.[2]

[1] The motion was lost by a majority of 29; the numbers being, for
it 56, against it 85. — ED.

[2] The following letter to Dr. Parr, in acknowledgment of this present, is taken from Dr. Johnstone's publication of Dr. Parr's Memoirs
and Correspondence. — ED.

" Russell Square, June 23. 1817.

" My dear Sir,

" Lady Romilly informed you of the safe arrival of your servant
with the plate, and he will, probably, before you receive my letter, have
got safe back to Hatton.   When I saw the full display of your magnificent present, I was very much dazzled with its splendour.   It very
far surpasses what I had expected, from your account of it, in beauty
and in value.   Rich, however, and magnificent as it is, its greatest
value in my eyes will always be, that it was yours ; that I received it
as a present from you ; and that it will remain with me a splendid
memorial of the good opinion which a man, whom I have so honoured and respected as I have you, is kind and partial enough to
entertain of me.   It is impossible that I should ever behold it without
a feeling of pride, at having been so honoured by you; and I have the
greatest satisfaction in reflecting that, when I shall have long been in
my grave, it will still continue the evidence in my family of the estimation in which I was held by Dr. Parr.   That you may long live in the
enjoyment of all the happiness you can desire, and that I may never
forfeit any part of your good opinion and your friendship, are the sincerest wishes of my heart.   I remain, dear Sir, with great gratitude and
warm affection, your most sincere and faithful friend and servant,

" SAML. ROMILLY."

Curwen's
Bill re-
specting
tithes
drawn by
Baron
Wood.

Curwen moved for leave to bring in a Bill to amend the law with respect to tithes. He understands little of the matter himself; and what he is doing is at the suggestion of Mr. Baron Wood, who has already drawn for him the Bill which he intends to bring in. The principal objects of it are, as I understand them, to authorize the receiving usage as evidence of a real composition, where the deed itself cannot be produced, and as evidence of exemptions or discharges from tithes claimed under dissolved monasteries; and to allow of presumptions of grants and conveyances of tithes from long usage as against lay impropriators. I spoke in support of the Bill as far as I understood these to be its objects.* Sir Wm. Scott, who, as Member for the University of Oxford, conceives himself bound to watch with great jealousy every innovation with respect to ecclesiastical property, expressed great doubt about the Bill, and reserved to himself a right to oppose it in its future stages, though he acquiesced in its being brought in.

On the same day, on a motion of Sir Egerton Brydges, for leave to bring in a Bill to alter and amend the Act of the King [54 Geo. 3. c. 156.] respecting the copyrights of authors, I expressed my disapprobation of that clause of the Act which makes it necessary for authors, whether they desire to derive benefit from the Act or not, to give printed copies of every work they publish to the Universi-

* A few days after this, Baron Wood sent me a little tract he has printed, entitled " Observations on Tithes and Tithe Law," with a note, in which he told me, that he hoped I should support the Bill in all its future stages.

ties and other public bodies, as a most unjustifiable tax upon literature.

20th, *Fri.* I presented a petition to the House of Commons against the further suspension of the Habeas Corpus, signed by 1400 of the inhabitants of Hull. The petition occasioned some debate on the Bill, and on the conduct of Government with respect to the persons who had been arrested and prosecuted, particularly those in Scotland; in the course of which, the conduct of the Lord Advocate, in preferring three different indictments for the same offence, was by some Members (particularly Lord Archibald Hamilton, Brougham, and Finlay) much censured. I took occasion to observe, that I had heard that the Lord Advocate, though he had preferred three indictments against the same prisoner successively for felony (the two first being held to be bad), had every time procured him to be committed on a charge of treason, that he might be confined in the Castle of Edinburgh, and under closer confinement than he could be if only charged with felony. The Ministers professed to be ignorant of the matter, and the Lord Advocate was absent.

23d, *Mon.* The Act for farther suspending the Habeas Corpus having been brought down from the Lords last Friday, was, on this day, read a first time in the House of Commons. A long debate took place, in which I opposed the Bill to the best of my abilities, and in a speech of some length, which was very favourably listened to.[1]

Marginal notes: Petition against suspension of the Habeas Corpus. The Lord Advocate of Scotland. Habeas Corpus Suspension Bill.

---

[1] On the division, the numbers were, for the first reading of the Bill 276, against it 111; majority 165. — ED.

25th, *Wed.*   I submitted to the House of Commons some motions on the subject of Lord Sidmouth's circular letter to the lieutenants of counties, written on the 27th of March last.   I moved, as Lord Grey had before done in the House of Lords, for a copy of the case upon which the opinion of the law officers had been given; and I moved two resolutions besides, pointing out and censuring the unconstitutional nature of that proceeding.   The view which I took of the case is embodied in these resolutions.   The letter is in these words : —

Lord Sidmouth's circular letter to the lieutenants of counties.

" As it is of the greatest importance to prevent, as far as possible, the circulation of blasphemous and seditious pamphlets and writings, of which, for a considerable time past, great numbers have been sold and distributed throughout the country, I have thought it my duty to consult the law servants of the Crown, whether an individual found selling, or in any way publishing such pamphlets or writings, might be brought immediately before a justice of the peace, under a warrant issued for the purpose, to answer for his conduct. The law officers, having accordingly taken this matter into their consideration, have notified to me their opinion, that a justice of the peace may issue a warrant to apprehend a person charged before him upon oath with the publication of libels of the nature in question, and compel him to give bail to answer the charge. Under these circumstances, I beg leave to call your Lordship's attention very particularly to this subject; and I have

to request that, if your Lordship should not propose to attend in person at the next general quarter sessions of the peace, to be holden in and for
the county under your Lordship's charge, you
would make known to the chairman of such sessions
the substance of this communication, in order that
he may recommend to the several magistrates to
act thereupon, *in all cases* where any person shall
be found offending against the law in the manner
above mentioned. I beg leave to add, that persons
vending pamphlets or other publications in the
manner alluded to, should be considered as coming
under the provisions of the Hawkers' and Pedlars'
Act, and be dealt with accordingly, unless they
show that they are furnished with a licence, as required by the said Act. I have the honour to be, &c.
" SIDMOUTH."

The resolutions which I moved were,—" That
it is highly prejudicial to the due administration
of justice for a Minister of the Crown to interfere
with the magistrates of the country in cases in
which a discretion is supposed to be by law
vested in them, by recommending or suggesting to
them how that discretion should be exercised.
Secondly, That it tends to the subversion of justice,
and is a dangerous extension of the prerogative,
for a Minister of the Crown to take upon himself
to declare in his official character to the magistracy
what he conceives to be the law of the land ; and
such an exercise of authority is the more alarming,
when the law so declared deeply affects the security of the subject and the liberty of the press,

Resolutions
moved
upon it.

and is promulgated on no better authority than the opinions of the law officers of the Crown." The motion for the copy of the case was negatived; and the resolutions were got rid of by the previous question, moved by the Attorney-General.[1]   I felt this to be a matter of considerable importance, and took great pains to point out *, at very considerable length, the mischief of allowing the executive power to assume to itself the exercise of a discretion vested by law in judicial officers; and to presume in matters, if doubtful, to solve these doubts, and pronounce what the law is. The new Solicitor-General[2] took part in the debate; but he confined his speech to the question of law, as to the power of magistrates to hold to bail for a libel before indictment.

Wrongous Imprisonment Act. Suspension Bill in Scotland.

26th, *Th.* On the Bill for the further suspension of the Habeas Corpus, Lord Folkestone moved in the Committee to expunge the clause which extends the Bill to Scotland. I supported his motion, and contended, that the last Report of the Secret Committee, which afforded the only grounds on which the present measure was proposed, did not take the least notice of Scotland; and, as it had been admitted by the Ministers that it had not been found necessary in a single instance to

---

* The *Times* newspaper, in giving an account of this speech, mistaking something that I said of the appointment of the new Solicitor-General, made me pay a high compliment to Garrow for his independence, &c. &c., though nothing could be farther from my intention than to pay him any compliment; and I never named him or alluded to him.

---

[1] By a majority of 108; the numbers being, for the resolutions 49, against them 157. — Ed.

[2] Sir Robert Gifford; Sir Samuel Shepherd having been promoted to the Attorney-Generalship. — Ed.

exercise in Scotland the authority given them by the Act which was about to expire, there could be no reason for continuing it in that part of the kingdom. No answer was given to these observations, but Lord Folkestone's motion was rejected.[1]

27th, *Fri.* This was the third reading of the suspension of the Habeas Corpus Bill, and a long debate on it took place.[2] The Lord Advocate of Scotland was in the House, and just as the question was about to be put, at near one o'clock in the morning, he started up and said, he had been all night waiting in his place, expecting to hear the charges preferred against him, which he understood had been brought forward in his absence, and he complained of the unfairness of so attacking him behind his back, and saying nothing when he was present to defend himself. He seems to have thought that all other matters, as being of far inferior consideration, ought to have been laid aside the moment it was discovered that he was in the House. Talk no longer about the liberties of the nation or the preservation of the Constitution, for behold, the Lord Advocate in his place, and ready to enter upon his defence! His defence was indeed a singular one. He admitted the fact of his having caused the prisoners at first, and after each indictment, to be committed on a charge of treason; but he represented the committing them at the same time on the two charges of treason and felony as having been done for their benefit and

M'Conochie Lord Advocate of Scotland.

---

[1] By a majority of 81; the numbers being, against Lord Folkestone's motion 129, in favour of it 48. — ED.

[2] The Bill was carried by a majority of 130: for it 195, against it 65. — ED.

protection, and to prevent the possibility of their
being detained as long as the prosecutor might have
detained them without bringing them to trial, if the
commitments had followed each other at intervals,
instead of being contemporaneous. The sum of
which, if I understood him, was, that he had pro-
tected the prisoner against an abuse of power by
himself; but surely he might have trusted himself not to have recourse against the prisoner
to dilatory proceedings, for the mere purpose of
oppression and vexation. If it was *not intended* to
try them for treason, why were they three times
committed on such a charge? and if they *were*
to be tried for treason, why were indictments first
preferred against them for felony? With respect to
the charge brought against him by Lord Archibald
Hamilton, he denied that the two first indictments
he had preferred had been quashed as being bad;
but Brougham, who had in his pocket the printed
account of these proceedings, proved his Lordship's
statement to be very incorrect.* The Lord Advocate said that he had come from Scotland purposely
to answer these imputations. It was certainly the
general opinion that he had much better have
stayed where he was. He has indeed made a very
poor figure both here and in Edinburgh, where
he has gone on from one blunder to another in the
whole course of his state prosecutions. It appears
strange that a man of such limited abilities should
have been raised to so important a situation; but
The Scotch the truth is, that all the men at the Scotch Bar,
bar.

* On the third indictment, one of these men, M'Kinlay, was
brought to trial in July, and was acquitted, after having suffered a close
imprisonment of many months.

who are most considerable for learning, talents, and reputation, are in opposition to Government; such as Clerk, Cranstoun, Jeffrey, Murray, Moncreiff, Thomson, and Grant.

29th, *Sun.* Dined at Richard Wilson's, at Fulham. Met there Pionkowski, the Pole, who was with Bonaparte at Elba, attended him on his entry into France, and came over with him to England. He was not allowed to accompany Bonaparte to St. Helena, but was permitted afterwards to join him, and was with him a year at St. Helena. I had a good deal of conversation with him. He says that Bonaparte's sole occupation is the writing his memoirs, to which he devotes a great deal of time every day, and he makes his attendants copy out fair what he writes. Pionkowski complains that Bonaparte is treated with great insolence and harshness by Sir Hudson Lowe, and is exposed to great hardships. It must be observed, however, that he is an enthusiastic admirer of Bonaparte, and seems disposed to exaggerate.

Pionkowski's account of Bonaparte.

30th, *Mon.* The Act for farther suspending the Habeas Corpus Act received the Royal assent.

The same night Mr. Ponsonby was seized, in the House of Commons, with an apoplexy, of which he died on Tuesday, July 7th. He was a very honest man, had many excellent qualities, and possessed very considerable talents; but he was, by no means, fit for the situation which he has for ten years occupied — that of leader of the party of Opposition.

Mr. Ponsonby.

July 9th, *Wed.* By a motion for papers, I brought to the notice of the House of Commons a very flagrant instance of the inefficacy of West In-

Dominica grand jury present-ment.

x 2

dian laws for the protection of slaves. A man of
the name of Bermingham had brought some of his
slaves to trial, in the island of Dominica, for an offence of which the magistrates before whom they
were brought acquitted them. After their acquittal, their master brought them out into the market-
place, and, of his own authority, inflicted upon
them the same punishment as they would have
suffered by law, if they had been found guilty.
For this offence an indictment was preferred against
him. The grand jury, by a majority of two, threw
out the bill, it being understood that ten of the
grand jury were for finding it a true bill, and twelve
for rejecting it. At the same Court, which was
held in February last, another indictment was preferred against one Le Guay, for cruel treatment of
a female slave, whom, though pregnant, he had
loaded with irons, and beaten with such violence
that he had broken her arm. This bill, too, the
grand jury threw out. There was a third bill, preferred against one M'Corry, for cruel treatment of
a slave, the circumstances of which I am not informed of ; but this, as well as the other bills, had
the sanction of the Attorney-General, and was preferred by his direction, and was signed by himself :
this bill was also thrown out by the grand jury.
But they were not satisfied with this, but thought
proper to present, as a nuisance, the preferring indictments against individuals for cruelty towards
slaves. The presentment, after presenting the bad
state of the jail, proceeds in these words : — " The
grand jury have further to present the dangerous *

---

* As if the danger were not from rendering the slaves desperate
by making them sensible that they had no protection from the laws.

consequences which are likely to occur from the number of indictments* for unmerited punishments inflicted on negroes by their owners, managers, or employers, which have been laid before them this day, unsupported by any evidence whatsoever.† On the contrary, it appeared from the evidence that in *some* of the cases the negroes merited the punishment they received." In my statement I omitted the mention of any names. I have no doubt of the accuracy of the facts stated by me, as I have seen them detailed in a letter from Archibald Gloster, the Chief Justice of the island. It was only last term that, in the case of the King *v.* Hatchard, the Court of King's Bench declared that it was a libel to state of any West Indian grand jury that they would not find a bill of indictment against a person guilty of cruel treatment of his slaves.

The Act of the 51st of the King, to prevent arrests on mesne process for debts of less amount than 15*l.* being to expire at the close of the present Session, I brought a Bill into the House of Commons to continue it for six years, which passed both Houses without opposition.

Statute 51 G. III. c. 124. to prevent arrests for small debts, continued.

12th, *Sa.* Parliament was prorogued.

Parliament prorogued.

I have given a closer attendance in the House of Commons, and have taken a greater part in the debates during this Session, than I have done in any preceding one. It was my duty to do so; for, never since I have been a Member of the

---

* There were only the three already mentioned.
† The evidence on the first indictment had been sufficient to satisfy ten of the grand jury.

House, has any subject come before Parliament of nearly the importance of that which has constituted the great business of the Session — the suspension of the Habeas Corpus Act. I felt deeply the loss which the public has sustained by the deaths of Horner and of Whitbread; who, if they had lived and had enjoyed health, would no doubt have been the most powerful opposers of that unnecessary and most unconstitutional measure; which has established a precedent of tyranny, of which, it is to be feared, the worst use will, in after times, be made. Thinned as the ranks of Opposition have lately been, it becomes each of us who remain to do all we can to resist the pernicious measures of Government. The exertions I have made, to my own very great personal inconvenience, and to the great interruption of my professional occupations, and consequently with no small pecuniary sacrifices, will, I make no doubt, be ascribed by many persons to an eager desire to turn out the present administration, and to obtain for myself the office of Lord Chancellor, to which it may naturally enough be supposed that I should in such an event aspire. How little do those who ascribe my conduct to such motives know me! With the utmost sincerity I can declare that I have no such ambition. I am deeply impressed with the conviction that that high station would add nothing to my happiness, or even to my reputation. Already I have attained the very summit of my wishes. The happiness of my present condition cannot be increased: it may be essentially impaired. I am at the present moment completely independent both of the favours and of the frowns of Government. The large income which I enjoy, and which is equal to all my wishes, has been entirely produced by my own industry and exertion; for no portion of it am I indebted to the Crown: of no particle of it is it in the power of the Crown to deprive me. The labours of my profession, great as they are, yet leave me some leisure both for domestic and even for literary enjoyments. In those enjoyments, in the retirement of my study, in the bosom of my family, in the affection of my relations, in the kindness of my friends, in the good-will of my fellow citizens, in the uncourted popularity which I know that I enjoy, I find all the good that human life can supply; and I am not, whatever others may think of me, so blinded by a preposterous ambition as to wish to change, or even to risk,

> " These sacred and homefelt delights,
>   This sober certainty of waking bliss,"

for the pomp, and parade, and splendid restraints of office; for the homage and applause of devoted but interested dependants; for that admiration which the splendour of a high station, by whomsoever possessed, is always certain to command; and for a much larger, but a precarious, income, which must bring with it the necessity of a much larger expense. The highest office and the greatest dignity that the Crown has to bestow might make me miserable: it is impossible that it could render me happier than I already am. One great source of misery to me in such a situation, the public, and even my most intimate friends, little suspect:

it is the consciousness that I am not qualified to discharge properly its most important duties. I have neither that knowledge in my profession, nor those gifts of nature, which such duties demand. Destitute of all talents I know that I am not. The faculties which I do possess I believe I fully and justly appreciate; but in those which are most essential to a Judge, in strength of memory, and in the power of fixing the attention on one single object, and abstracting the mind from all other considerations, I know myself to be most lamentably and irremediably deficient. Often in earlier life, when I was looking up to that eminent station as that to which I might one day be raised, and when I was planning, and enjoying by anticipation, essential reforms to be effected, and beneficial laws to be passed, I have been haunted by a deep sense of my disqualifications; and, contrasting these with the erroneous opinions which others entertained of me, I have thought how soon, if I were seated on the Bench, I should undeceive my too partial friends and a mistaken public; and with what truth there might be said of me something of the same kind as was observed of Galba — "omnium consensu capax Imperii, nisi imperâsset."

19th, *Sat.* Went to Cumberland Lodge in the evening, and stayed there till Monday morning, the 21st.

26th, *Sat.* Again at Cumberland Lodge; returned the 28th.

Newspaper misrepresentations

August 13th. The misrepresentations made by the newspaper reporters of what passes in the Court

of Chancery are so frequent, that it would be end- of the pro-
less to notice them.　But some which have ap- ceedings in
peared lately are of so extraordinary a nature that Chancery.
they cannot be accounted for by misconception,
but seem evidently the effect of design and system.
The *Morning Chronicle* has been endeavouring to
justify or extenuate the Chancellor's unexampled
and cruel delays; and for this purpose, it has sometimes represented me, and sometimes Sir Arthur
Piggott, as praising him in high and extravagant
terms for the mode in which he discharges the
duties of his office.　At other times it makes the
Chancellor himself express the painful anxiety he
feels to do justice, and the hours he consumes in
endeavouring to discover the truth of each case.
These representations, however, are mere fictions.
Not only the expressions contained in these newspapers were never used, but nothing passed which
could afford a pretext for pretending that they had
been used.　The substance as well as the language,
the panegyrics and the apology, are all pure invention.

24th, *Sun.*　I left town for Tanhurst.

After passing a fortnight at Tanhurst, I set out
(*Sept.* 8th), with my dear Anne and Sophy, to pay
a few visits.　The first was to my friend Phelps,
at Chevenage, a house which he has lately taken
near Tetbury, in Gloucestershire.　In his neighbourhood, or, at least, within a morning's ride, are
Dursley, Berkeley Castle, Frocester Hill, and the
Vale of Rodborough.　We visited all these places,
and passed our time most agreeably; and, on the
14th of September, left Chevenage for Bowood.

We stayed there ten days. The amiable disposition of Lord and Lady Lansdowne always renders this place delightful to their guests. To me, besides the enjoyment of the present moment, there is always added, when I am at Bowood, a thousand pleasing recollections of past times; of the happy days I have spent, of the various society of distinguished persons I have enjoyed, of the friendships I have formed, here; and, above all, that it was here that I first saw and became known to my dearest Anne. If I had not chanced to meet with her here, there is no probability that I ever should have seen her; for she had never been, nor was likely, unmarried, ever to have come, to London. To what accidental causes are the most important occurrences of our lives sometimes to be traced! Some miles from Bowood is the form of a white horse, grotesquely cut out upon the downs, and forming a land-mark to a wide extent of country. To that object it is that I owe all the real happiness of my life. In the year 1796, I made a visit to Bowood. My dear Anne, who had been staying there some weeks, with her father and her sisters, was about to leave it. The day fixed for their departure was the eve of that on which I arrived; and, if nothing had occurred to disappoint their purpose, I never should have seen her. But it happened that, on the preceding day, she was one of an equestrian party which was made to visit this curious object; she over-heated herself by her ride; a violent cold and pain in her face was the consequence. Her father found it indispensably necessary to defer his journey for several days, and in the mean time I arrived. I saw in her the most beautiful and accomplished creature that ever blessed the sight and understanding of man. A most intelligent mind, an uncommonly correct judgment, a lively imagination, a cheerful disposition, a noble and generous way of thinking, an elevation and heroism of character, and a warmth and tenderness of affection such as is rarely found even in her sex, were among her extraordinary endowments. I was captivated alike by the beauties of her person and the charms of her mind. A mutual attachment was formed between us, which, at the end of a little more than a year, was consecrated by marriage. All the happiness I have known in her beloved society, all the many and exquisite enjoyments which my dear children have afforded me, even my extraordinary success in my profession, the labours of which, if my life had not been so cheered and exhilarated, I never could have undergone, — all are to be traced to this trivial cause.

Our last visit was to my old and most valuable friend Jeremy Bentham, at Ford Abbey, in the neighbourhood of Chard ; a house which he rents, and which once belonged to Prideaux, the Attorney General of the Commonwealth. I was not a little surprized to find in what a palace my friend was lodged. The grandeur and stateliness of the buildings form as strange a contrast to his philosophy, as the number and spaciousness of the apartments, the hall, the chapel, the corridors, and the cloisters, do to the modesty and scantiness of his domestic establishment. We found him passing his time, as he has always been passing it since I have

Ford Abbey.

Bentham.

known him, which is now more than thirty years, closely applying himself for six or eight hours a day in writing upon laws and legislation, and in composing his Civil and Criminal Codes; and spending the remaining hours of every day in reading, or taking exercise by way of fitting himself for his labours, or, to use his own strangely invented phraseology, taking his ante-jentacular and post-prandial walks, to prepare himself for his task of codification. There is something burlesque enough in this language; but it is impossible to know Bentham, and to have witnessed his benevolence, his disinterestedness, and the zeal with which he has devoted his whole life to the service of his fellow creatures, without admiring and revering him.[1]

[1] The following letter from Sir S. Romilly was written from Tanhurst on October 2. 1817. — ED.

" Dear Dumont,
" Your letter of the 11th September found me, not as you supposed it would, at this place surrounded by my children, and in the daily contemplation of that beautiful country which is here spread out before us, but rambling about upon a little excursion. We were induced to make it, not to search for greater happiness than we were enjoying at home (for that we did not hope for), but to satisfy some promises we had made to visit some of our friends. We are now, however, returned, and I have the prospect of enjoying for three weeks or a month this earthly paradise (for such it is to me), before my usual labours recommence. One of our visits was to Bowood, — a place which I always see with delight, not only on account of the kindness and excellent qualities of its present owners, but of the many pleasing recollections of past times with which it is in my mind always associated. You must well know, my dear Dumont, how great a part you must have had in those recollections. The days we have passed there, and the delightful walks we have taken together, can never be effaced from the memory of either of us; but, above all, it is because I there first saw my dearest Anne that I never see or think of Bowood but as of the cause of all the real happiness that I have enjoyed in life. Another of our visits was to Ford Abbey. I had heard of it only as of a place that had fallen into decay, and whose gloomy appearance had produced such an effect upon the imaginations of the servants, that they never ventured into some of the apartments, from terror of spirits, with which they supposed them to be haunted. I was much surprised, therefore, by the cheerfulness, and still more by the magnificence, of the house — a palace I should

30th.   We returned to Tanhurst.
From the 16th to the 25th of *October* inclusive,

---

rather call it, for it is much more princely than many mansions which pass by that name.   The front of it extends no less than 250 feet.   To the remains of the monastery, which are very considerable, and are of Gothic architecture, have been added, about the time of Edward VI. or Queen Elizabeth, a great pile of building, broken into different parts, and very richly ornamented, which have a most striking and beautiful effect ; and the pleasure grounds are rendered as gay as a great profusion of flowers can make them.   The rooms are spacious, and some of them splendidly furnished and enriched with tapestry, which is some of the best that I have ever seen in England.   In the midst of all this luxury, we found Bentham leading his usual life, — taking what he calls his ante-jentacular and post-prandial walks regularly every day, and as regularly devoting six or seven hours to his labours of codification. The society we found and left with him were, Mill and his family, and a Mr. Place, an acquaintance which he has, I believe, made since you left us.   Place had been with him about three weeks, and was to quit him a few days after us.   He is a very extraordinary person : by trade he is a master tailor, and keeps a shop at Charing Cross.   This situation — a humble one enough — has, however, been to him a great rise in life, for he began his career in the lowest condition.   He is self-educated, has learned a great deal, has a very strong natural understanding, and possesses great influence in Westminster — such influence as almost to determine the elections for Members of Parliament.   I need hardly say that he is a great admirer and disciple of Bentham's.   Bentham is extremely anxious to see you ; and persuades himself not only that he should be of great use to you, in assisting you to frame the Geneva Code, but that it is hardly possible that you can do without his assistance.   On the subject of procedure, he says, and I think with truth, that it requires experience, which you cannot have had, to form proper rules ; and he thinks that the English law, though bad as a system, is excellent as containing a great collection of facts and an immense store-house of materials for legislation.   In short, he has quite set his heart upon seeing you here ; and I am too much interested that you should come, not warmly to second his request.   He and Mill wrote you a joint letter upon the subject, which he is extremely apprehensive has been lost.   He is just about to publish a work which contains some excellent observations on the importance of substituting a written code in the place of an unwritten common law.   It is entitled ' *Papers relative to Codification and Public Instruction*,' and consists of letters written at different times upon the subject to the Emperor Alexander ; to Madison, President of the United States ; and to the People of America.   The style is obscure, and many things said against England and its Government with great bitterness and asperity, probably as a means of paying court to the Americans, but which, as the book is to be published in London, are, I think, very injudicious.

" You will have seen Miss Vernon, Miss Fox, Whishaw, and Lens, and they undoubtedly will have told you more news of your London friends than I can do.   Ever, dear Dumont, most sincerely and affectionately yours."

a special commission sat at Derby for the trial of
the persons concerned in the outrages committed
in that county in June last. Four men were separately tried and convicted of high treason. After
their conviction, nineteen others, who had before
pleaded not guilty, withdrew that plea and pleaded
guilty, it being understood that they would not be
punished with death. There were twelve other
persons against whom bills had been found; but
the Crown declined producing any evidence against
them, and they were consequently acquitted. Of
the four men who had been tried and convicted,
three (Brandreth, Turner, and Ludlam) were executed.

Nov. 2d, *Sun.* I returned to town from Tanhurst.

6th.   Princess Charlotte, the only child of the
Regent, was last night delivered of a dead child;
and four hours after, at half-after two o'clock this
morning, herself died.

11th.   The death of the Princess is very generally felt, and acknowledged to be a great public
calamity. Much was not known of her, but the
little that was known was favourable to her character.   Her domestic retirement, and the warm affection which seemed to unite her to the Prince,
her husband, had greatly endeared her to the public.   Whether there was much chance, if she had
lived, of a Whig administration again being the
government of this country, I do not know; but
that there is no prospect now of such an event
taking place in a long series of years, cannot be
doubted. This great change in the order of succession to the throne, will, it is probable, have a

very sensible effect upon the Opposition. In all likelihood, it will both thin their ranks and relax their efforts. Upon me it will not have the slightest influence. As a desire of getting into office has never been among the motives which have governed my public conduct, I can, in the present state of affairs, and in the prospect of what is to come, only see stronger ground than I ever discerned before for persevering in that course which I have hitherto pursued.

Dec. Sir John Egerton, one of the members for Chester, having, by a public advertisement, signified his intention not to offer himself as a candidate at the next election, in consequence of the dissatisfaction which he understood that his conduct, in voting for the suspension of the Habeas Corpus, had given his constituents; some of the inhabitants of Chester thought proper, without any communication with me, and without my being personally known to any individual there, to propose me as a proper person to represent the city in Parliament : and in a Chester newspaper of the 20th December, called the " Chester Guardian and Cambrian Intelligencer," appeared an advertisement in these words : — " The Freemen of Chester are hereby informed, that an invitation to Sir Samuel Romilly to become one of our Representatives in Parliament will be ready for signature at 10 o'clock on Saturday morning." Then follows the name of the place where the invitation lay, and a great many praises of me, and a statement that an early canvass for me would be undertaken.

Proposed invitation to me to represent Chester in Parliament.

22d. I received a letter dated Chester, the 20th, from Mr. Joseph Swanwick, describing himself as chairman of the committee, and which, except as to what is complimentary to me, is as follows: "You have probably noticed the conduct of this city on the late suspension acts, and the fact of Sir John Egerton's resignation in consequence of the acknowledged displeasure of his constituents for his conduct on that question. Sir John was seated after a very severe struggle with the Grosvenor interest, and it was generally imagined that the influence of that family would be again exerted in its full force to carry two members for Chester. But some of those who, while they admired his Lordship's political conduct, were still strongly attached to the independence of the city, have had a most satisfactory explanation with his Lordship upon the subject; and he has pledged himself not to oppose the introduction of a member of liberal principles, but, on the contrary, if he should appear to meet the approbation of the citizens, to give him his decided support. In these circumstances our eyes were naturally directed towards yourself," &c. He then goes on to say that Sir John Egerton's friends had begun a brisk canvass in his favour, and that therefore they had had no choice but to announce my name, or to allow many votes to be engaged; that they wished to know my sentiments on the subject, and hoped that there did not exist any irremovable obstacle to my representing Chester in Parliament. I returned an answer in these words : —

" Russell Square, Dec. 23. 1817.

" Sir, — I received yesterday, but too late to answer it by return of post, the letter which you did me the honor to write on the 20th instant. I can hardly express to you how much I am gratified at finding my public conduct approved and applauded by the citizens of Chester. To represent so very respectable a body of constituents in Parliament, I should consider as one of the highest honors that could be conferred on me, and as the best reward I could receive for any endeavours that I may have used to serve the public ; and yet that honor and that reward, highly as I should prize them, I shall find myself obliged most respectfully and reluctantly to decline, if, as I fear is the case, it cannot be obtained without offering myself as a candidate and soliciting the votes of the electors. I have the honour to be, Sir," &c.

I afterwards received another letter from Mr. Swanwick in these words : —

" Chester, Dec. 29. 1817.

" Sir, — I am directed to acknowledge the receipt of your very obliging communication of the 23d inst., and to say how much we should have deemed ourselves honoured to have returned you member for Chester on strictly constitutional principles, and by constitutional means. We conceived that the foreground was perfectly clear ; that all parties fully understood each other ; and that the only opponent we had to contend with, was the ministerial interest in the city. In this it appears

that we have been mistaken, and that it is not
impossible a second member of the Grosvenor
family may be brought forward at the ensuing
election. We cannot express to you, Sir, the chagrin and disappointment with which this turn of
affairs has affected us, not only as it immediately
interferes with our flattering prospect of connexion
with yourself, but as it involves the character of
our city for principle and consistency. We can
assure you, that we have not acted upon light
grounds : direct interviews with Lord Grosvenor,
in the presence of his confidential agents, convinced
both them and us, that the General was not to be
brought forward, and that our nomination was perfectly agreeable to his Lordship ; but, owing to
unpleasant rumours, we again saw Lord Grosvenor
on Saturday evening last, when it appeared by no
means so certain, that General Grosvenor would
be withdrawn. Under these circumstances, with
the detail of which we will not trouble you, we
thought ourselves called upon to close our inter-
course on this subject with his Lordship. We have
cautiously abstained from implicating you in the
transaction any further than as the object of our
best hopes and most deliberate choice. We shall
ourselves look closely to events, but cannot be
guilty of the injustice of exciting expectation which
we cannot fairly hope to realize, and which may
prevent you from paying attention to applications
from other quarters, where the esteem and admiration of your fellow citizens may have fewer obstacles to contend with in showing themselves. With
the most fervent wishes that health and vigour of

mind may long enable you to serve and adorn our common country,

"I remain, Sir, your most obedient servant,
        "Joseph Swanwick,
                "Chairman of the Committee."

My answer to this letter was as follows : —

"Russell Square, Jan. 1. 1818.   My answer.

"Sir, — My last letter will undoubtedly have apprized you that, though nothing would be more gratifying to me than to represent the city of Chester in Parliament, I had formed no sanguine expectation that that honour would ever be conferred upon me. Your favour of the 29th of last month, therefore, has caused me no disappointment. For the very kind manner in which you have addressed me on this occasion, I beg, Sir, you would accept my best acknowledgments. I am proud of the good opinions of those citizens of Chester who were desirous that I should be their representative, and I shall be always most grateful for their good wishes. I have the honour to be," &c.

1818.

8th, *Jan.* WHILE I was on my visit to Bentham last autumn, at Ford Abbey, he gave me a little work he had just printed, and to which he has affixed one of his quaint titles, — " Papers relative to codification and public instruction; including correspondences with the Russian Emperor, and divers constituted authorities in the American United States." I amused myself, after my return to Tanhurst, with writing a paper on this work, which I have since given to Brougham, to insert in the Edinburgh Review, and it has accordingly appeared in the number which has just been published, and which is the Review for November last. My principal object in writing it was to draw the attention of the public to those evils which appear to me to be inseparable from an unwritten law, such as is the Common Law of England. I have spoken in it of Bentham with all the respect and admiration which I entertain of him, but I have thought myself bound not to disguise his faults. I shall be extremely concerned if what I have said should give him any offence.

23rd. Sir William Grant has resigned the office of Master of the Rolls, to the extreme regret of all those who practised in his court, and to the great misfortune of the public. His eminent qualities as a judge, his patience, his impartiality, his courtesy to the bar, his despatch, and the masterly style in which his judgments were pronounced, would at any time have entitled him to the highest praise ; but his mode of administering justice appeared to the greater advantage, by the contrast they afforded to the tardy and most unsatisfactory proceedings both of the Chancellor and the Vice-Chancellor. Sir Thomas Plumer succeeds Grant at the Rolls, and Leach is to be Vice-Chancellor in the place of Sir Thomas Plumer. I had before intended to discontinue my attendance at the Rolls when the next session of Parliament commenced ; but if I had had no such previous intention, this change would have determined me. Plumer has great anxiety to do the *Sir Thomas Plumer.* duties of his office to the satisfaction of every one, and most beneficially for the suitors ; but they are duties which he is wholly incapable of discharging. There is so general a sense of this in the profession, that, if Leach disposes of the business which will come before him with the expedition which is expected from him, very few causes will probably be hereafter set down at the Rolls. The number of causes entered there for hearing has been of late years unusually great ; so great, that, notwithstanding Sir William Grant's great despatch, he has left an arrear of more than 500 causes. Causes were set down there with a twofold object ; — that Sir William Grant might hear, and that Sir Thomas Plumer might not hear them. Leach, *Sir John Leach.* though with a bad judgment, and with little learning in his profession, will, in the present state of the court, be a very useful judge. He is very quick ;

he has few doubts; he will decide with great despatch; and will not, like the two other judges of the court, hesitate and delay his judgments in the plainest cases.   I shall not be surprised if, in a few years, the contrast between Leach's despatch and the Chancellor's delay becomes so striking, that his Lordship will find it difficult to retain his office.   That Leach will, by his extraordinary presumption, involve himself in some ridiculous difficulties, is not at all improbable.   He dined a few days ago in a company of fourteen persons, all of the profession, and some the intimate friends of Sir William Grant.   In the course of conversation, it was said, that that gentleman's leisure might have been very usefully employed, if he had been a member of the House of Lords, in assisting the Chancellor in the hearing of appeals in that House; upon which Leach said to one of Sir William Grant's friends, " If you will undertake that he will give that assistance to the Lord Chancellor, I will undertake that he shall be made a peer."   This was repeated to me in the same words by three persons who were present at the dinner.

Meeting of Parliament.   27th, *Tu.*   Parliament met.   Being fully convinced that the late suspension of the Habeas Corpus was a most unnecessary and mischievous measure, and that it will be a most dangerous precedent, I took this the first opportunity of the House of Commons meeting to call the attention of the House to what had passed during the recess; — to the acquittal of the prisoners who had been apprehended at Manchester, without Government even offering any evidence against them; —

to the trial of M'Kinlay, in Scotland, who was also acquitted; to the nature of the case proved in evidence upon the trials at Derby; and to the three late extraordinary trials of Hone; to show how little foundation there was for the exaggerated statements which had formerly been made, and how ill the suspension of the Habeas Corpus was adapted as a remedy for the evils which really did exist.

Lord Althorp intended to have given notice of a motion for the next day to repeal the Suspension Act, but Ministers themselves announced their intention to move for its repeal.

28th, *Wed.* Accordingly, Lord Sidmouth this day brought a Bill into the House of Lords for its repeal, which was read three times on the same day; and on *Thursday, January* 29th, it was brought down to the Commons, and there read three times and passed. Ministers were desirous that there should be no discussion on it, and in that wish the Opposition, in my opinion not very wisely, acquiesced. I took occasion, however, to observe upon the conduct of Government, which had postponed the meeting of Parliament to so late a period, that it had been impossible to repeal the Act till after the time when the Ministers themselves admitted that it had ceased to be necessary. In truth, there had been no interruption of the public tranquillity at any time since the month of June last; a remarkable period, for it was in that month of June that the conduct of Government in employing spies and informers had been exposed and condemned in the House of Commons. From

The Act for the suspension of the Habeas Corpus repealed.

that time, Government had ceased to employ such instruments ; and, from the time when they ceased to be employed, all the signs of disaffection which had manifested themselves in different parts of the country had ceased.

30th, *Fri.* I dined at Stephen's, at Knightsbridge, with Wilberforce, Brougham, Macaulay, Mackintosh, William Smith, and Harrison. The object of our meeting was, to consider in what way the unhappy condition of the negroes in the West Indies can be most advantageously brought before Parliament, with a view to some legislative measure being adopted for their relief.

31st, *Sat.* The Royal Assent given to the Bill to repeal the Suspension Act.

Feb. 5th, *Th.* Papers relative to the state of the country have, by order of the Regent, been presented to both Houses of Parliament, sealed up : and this day it was moved by Lord Castlereagh, that they should be referred to a secret committee to be named by ballot. I joined with others in opposing this.[1] The speech from the throne, and the recent repeal of the Suspension Act, proved that no legislative measure was meant to be founded on the report of the proposed committee, except an Act of Indemnity to the Ministers : and, for such an inquiry, nothing could be more improper than that the Ministers should themselves name the committee, which they would do if it was to be appointed by ballot. I took this occasion to en-

---

[1] On the question, that the Committee be chosen by the way of ballot, the numbers were, — ayes, 102 ; noes, 29 ; majority in favour of Ministers, 73. — ED.

large upon the consequences which may hereafter be apprehended from such a precedent as that which the late suspension of the Habeas Corpus has established.

10th, *Tu.* Lord Archibald Hamilton moved, in the House of Commons, for the production of the record of Andrew M'Kinlay, before the Court of Justiciary in Scotland, for the purpose of bringing under the view of the House the conduct of the law officers of the Crown, in grossly tampering with a witness of the name of Campbell, produced for the Crown, and whose evidence was, on that ground, rejected by the Court. I supported the motion, and spoke in answer to Lord Castlereagh and the Lord Advocate.   *Law officers in Scotland*

11th, *Wed.* Mr. Fazakerly moved, " That it be an instruction to the Secret Committee to inquire and report whether any steps had been taken to detect and punish the spies employed by Ministers, who by their conduct had encouraged the evils they were only to detect." I spoke in support of the motion.   *Spies.*

17th, *Tu.* I took part in the debate on Lord Folkestone's motion, to refer the petitions of persons, complaining of the hardships they had suffered by imprisonment during the late suspension of the Habeas Corpus, to a committee.[1]

18th, *Wed.* I was examined as a witness before the Committee of the House of Commons, appointed to inquire into the Bankrupt Laws; and

---

[1] This and the two preceding motions were lost by large majorities. — ED.

Bankrupt
laws.

I stated very fully my notions of the mischievous tendency of many of the provisions in the present laws relating to bankruptcy. My evidence will, as matter of course, be printed.*

Curwen's
Bill to
amend the
law of
tithes.

19th, *Th.* The Bill which Mr. Curwen brought last Session into the House of Commons, to amend the laws relating to tithes†, was brought in so late in the Session, that it was impossible to carry it through all its regular stages; it was therefore merely printed and read a second time; and he, this day, again moved for leave to bring in his Bill. Sir William Scott said that he should not oppose its being brought in; but he made a speech, which could have no other object than to raise the strongest prejudice that he could against it. In the most solemn manner he called upon the House to consider the danger of making any alteration in the laws respecting tithes; to reflect that the Church was not represented among them; and to recollect what dangerous and mischievous notions some persons were desirous of propagating with respect to this species of property: and he read a number of passages from different petitions, presented in the last Session of Parliament, complaining of tithes as a great grievance. On what he knew to be the real objects of the Bill, he did not say a syllable. I endeavoured to remove the false and most unjust impression which his speech was calculated to make, and stated what were the evils which the Bill was intended to remedy. I said that

* It has since been printed at length in the Report of the Committee.

† Vide *antè*, p. 300.

I did not approve of all the provisions of the Bill, if it was to be the same as that which was brought in in the last Session ; but that, on the whole, the Bill would effect a most important improvement in the law. Peel, the other Member for the University of Oxford, and Smyth, one of the Members for the University of Cambridge, reserved to themselves a right to object to the Bill when it should be brought in.

25th, *Wed.* Leave was given me by the House of Commons to bring in a Bill to repeal the Act of King William, which punishes shoplifting with death. In the course of the observations which I made* on this occasion, I noticed the bad effects produced by frequent executions, particularly in the case of forgery.[1] For that crime the sentence was seldom remitted ; and yet, under this excessive severity, the crime was rapidly increasing. Though the Crown seldom pardoned, the Bank had power, under a recent Act of Parliament (41 Geo. III. c. 39.), to prosecute what was really a capital crime (the uttering Bank notes, knowing them to be forged) in such a manner as to subject the offender only to transportation. The same uncertainty of punishment therefore, prevailed in this as in other crimes, and the many lives that were sacrificed were taken away without any benefit to the public. I was the rather induced to bring this matter to the notice of the House, at the present moment,

Shoplifting Act. Capital punishments.

* The *Morning Chronicle* contained a tolerably accurate account of this speech.

---

[1] The punishment of death for forgery has since been abolished by 11 Geo. IV. & 1 Will. IV c. 66., and 7 Will. IV. & 1 Vict. c. 84. — ED.

because a considerable impression has been made upon men's minds by some late executions. A week ago, two women were hanged in London for forgery; and on this day two boys were to have been executed for the same crime, and were saved by a discovery, made only two days ago, that they had been employed to commit the offence by a villain, who afterwards gave information against them, and caused them to be apprehended.

27th, *Fri.* Dined at Mr. John Smith's (the Member for Nottingham). Among the company **Mrs. Fry.** I met there was Mrs. Fry *, who has now for about a year most generously devoted herself to the care and improvement of the female prisoners in Newgate. She is the wife of a rich banker in the City; and it is from pure motives of humanity and religion that she has been induced to make such a sacrifice of her time and her comforts. By the accounts of those who knew the prison in its former state, the reforms she has effected are the most important and complete. I learned from her some **Bad effects** curious facts respecting the effects produced by **of capital** capital punishments. Her observations are the **punish-** **ments for** more valuable, as she has had such opportunities **light of-** of seeing and conversing with the prisoners. She **fences.** told me that there prevails among them a very strong and general sense of the great injustice of punishing mere thefts and forgeries in the same manner as murders: that it is frequently said by them, that the crimes of which they have been guilty are nothing, when compared with the crimes

* Wilberforce, and my excellent friend the benevolent William Allen, the Quaker, were also of the party.

of Government towards themselves: that they have only been thieves, but that their governors are murderers. There is an opinion, too, very prevalent among them, that those who suffer under such unjust and cruel sentences are sure of their salvation : their sufferings they have had in this life, and they will be rewarded in that which is to come. All the crimes they have committed, they say, are more than expiated by the cruel wrongs they are made to endure. She spoke of the docility she had found, and the gratitude she had experienced from the female prisoners, though they were the most profligate and abandoned of their sex. Kind treatment and regulations, though of restraint, yet obviously framed for their benefit, seem to have been alike new to them ; and to have called forth, even in the most depraved, grateful and generous feelings.

March 11th, *Wed.*   In the House of Commons, on the question whether the House should go into a Committee on the Bill to indemnify Ministers and magistrates for their late proceedings, I opposed the Bill in a speech of considerable length.[1] It was the only opportunity I could properly avail myself of to oppose it. It was at a most inconvenient time to myself that I had to do it, and I spoke under very great anxiety of mind ; my dear Anne being extremely ill.

The Indemnity Bill.

16th, *Mon.* On the motion for the second reading of the Bill for the amendment of the law relating to tithes, which has been drawn by Baron

---

[1] The question was carried by a majority of 173 : the numbers being, for it, 238 ; against it, 65. — Ed.

Wood, and has been brought into the House of Commons by Mr. Curwen, I spoke in support of the Bill. I expressed my approbation of the general objects of the Bill; though I stated that I objected to the clause respecting the trying of issues upon moduses, and that I thought there were other clauses which might require alteration. The only speakers against the Bill were Sir William Scott and Mr. Peel, the two Members for the University of Oxford, and Mr. Smyth, one of the Members for the University of Cambridge, and Mr. Wetherell. The Attorney and Solicitor General, however, and all the ministerial members, voted against the Bill, and, accordingly, it was lost. It was a very thin House, there being only 15 for the Bill, and 40 odd[1] against it. I did not stay to vote, being anxious to get home on account of the illness which my dearest Anne still continues to labour under.

19th, *Th.* My Bill to abolish the punishment of death for shoplifting went through the Committee. Mr. Peel, the Irish Secretary, has undertaken, if the Bill should pass, to bring in a Bill to repeal the Irish Acts of Queen Anne and George II. to the same effect; and he this day brought in a Bill to repeal the Irish Act which punishes with death the stealing goods to the amount of five shillings privily from the person.

22d, *Easter Sunday.* I am spending these holidays in town; my dear Anne continuing too ill to allow of her going to Tanhurst, though she is, I hope, recovering.

---

[1] The number was 44. — Ed.

23d, *Mon.*   A letter from my good friend Du- Dumont's
letter.
mont, from Geneva, of the 12th of this month,
reached me to-day, and brought me the good news
of his intending to come to us in May.   He tells
me that my article in the *Edinburgh Review*, upon
Bentham, has been of some advantage to him, and,
what he considers as much more important, to the
project of a new code.   " Bentham," he says, " ne
sera jamais mieux loué, mais la critique blesse plus
que les éloges ne flattent, et surtout quand on est
au point de prendre les défauts de style pour des
qualités.   Pour ce qui me concerne*, je n'y trouve
à redire qu'une prévention trop favorable, mais il
ne faut plus parler de sacrifice d'amour propre, car,
d'être ainsi loué c'est avoir fait ce me semble un
gain usuraire.   Heureusement la tête ne m'en a
pas tournée ; et puis on ne me gâte pas à Genève.
Il est pourtant vrai que l'article, qui a été beaucoup lu ici et dont on a beaucoup parlé, m'a été
très-avantageux, et qu'il est venu le plus à propos
du monde.   On s'étoit gendarmé contre moi le
plus injustement possible ; j'en avois pris et montré
de l'humeur et avec raison ; mais un on deux discours m'ont rétabli dans toute la faveur de l'assemblée, et ont même été accueillis avec exagération.
Tout cela ne signifie rien.   L'essentiel est notre
Code.   Le mot flatteur sur Genève † a eu son
effet.   *Possunt quia posse videntur.*   Je suis toute-
fois bien eloigné de compter sur la réussite de notre
travail," &c.

25th, *Wed.*   Roget took me with him to Dept-
ford to see the vessels which are about to sail to

---

* Edinburgh Review, vol. xxix. p. 237.   † Ibid. p. 236.

the North Pole, and in search of the North-West passage. We were on board the Dorothea, Captain Buchan, destined to the first, and the Isabella to the latter, of these expeditions. We had much conversation with Captain Buchan, and with Lieutenant Franklin, who commands the Trent.

April 5th, *Su.* Bentham wrote, some little time ago, and printed a work, which he has entitled " Church-of-Englandism and its Catechism examined." He allowed me to see it after it was printed. The work is written against the National School Society, whose aim is to proscribe all education of the poor, except that in which the religion of the Church of England forms an essential part; and the work, therefore, undertakes to prove, that Church-of-Englandism is wholly different from true Christianity, as it is to be learned from the gospel. The subject, however, is treated with so much levity and irreverence that it cannot fail to shock all persons who have any sense of religion. I had prevailed on Bentham till now not to publish it. He desired me to strike out the passages I thought most likely to give offence ; but they were so numerous that I was obliged to decline the task ; and I understood that he had given up all thoughts of publishing the work. To my astonishment, however, I learned yesterday that it had been advertised the day before with his name, and had been publicly sold. I have made a point of seeing him to-day, and, by the strong representation I have made to him of the extreme danger of his being prosecuted and convicted of a libel, I have prevailed on him to promise imme-

diately to suspend, if not to stop altogether, any
further sale of the book.

11th, *Sat.* My dear Anne set out for Brighton
for the recovery of her health.

14th, *Tu.* On the third reading of the Bill for
abolishing the punishment of death for the crime
of privately stealing in shops, the Attorney-General objected to the preamble, as stating what he
was pleased to call mere abstract principles, which,
if once adopted by the legislature, might lead to
great alterations in the law.[1] The House appeared,
however, on some little discussion which took
place, so decidedly against him, that he did not
venture to call for a division, and the Bill passed
without the amendment he had suggested. The
preamble is in the words of a preamble to a former
Bill which I brought in, and which, on the objections of Sir Thomas Plumer, I was then obliged
to give up.*

22d, *Wed.* By a motion for papers which I
made this day in the House of Commons, I
brought to the notice of the House some occurrences which have lately taken place in the islands
of Dominica and Nevis. My principal object was
to revive, if I could, some portion of that lively
interest which the public, a few years ago, took in
the condition of the slaves in the West Indies.
The cause of that unhappy class of mankind has

The Shop-lifting Act.

Its pre-amble.

Condition of the slaves in the West Indies.

* Vide *suprà*, Vol. II. p. 251.

[1] The criminal law has undergone considerable changes from that
time down to the first year of the present reign. By statutes
7 Will. IV. and 1 Vict. c. 84, 5, 6, 7, 8, 9, and 91, the punishment of
death is abolished in all cases of crimes not accompanied by personal
violence, or which do not, by their immediate consequences, endanger
life. — ED.

lately lost ground in England very considerably. Various circumstances have conspired to bring this about. It is now about a year and a half ago, that the African Institution published (certainly with great levity) a story which had been communicated to them of the cruel treatment of a slave in Antigua, and of the grand jury having thrown out a Bill of indictment which was preferred against the author of the cruelty. For this story there appeared to be no foundation; and a prosecution having been instituted against the printer of the society, he was convicted and a fine was imposed on him. From this single instance, the public were earnestly exhorted to believe that all the accounts which had been published of West Indian severities were fabrications and calumnies. The attempt, in the last year, to carry the Registry Bill had roused a very general and a very vehement opposition in the West Indian interest. The very mention of such a measure, it was pretended, had excited a spirit of revolt among the negroes; and the most terrible consequences were predicted if the Bill should be persevered in. To these real or affected alarms the unhappy disturbances which broke out in Barbadoes, though they were not in any manner connected with this subject, appeared to give countenance. In the mean time, no pains have been spared to raise a cry against Mr. Wilberforce, and the other friends of the slaves in this country. Numerous pamphlets have been published by Marryat and other agents of the islands. Most of the newspapers have been gained over by them; and the tendency of the paragraphs with which these are continually supplied, are to excite for the poor defamed planters, overseers, and managers of West India estates, that compassion which used once to be felt for the negroes. It has become extremely difficult to counteract the effects of this powerful combination. By means of the press it is hardly possible : the Judges of the King's Bench having, when they passed sentence on Hatchard ('the printer of the African Institution), declared that it was a libel to say of a West Indian grand jury that they were disposed to refuse justice to an injured individual. No man can venture to write in defence of the negroes without exposing himself to a prosecution ; for all the severities and cruelties to which they are subjected are to be traced to the injustice of their legislatures and tribunals. It seems, therefore, to be only in Parliament that, in the present circumstances, facts respecting the conduct of the courts of justice in the West Indies, however well authenticated, can with any security be stated. The transactions which I took this opportunity of bringing before the House are partly connected with those which I stated, and on which I moved for papers late in the last session.   After the grand jury of Dominica had not only thrown out the Bills that had been preferred against masters for cruelty towards their slaves, but had presented the preferring such Bills to them as a nuisance, the governor determined to try whether justice could not be obtained for injured slaves without the intervention of a grand jury.   Accordingly, by his direction, the Attorney-General of the

Misconduct of the grand jury at Dominica.

Miscon-
duct of
pettyjuries. island filed three several informations against persons for making their slaves work in chains and
with iron collars round their necks, against the
positive terms of an Act of Assembly.   The facts
were clearly proved, but all the defendants were
acquitted; and the grand jury again presented, as
a matter dangerous to the community, the interposition of the executive government between
master and slave.   The court, however, refused to
receive this presentment, and it was withdrawn.
In addition to this state of the administration of
justice, I brought under the view of the House
Supposed
state of the
law in Do-
minica with
respect to
the galley
gang. what is represented to be, and is acted upon as,
the law of the island.   At Dominica, as well as in
some other of the West India Islands, there is
what is called a public chain, in which slaves
convicted of crimes are sentenced to labour.
To this public chain, masters assume a right of
sending their slaves for any private offence of
which they may think them guilty.   The Governor
(Mr. Maxwell) was desirous of remitting the
punishment of some of those slaves; but he was
told that it was not within his authority.   In this
difficulty he consulted Mr. Glanville, the Attorney-
General of the island; but that gentleman gave it
as his opinion that, although the Governor might
by the Royal prerogative pardon slaves who had
been judicially condemned to this punishment, yet
he had no power whatever to release any slave
who, without any public investigation or even any
imputed crime, had been sentenced by the sole
will of his master to this most severe doom.   Such
unhappy creatures must, according to this Attor-

ney-General's opinion, endure the punishment (and it is one of excessive severity) for their whole lives, unless it shall be the pleasure of their masters to remit it. I adverted, too, to the law of Dominica, which imposes restrictions and a very heavy tax on the manumission of slaves; and to another law which declares, that no person of colour who lands in the island shall be considered as free, unless he produces a certificate of his freedom, and pays a duty. The Colonists are jealous of the interposition of the British legislature in any of the internal affairs of their islands. They pretend that such an interposition is a violation of the most sacred principles of our Constitution; and we here find the men who so loudly profess that they have imbibed the spirit of the British Constitution, inverting one of its most sacred principles. A slave no sooner sets his foot on the shores of Great Britain than he becomes free; while in Dominica, when a free negro lands upon their coast, he instantly sinks into a slave, and it is only by money that he can redeem himself from that degraded condition. I discussed at some length this pretension of the West Indians to the exclusive right of making laws for their own government, and for the regulations of their slaves; and showed how contrary it was to the practice of past times, and how inconsistent with the state and condition of the great mass of the population of the islands. It has never, indeed, been without indignation that I have heard these boasted claims of independence, and this vindication of political rights, on the part of the West Indians; some of

Law of Dominica upon manumission.

whom even pretend that they have a much keener sense and a more ardent love of liberty than mere Englishmen can pretend to. In this spirit I have seen cited in some of their pamphlets a passage of Burke's, in which he says that " Masters of slaves are by far the most proud and jealous of their freedom. Freedom," he adds, " is to them not only an enjoyment, but a kind of rank and privilege. Not seeing there that freedom, as in countries where it is a common blessing, and as broad and general as the air, may be united with much abject toil, with great misery, with all the exterior of servitude, liberty looks among them like something that is more noble and liberal." On such authority, these West Indian declaimers arrogate to themselves a love of liberty which is more enthusiastic, and as it were of a sublimer nature than can animate us. They do not perceive that as far as the spirit of West Indian differs from that of an English love of liberty, it is by having a mixture of some of the worst of human passions; pride, disdain, a love of dominion, a superiority not founded on merit and on a successful emulation, but on the base and abject condition of all around us. A genuine love of liberty is not a little selfish feeling confined to ourselves and to the contracted circle of our privileged associates; it expands itself to all without distinction who are under the protection of the same state. It is as indignant at that injustice which we see done to others, as at that which we feel pressing upon ourselves. It delights in the security of the meanest peasant in the land; and even rejoices that it is unable to exercise, as it is secure from suffering, an unjust dominion : while that too ardent, that impetuous love of liberty, is, in truth, an excess of self-love, a desire of authority, an impatience of control, a disdain of subordination.

> " Licence they mean when they cry liberty;
> For who loves that, must first be wise and good ;
> But from that mark how far they rove we see."

I took occasion, in the course of what I said in the House on the motion, to mention what has lately happened at Nevis, in the case of one Huggins, a man whose character for cruelty towards his slaves was some years ago made notorious to the House and to the public. He was lately tried at Nevis, for cruel treatment of certain slaves who were under his charge, as attorney to an absent proprietor. He had caused 100 lashes, with the usual instrument of punishment, a cartwhip, to be inflicted on two very young lads ; and he had been barbarous enough to inflict twenty lashes on the sister and a female cousin of the poor youths, because they had shed tears at witnessing their tortures. The case was clearly proved on the trial, no witness was called for the defendant, and yet he was acquitted. I was very sure of the accuracy of the facts I stated ; those relating to Dominica being stated in letters from the Governor, which were put into my hands, and those which respected Nevis being communicated to me by one of the counsel for the prosecution.

Cruel treatment of slaves by Huggins at Nevis.

His acquittal.

30th, *Th.* Mr. Sturges Bourne moved for, and obtained leave to bring a Bill into Parliament to alter the Poor Laws, as far as they relate to settle-

Poor laws. Settlements

ments; and to declare that a three years' residence shall alone give a settlement. I expressed in the House my approbation of this measure. Nothing can be more impolitic, and in many cases more cruel, than the present law; according to which, a man may have resided and exercised his industry for twenty years in a parish without gaining a settlement, and may, at the pleasure of the parish officers, the moment he stands in need of a little temporary relief, be removable, with his wife and all his children, perhaps to some remote part of the kingdom, amongst strangers, where he can find no occupation, and where he, with his family, may be destined to become the inhabitants of a workhouse.

Rewards on convictions.

May 4th, *Mon.* On Mr. Bennet's Bill, to abolish the parliamentary rewards which are given on conviction of certain offenders, I spoke, and I opposed an amendment of the Attorney-General.

Alien Bill.

5th, *Tu.* Lord Castlereagh moved for leave to bring in a Bill to continue the Alien Act for two years longer. The members who generally are in opposition to the Ministry were disposed to postpone making their objections to this measure to some future stage of it. Thinking, however, that it ought to be opposed in every stage, I shortly stated my objections to it, and I divided the House.[1]

Whitsuntide.

10th, *Whitsunday.* I set out for Brighthelmstone with my three youngest boys, whom I sent for from school for the purpose. John and Edward had gone before, so that I had all my children with me at Brighthelmstone except William.

[1] The numbers were, — for the first reading of the Bill, 55; against it, 18; majority, 37. — Ed.

I found my dearest Anne very much recovered, and I spent my short vacation most happily. It was much too short; for I was obliged to return to attend a claim of peerage in the House of Lords on Thursday.

16*th, Sat.* My dear Anne returned.

18th, *Mon.* Mr. George Bankes has brought a Bill into Parliament to prohibit, under certain penalties, the buying of game. To-day, on the second reading of it, several members, who are enemies to the system of the present Game Laws, opposed it. I am myself very much an enemy to those laws; but, because I am an enemy to them, I approve, and spoke in support of, Mr. Bankes's Bill. The present system is a most pernicious one, and is productive of great misery and of enormous crimes. It consists of a very rigorous body of criminal law, but of criminal law which has so little the sanction of public opinion, that no man is thought the worse of, by persons in his own rank of life, for incurring its penalties. The imprisonment, however, which detected poachers are made to undergo, the idle and dissolute habits of life they contract, and the desperate and ferocious spirit which the very severities they are exposed to excite in them, form by degrees a large body of men ready for the commission of the most enormous crimes; and though the Game Laws cannot be considered as the principal, yet they certainly form one, and not the most inconsiderable, of the various causes of that terrible increase of crimes which we have lately witnessed.* What renders

Game laws. Prohibition of buying game.

* In 1806, the number of persons committed for trial in England and

this system the more mischievous is, in my opinion, the very circumstance that, while the selling of game is punished as a crime, the buying it is allowed to pass with complete impunity. If there were no buyers, there could be no sellers. It is the buyers of game who encourage and make poachers, though among these buyers are often the most rigid enforcers of the Game Laws.[1]

Proposed repeal of the Septennial Act.
19th, *Tu.* On a motion of Sir Robert Heron's to repeal the Septennial Act, and restore triennial Parliaments, I spoke shortly in support of the motion.[2]

Alien Bill.
On the same day, in a debate[3] which took place upon going into the Committee on the Alien Bill, I opposed the Bill. Sergeant Copley[4], who, after having long expressed sentiments hostile to the Ministry, has lately come into Parliament for a Government borough, answered me; and Sir James Mackintosh, in an admirable speech, answered Sergeant Copley.

Committee on the cruel treatment of slaves in Nevis.
20th, *Wed.* On my motion, a select Committee was appointed to consider the papers lately laid before the House of Commons, relative to the treatment of slaves in the island of Nevis, — the papers which I had moved for on the 22d of last month.

Wales was 4346; from that time the number has gone on increasing almost every year; and in the last year (1817) it was 13,932.

---

[1] In 1831, the sale of game was made legal. See 1 & 2 Will. IV. c. 32. — ED.

[2] The motion was lost by a majority of 75 : — the numbers being, ayes, 42; noes, 117. — ED.

[3] The numbers on the division were — ayes, 99; noes, 32; majority in favour of going into Committee, 67. — ED.

[4] Now Lord Lyndhurst. — ED.

21st, *Th.* I very warmly supported in the House of Commons a motion of Mr. Bennet's, for referring to a Committee the petitions of two booksellers at Warrington. The cases stated by them (the material facts of which were not denied) appeared to me to be the more important, as they afforded a practical illustration of the mischiefs which were to be expected from Lord Sidmouth's circular letter of the last year to the magistrates on the subject of libels. These two men had been carried before a justice of the peace, charged with publishing libels; and, not being able to find bail, had been sent in irons to the House of Correction, and there kept to hard labour till the Quarter Sessions, at which they would have been tried, if the Attorney-General had not by certiorari removed the indictments into the King's Bench. Their houses too had been searched, and their papers and books seized and carried away. A proceeding so outrageous and so illegal would, a few years ago, have been thought incredible. The House, however, on such a case being brought before it, refused, by a considerable majority[1], even to institute any inquiry.

Persons charged with libels put in irons and kept to hard labour in the House of Correction before trial.

Their houses searched for papers.

22d, *Fri.* On the third reading of the Alien Bill, I moved, as an amendment, that the Bill should not extend to any alien who was resident in this country on the 1st of January, 1814, and had ever since continued to reside here. This amendment, as well as one moved by another member, that it should not extend to the wives of natural-born subjects, was rejected by the House.

Amendments to the Alien Bill moved and rejected.

[1] A majority of 73 to 17. — ED.

Case of a
slave mur-
dered in
St. Kitt's by
a clergy-
man of the
name of
Henry
Rawlins.

June 3d, *Wed.*   I brought under the notice of the House of Commons another case of horrible barbarity in one of the West India Islands. A negro slave in St. Christopher's had run away. He was brought back to the plantation he belonged to, flogged, and made to pass the night chained to another runaway slave who had been punished like himself. The next morning he was brought out into the field with the rest of the gang, and was compelled to work chained as he was to his companion. After some time, the wretched creature, exhausted with hunger, fatigue, and pain, sunk to the ground. The manager, a clergyman of the name of Henry Rawlins, commanded two drivers to flog him till he rose and resumed his labours. From the cruelties thus inflicted on him, he died in a few hours, being still chained to his fellow slave. He was buried the same day without any coroner having sat upon his body, although, by a law of the island, an inquisition is to be held on every slave who dies without having been previously seen by a physician. The affair, however, having made some noise in the island, the body was dug up, and a coroner's inquest was held upon it. The body bore every mark of violence upon it, and the teeth of the unhappy creature appeared to

have been recently broken : but the jury found by their verdict, that he died by the visitation of God.

Still, however, the matter had become so much the subject of conversation, that it was found necessary to indict one of the drivers for murder. In the course of his trial, it had been at first sworn by the slave to whom the deceased had been chained, that Rawlins was not present when the punishment was inflicted; though it afterwards came out in evidence, not only that Rawlins was present, but that he actually took the whip out of the driver's hand and flogged the slaves himself. On this evidence the driver was acquitted, and Rawlins himself was brought to trial. The facts were proved, and yet Rawlins was acquitted of the murder, but convicted of manslaughter. Thus convicted, the sentence on him was only that he should pay a fine of 200*l.*, and be imprisoned for three months. In bringing this matter to the view of the public, I had (and so I stated to the House) principally in view to show the manner in which justice was administered in some of the West India Islands, in cases in which slaves were concerned. A more complete picture of this could hardly be exhibited than what appeared in the gross misconduct of the Coroner's Jury, who had endeavoured to stifle all inquiry, by finding, upon their oaths and against the evidence of their senses, that a man so cruelly murdered had died a natural death; in the verdict of the Petty Jury, who had found such an atrocious murder to be manslaughter; and in the sentence of the Court, who, for so aggravated a manslaughter, if manslaughter it was, had passed the mild sentence of a three months' imprisonment and a fine of only 200*l.* My motion, which was agreed to, was only for copies of the depositions taken before the Coroner; the minutes of the evidence upon the two trials having been before, at my instance, laid before the House and printed.

On the same day, on a question of agreeing to

Misconduct of the Petty Jury and of the Court.

the amendments made by the Lords to Brougham's Bill for appointing Commissioners to enquire into abuses of charitable foundations, — much having been said respecting the remedy for such abuses, which already existed in the Court of Chancery, and Lord Castlereagh having called upon me to vindicate the Court from the imputations which he said Brougham had cast upon it, — I stated that an effectual remedy for such abuses certainly could not be found in the Court of Chancery; that the proceedings were so slow and so expensive in the cases of informations, that it required an extraordinary degree of public spirit, and a determination to make great sacrifices of money and of personal labour and convenience, for any person to become a relator in such a proceeding ; and that the summary remedy, which had been provided by the Bill I brought in a few years ago, was limited to cases where the charity lands had not got into the hands of third persons, but remained with the trustees.

The law respecting Usury is productive of great injustice, as it applies to promissory notes and bills of exchange. Such securities, as well as all others, if given for an usurious consideration, or upon an usurious contract, are, by the statute of Queen Anne, made absolutely void. The nature, however, of negotiable securities (which are assignable by indorsement, and where an indorsee, who discounts them, can have no means of ascertaining what the original contract was upon which they were given) makes this, with respect to these commercial transactions, a most unjust law.   To remedy this evil,

I lately brought into the House of Commons a Bill to declare that no negotiable security, given after the passing of the Act, should be void in the hands of a *bonâ fide* indorsee, who, at the time of discounting it, had not notice that it was usurious. The Bill passed the Commons without opposition, and will pass the Lords; for the Chancellor, to whom I mentioned the subject before I brought the Bill in, approves of it. He has indeed endeavoured to render the Bill more efficacious than it appeared to him that it would be in its original form, by adding in the House of Lords the word " actual " before the word " notice," in order to prevent any question that might arise as to an indorsee, who takes a Bill after it has become due, having constructive or implied notice. I have been asked why I did not extend this Bill to negotiable securities given for gaming debts. The injustice is, indeed, apparently as great in one case as in the other; but, in the experience which I have had, I have scarcely, I think, met with an instance of a note given for a gaming debt being really negotiated to a *bonâ fide* indorsee. The holders of such bills are almost always acting in collusion with the original payee.

5th, *Fri.* After the Alien Bill had passed the House of Commons, the Ministers discovered that, by an act of the Scottish Parliament, passed in 1695, all foreigners who acquired stock in the Bank of Scotland to a certain amount, became naturalized subjects, and that lately a good many foreigners had purchased such stock. They therefore, in the House of Lords, added a clause to the Bill, declaring that no foreigner who had, since the 28th

Clause added in the House of Lords to the Alien Bill, taking away the right of naturalization from persons who had become recent purchasers of of April last, or who should in future become a proprietor of such stock, should by means thereof be naturalized. This amendment of the Lords was taken to-day into consideration in the House of Commons. I opposed it, as being unjust towards the persons who, on the faith of a Scottish Act of Parliament, confirmed by five different British statutes since the Union, had invested their money in the purchase of stock, and were to be thus violently deprived of the advantages which had induced them to make the purchase; as being an *ex post facto* law, and therefore repugnant to all true principles of legislation; and as being contrary to all parliamentary usage, and, in substance, a tacking by the Lords of a new and distinct Bill to that which the Commons had sent up to them. To a Bill to *continue* an existing law, the Lords add, in the form of a clause, a Bill to *repeal* an existing law; and, by merely adding it as a clause, they allow of only one question being put upon it in the Commons, and deprive them of the several opportunities which they would have had of considering it in its different stages if it had come down to them in the form of a Bill. In addition to these objections, I observed, that the amendment was one which the Commons could not agree to without giving up one of their most important privileges — that of originating Money Bills. The effect of the amendment is, from the time of passing it, to subject all the individuals, whom it deprives of the naturalization they have acquired, to the Alien duties; and, if any of them have purchased estates, to have their lands forfeited to the Crown, as the property of aliens. As it was understood that Parliament was to be prorogued the next day, and immediately afterwards dissolved, I took occasion to remind the House, in this the last hour as it were of its existence, of the account which it had to render to the nation of the important trust committed to it. After passing shortly in review the most important acts of the Parliament, — the Habeas Corpus twice suspended ; the Act of Indemnity ; the disregarded and despised complaints of those who have suffered under the exercise of ministerial authority; the sanction given to Lord Sidmouth's celebrated circular letter, to the severities exercised over men who were only accused of publishing political libels, and to the systematic employment by Government of spies and informers; the Alien Bill, by which, even in time of peace, we had shut our ports against foreigners flying from persecution in their own country, and seeking with us an asylum ; and, to crown all, this last violation of all principles of law and of the Constitution, this great act of signal injustice ; — I concluded by expressing my fervent hope that England would never see another Parliament as regardless of the liberties of the people, and of the best interests of mankind, as the present.[1]

[1] The following is the report of the concluding passages of the speech referred to, as given in Hansard's *Parl. Debates*, vol. xxxviii. p. 1275. — Ed.

"I do not know what course the House is about to take on this subject, although I cannot help suspecting what that course will be —a course utterly unwarrantable to the individuals more immediately concerned, and utterly repugnant to the spirit of all parliamentary proceeding. Deeply involved as our privileges are in this question, yet, as this Parliament will, in all probability, be dissolved in a very short period, I fear its last act will be an act of signal injustice. Such,

The objection founded on the privilege of the Commons to originate all Money Bills, appeared to the House to have great weight ; and the Speaker having expressed his opinion that the clause came directly within the rule, the House resolved not to agree to the amendment. This must very much disconcert the Ministers' plans. They must either give up their clause altogether, or bring in a new

The clause rejected by the Commons.

Sir, will be a fit close for the greater part of our proceedings. Apprehending that we are within a very few hours of the termination of our political existence, before the moment of dissolution arrives, let us recollect for what deeds we have to account : — Let us recollect that we are the Parliament which, for the first time in the history of this country, twice suspended the Habeas Corpus Act in a period of profound peace : — Let us recollect that we are the confiding Parliament which entrusted His Majesty's Ministers with the authority emanating from that suspension, in expectation that, when it was no longer wanted, they would call Parliament together to surrender it into their hands, — which those Ministers did not do, although they subsequently acknowledged that the necessity for retaining that power had long ceased to exist : — Let us recollect that we are the same Parliament which consented to indemnify His Majesty's Ministers for the abuses and violations of the laws of which they had been guilty, in the exercise of the authority vested in them : — Let us recollect that we are the same Parliament which refused to inquire into the grievances stated in the numerous petitions and memorials with which our table groaned; that we turned a deaf ear to the complaints of the oppressed ; that we even amused ourselves with their sufferings : — Let us recollect that we are the same Parliament which sanctioned the use of spies and informers by the British Government; debasing that Government, once so celebrated for good faith and honour, into a condition lower in character than that of the ancient French police : — Let us recollect that we are the same Parliament which sanctioned the issuing of a circular letter to the magistracy of the country, by a Secretary of State, urging them to hold persons to bail for libel, before an indictment was found : — Let us recollect that we are the same Parliament which sanctioned the sending out of the opinion of the King's Attorney-General and the King's Solicitor-General as the law of the land : — Let us recollect that we are the same Parliament which sanctioned the shutting of the ports of this once hospitable nation to unfortunate Foreigners, flying from persecution in their own country.

" This, Sir, is what we have done ; and we are about to crown all by the present most violent and most unjustifiable act. Who our successors may be I know not ; but God grant that this country may never see another Parliament so regardless of the liberties and rights of the people, and of the principles of general justice, as this Parliament has been."

Bill, which will necessarily postpone for some days the dissolution of Parliament.

8th, *Mon.* The Ministers have brought a Bill into the House of Commons, to declare that the purchasing stock of the Bank of Scotland shall not have the effect of naturalizing the purchaser; but they have given the Bill merely a prospective operation, and it is to be in force only till the 25th of next March.

A new Bill brought in, but not retrospective.

The foreigners, therefore, who have already purchased stock since the 28th of April (and it seems they are only 94 in number) are left in undisturbed possession of their naturalization. The Bill was read three times in one day, and sent up to the Lords.

An immediate dissolution of Parliament is now certain. It is decided that I am not to come in again for Arundel. The Duke of Norfolk has been very anxious to bring me in, but he has found it impossible, without leaving out his brother, Lord Henry Howard. Sir Arthur Piggott has, in a letter which I have seen, pressed the Duke to suffer him to retire to make room for me, but the Duke would not consent to leave out so old and faithful a friend; and it has, I know, very much mortified the Duke, that, in consequence of his unavoidable arrangements with respect to his seats at Steyning and Horsham, he is unable to provide one for me. In the mean time, I have had very strong representations made to me to offer myself at several places of popular election, such as Liverpool, Coventry, Chester, Hull, Huntingdonshire, and Glamorganshire. I have been assured that my success at any of those places would be certain,

Expected dissolution of Parliament.

and that the expense would be very inconsiderable. I had determined not to accept any of those offers, or to put myself to any expense, or to offer myself as a candidate anywhere, when, on this day, a requisition was made to me by many electors of Westminster, to bring me in without trouble or expense; and I have accepted it.

9th, *Tu.* The Bill respecting the Bank of Scotland Stock passed the House of Lords.

Parliament dissolved.

10th, *Wed.* The Prince Regent from the throne dissolved the Parliament, without, as had been expected, any previous prorogation. As soon as the Court of Chancery rose to-day, I went out of town to Tanhurst. This is one of the great advantages that I have derived from giving up the Rolls. I shall now have a week entirely to myself, and which I can pass quietly in the country. I shall enjoy it the more from the contrast it forms to the bustle which will be going on in town respecting the approaching Westminster election.

I am requested to permit myself to be nominated as a candidate for Westminster.

The requisition which was made to me on Monday last did not take me quite by surprise. I had been asked, some days before, whether, if I were elected to represent the City of Westminster in Parliament, I would sit for it. My answer was that, if I were elected without any interference on my part either directly or indirectly, I should certainly think it my duty to accept the seat, but that I would not offer myself as a candidate, or take any step whatever towards securing my election. In accepting the offer thus made me, I have no pleasure whatever. It gratifies no vanity of mine, and, whatever be the result, it will contribute in no degree to my happiness.   I am acting solely under a strong sense of duty ; and those only who know how extremely disagreeable it is to me to present myself as an object of public notice, can judge what an irksome duty it is that I conceive myself to be discharging.

The Requisition, and my answer to it, were in the following words: —

" To Sir Samuel Romilly.

" Sir, — Anxious to see this populous and important city represented in Parliament by a person conspicuous in the country for talents and integrity, we, the undersigned inhabitants of Westminster, request you to permit us to put you in nomination at the ensuing election.   We farther request you to abstain from all personal attendance, trouble, and expense.   We require from you no pledge, since the uniform tenor of your honourable life, your known attachment to the Constitution, your zealous and unremitting efforts for the amelioration of the laws, the correction of abuses, and the support of the cause of freedom, justice, and humanity, wherever assailed, are a sure pledge to us of your qualifications for our service, in common with that of the country at large.

" We have the honour to be, Sir,

" Your faithful Servants.[1]

" Westminster, June 6th."

[1] This requisition, signed as follows, together with Sir S. R.'s answer to it, were inserted in the original MS., from a newspaper. — ED.

John Mackay.	Edward Jeffery.	George Lamb.
John Rodwell.	Robert Linerly.	James Stodart.
Wm. Allason.	Richard Tait.	Ligonier Thomas.
J. Arnold.	George Metcalfe.	George Lane.

" Gentlemen,

" In answer to the Requisition which I have this day had the honour to receive from you, I do not hesitate to say, that, though I should never have presumed to offer myself as a Candidate to represent the City of Westminster in Parliament, yet, if it should be the pleasure of a majority of the electors, without any solicitation or interference on my part, to choose me for one of their Representatives, I shall think that the highest honour has been conferred on me that it was possible for me to attain. I shall be proud to accept such an honour, and I shall endeavour to discharge, to the best of my abilities, the important duties which it will impose upon me.

" I have the honour to be, Gentlemen, with great respect, your most obedient and faithful Servant,

" SAMUEL ROMILLY.

" June 8. 1818."

Thomas Tomkison.
George Yonge.
A. Ritchie.
Thos. Wright and Co.
James Sutton.
John Wood.
Robert H. Evans.
G. Philips.
H. G. Bennet.
Daniel Giles.
Harvey Combe.
R. Payne Knight.
Ja. Perry.
Boyce Combe.
Cliff Ashmore.
J. Mills.
J. Fisher.
Robt. Spencer.
Geo. Bainbridge.
Th. Hughes.

Joseph Delafield.
J. Hammond.
Geo. Clarkson.
Rich. Henderson.
Henry Joyce.
Geo. Adcock.
Robt. Walpole.
James Chambers.
H. Donaldson.
P. Moore.
Henry Burgess.
J. Willis.
R. Griffin.
V. Knox.
T. Chamberlayne.
R. Whitcroft.
J. Oliphant.
R. W. Clarkson.
Jno. Nash.
Chas. Prater

Sefton.
J. T. Walker.
Nathaniel Roberts.
J. Dunn.
S. Yockney, Son, and Yockney.
John Paternoster.
George Austen.
W. H. Davis.
John Wilson.
John Smith.
James O. Pettitt.
William Vickery.
Keene and Horsford.
Richards and Son.
Christopher Allen.
Stephen Lewis.
T. Field and Son.
George Dawne.
Charles Smith.

17th, *Wed.* After staying a week at Tanhurst, I returned to town, but without my dear Anne. A very distressing increase of the indisposition with which she has been afflicted, obliged me to leave her behind me. Dumont, who is come from Geneva, and is passing some months in England, had come to visit us at Tanhurst, and returned with me to town. On my return, I find the preparations for the ensuing election for Westminster going on with great activity. •My friends are exerting themselves very strenuously on my behalf, and committees have been formed in the different parishes to canvass for me. At the pressing instance of Lord Holland, and of others who are very zealous and active for me, and whom I knew not how to refuse, I have consented to my son William joining the canvassers. It is with great reluctance that I have given this consent, for I can hardly think there is much consistency in refusing to solicit votes myself, and yet allowing my son to solicit them. Lord Holland is very desirous that I should go on the hustings during the election, but this I am fully determined not to do. I will ask no man for his vote either in private or in public, and shall neither be disappointed nor much elated, whatever be the result of the election.

The candidates are, — Captain Maxwell, who is supported by all the influence of Government; Hunt, my former competitor at Bristol, who can have no possible expectation of being elected, and who stands only that he may have an opportunity of making violent speeches, and abusing the men he once extolled; old Major Cartwright, who

Approaching election for Westminster.

The candidates.

seems to be put up by some absurd Radical re-
formers, without any hope or even wish of his own ;
and Douglas Kinnaird, a brother of Lord Kinnaird's, with whose name, till the present moment,
the public was wholly unacquainted, and who is
set up by a little committee of tradesmen, who
persuade themselves that they are all-powerful in
Westminster, and can bring in any man whom they
choose to propose as a colleague to Sir Francis
Burdett,— Sir Francis himself being, as they suppose, and I believe with very good reason, quite
sure of being elected.

The canvass for me has, I am told, been very
successful, and my friends express the greatest
confidence that I shall be elected. Burdett and
Kinnaird's Committee appear to be very angry at
my being named as a candidate, and have published
some violent hand-bills against me, in which they
accuse me of being a lawyer, one of the Whig
faction, and a person who sat on a committee
against the much-injured Princess of Wales. This
nonsense seems to have had very little effect; but
what I find has been of great disservice to me with
many of the electors, is the opinion which is
generally entertained that I was the author of Lord
Redesdale's Insolvent Debtors' Act. That notion
is likely, as I understand, to lose me many votes.

Com-
mencement
of the
election.

18th, *Th*. The election began. The show of
hands was in favour of me and of Hunt. A poll
was of course demanded ; and at the close of the
poll of this day, the numbers were, — Romilly,
189 ; Maxwell, 176 ; Burdett, 87 ; Kinnaird, 25 ;
Hunt, 14 ; Cartwright, 10.

19th, *Fri.* At the close of the poll to-day the numbers were,— Romilly, 825; Maxwell, 754; Burdett, 348; Kinnaird, 55; Hunt, 30; Cartwright, 18.

And 20th, *Sat.* Romilly, 1276; Maxwell, 1241; Burdett, 484; Kinnaird, 63; Hunt, 33; Cartwright, 20.

22nd, *Mon.* It being clear, from the state of the poll on Saturday, that Kinnaird had no chance of being elected, and that Burdett's Committee and his other friends were greatly endangering his election by canvassing for Kinnaird in opposition to me, they determined to withdraw that gentleman as a candidate, and to canvass for Burdett alone, and to endeavour by every exertion they could make to place him at the head of the poll. They accordingly sent an invitation to him, to present himself upon the hustings. This he declined doing, in a strange letter filled with quotations from Shakspeare, and which discovered very clearly his mortification (notwithstanding the indifference he has always affected on the subject) at seeing himself so low on the poll. It must indeed be mortifying to him; for, a few weeks ago, he imagined he could bring whom he pleased in with himself as Member for Westminster. He offered it, as I have been assured, to Mr. Fawkes, of Yorkshire, and pressed him to accept it; but that gentleman declined the honour intended him. In consequence of the exertions made, Burdett gained greatly on to-day's poll. The numbers at the close of it were, — Romilly, 1879; Maxwell, 1726; Burdett, 1263.

Kinnaird and Cartwright withdrawn as candidates.

23d, *Tu.* Burdett still gained upon the poll,

and got before Maxwell : at the close the numbers were, — Romilly, 2546; Burdett, 2171 ; Maxwell, 2169.   Captain Sir. Murray Maxwell has been grossly insulted by the populace every day of the election ; and to-day, as he was retiring from the hustings after the election was over, he was attacked by some ruffians and very severely hurt.

I have never been near the hustings, nor intend to go near them till the election is at an end.   I attend every day in the Court of Chancery, and go on with my business there as quietly as if there was no election in the kingdom.   To-day I dined with Rogers (the poet).   A very pleasant dinner with Crabbe (whom I had never before seen), Frere, and Jekyl.

24th, *Wed.*   Burdett continues advancing every day on the poll ; and his friends entertain no doubt that they will place him at the head.   Douglas Kinnaird, who, now that he is no longer a candidate, has come to the hustings to make speeches for Burdett, speaks of his being at the head of the poll as the only matter worth thinking about in the election.   "So that he comes in triumphantly on the car of reform, it is matter of indifference who may get up behind ;" this was one of his phrases. Other of Burdett's sanguine friends say they are sure of getting him several thousand votes above all the other candidates.   Knowing the exertions that are making by Government for Maxwell, they suppose that the contest will be between Maxwell and me ; and, with this knowledge, some of them, and amongst others Kinnaird, have requested many of the electors, if they would not give single votes for Burdett, to bestow their second votes on Maxwell rather than on me. At the close of the poll to-day, I had 3016 votes; Burdett, 2792; and Maxwell, 2598.

July 4th, *Sat.* This being the last day on which by the Act of Parliament the poll could be kept open, the election finally closed; and, notwithstanding the boasts of Burdett's friends, I was at the head of the poll, as I had been during the whole contest. The numbers were,—for me, 5339; for Burdett, 5238; for Maxwell, 4808; and for Hunt, (who, under every sort of disgrace, had continued a candidate to the end, some days polling one or two votes, and some days none,) 84. Though I had kept away from the hustings during the whole of the election, I thought myself bound to attend at the close of it to thank the electors. I addressed them in a short speech, which will be found at the end of this volume[1], and which was very favourably received.

Election closed.

[1] The following is the speech alluded to. — ED.
" As long as the contest which has just terminated was depending — as long as my appearance amongst you could be considered as a solicitation of your votes for an honour which, whatever the kind partiality of my friends may have induced them to think, I never presumed to imagine myself deserving of, I abstained from presenting myself to you ; but, now that the contest is at an end, — now that I have been chosen one of your representatives, and that I can address you by the endearing name of my constituents, — I hasten to appear before you, and to thank you for the honour you have done me, and the confidence you have placed in me. To be chosen by your free and unbiassed votes to represent this great, populous, independent, and enlightened city in Parliament, — to be selected from amongst public men to declare your will and express your sentiments on all the most important questions that can interest the community, — is, in my estimation, the highest honour to which, in this free State, any individual can be raised. It is an honour to which, notwithstanding the decision you have pronounced, I can still hardly venture to think that I had any just pretensions. The endeavours I have used to serve the public have, by the too indulgent partiality of others, been, I am sensible, in this place greatly over-rated ; and I ought rather to offer an apology for what has been said of me, than to claim the benefits of such a panegyric. I have,

The ceremony of chairing followed, which I would very willingly have dispensed with. It was settled, however, by those who had taken great pains to secure my election, that a chairing there must be; and there was no escaping it. The procession, which consisted of many carriages and horsemen, passed through the Strand, Pall Mall, and St. James's Street, to Burlington House, the residence of Lord George Cavendish; from which I soon got away by the garden door, and walked very quietly

---

indeed, endeavoured to be useful to the public; but my endeavours have seldom been successful. Such, however, as they are, it is those endeavours which alone have recommended me to your favour; for, though born and having passed my whole life amongst you, it is by my public conduct alone that I have become known to you. Gentlemen, I really have not words adequately to express the gratitude which I feel. I am sensible, however, that the thanks which it will become me to give, and which will be worthy of you to receive, are thanks not to be expressed in words, but in actions, — not in this place, but within the walls of the House of Commons. The Representative of Westminster should express his thanks by a faithful discharge of the sacred duties which you have imposed upon him; by a constant and vigilant attention to the public interests; by being a faithful guardian of the people's interest, and a bold assertor of their rights; by resisting all attacks, whether open or insidious, which may be made upon the liberty of the press, the trial by jury, and the Habeas Corpus — the great security of all our liberties; by defeating all attempts to substitute, in place of that government of law and justice to which Englishmen have been accustomed, a government supported by spies and informers; by endeavouring to restrain the lavish and improvident expenditure of public money; by opposing all new and oppressive taxes, and, above all, that grievous, unequal, and inquisitorial imposition, the income tax, if any attempt should be made in the new Parliament to revive it; by endeavouring to procure the abolition of useless and burthensome offices, a more equal representation of the people in Parliament, and a shorter duration of the Parliament's existence; by being the friend of religious as well as of civil liberty; by seeking to restore this country to the proud station which it held amongst nations when it was the secure asylum of those who were endeavouring to escape in foreign countries from religious or political persecution. These are the thanks which the electors of Westminster are entitled to expect; and when the time shall come that I shall have to render you an account of the trust you have committed to me, I trust in God that I shall be able to show that I have discharged it honestly and faithfully. Gentlemen, for myself I return you my sincerest thanks, and for the result of the election I offer you my warmest congratulations."

home unobserved by any one, though a short time
before I had been offered as a spectacle to the
immense crowd which thronged all the streets
through which the cavalcade had passed. Though
Sir Francis Burdett's friends were disappointed
and chagrined at his being second on the poll, and
deferred his chairing to a future day, yet no
symptom of dissatisfaction appeared in any part of
the crowd; but I was everywhere hailed with
shouts and congratulations.

Among the strange incidents which occurred
during the election, was the decided part which my
excellent friend, Jeremy Bentham, took against
me. He did not vote, indeed; but he wrote a hand-
bill, avowed and signed by him, in which he represented me to be a most unfit Member for Westminster, as being a lawyer, a Whig, and a friend
only to moderate reform. This hand-bill he sent
to Burdett's Committee; but, as it did not reach
them till after they had become sensible that they
had injured their cause by their abuse of me, they
refused to publish it. Some of my friends were
very angry with Bentham for this hostile interference against me. For myself, I feel not the least
resentment at it. Though a late, I know him to
be a very sincere, convert to the expediency of
universal suffrage; and he is too honest in his politics to suffer them to be influenced by any considerations of private friendship.

12th, *Sun.* Attended a meeting of the Opposition at Brookes's, at which it was determined
to request Tierney to consider himself as their
leader.

Bentham.

Dined the same day at the Duke of Sussex's, at Kensington Palace. It was a dinner which His Royal Highness was kind enough to give to celebrate my election.

19th, *Sun.* I took possession of a small cottage which I am to rent for a few weeks on Hampstead Heath. I shall only be able to get there in the evening, and must be in town early every morning to attend the Court of Chancery.

27th, *Mon.* I dined at Bentham's; a small but very pleasant party, consisting of the American Minister (Mr. Rush), Bentham, Brougham, Dumont, Mill, and Koe.

I have received numerous letters of congratulation from my friends, on the result of the Westminster election. The two which, from the view they take of the subject, are most worth preserving, are from my friend Creevey, at Brussels, and from Mr. Otter. Creevey's letter is as follows : —

Creevey's letter on the Westminster election.

" Dear Romilly,   " Brussels, July 13.

    " I am quite sure there is not a man in all England who rejoices more sincerely in your late triumph at Westminster than myself; and I write you this line to tell you so. Considering your uniform conduct in Parliament, and, above all, considering that faithful and courageous picture which you drew of the late Parliament at the close of its existence, your triumph over the court, and within its own walls, is almost beyond belief. Your election, too, will be a just and lasting reproach to the Whig aristocracy, who had made no arrangement for securing your continuance in Parliament, and who could never have anticipated this fortunate event *: and lastly, it is a great and signal triumph over the intemperate partizans of Burdett, who have been compelled for the first time in their lives to suspend their blackguard abuse and folly, from pure extorted deference to your own personal character ; so that your election is perfect in all ways, and ought to be an eternal lesson for politicians of all descriptions in time to come."

To save myself the trouble of copying Mr. Otter's letter, I annex it at the end of the book.[1]

Aug. 7th, *Fri.* I gave up the cottage at Hampstead.

Mr. Otter's letter.

---

* This is certainly an unjust reproach. I had no claims on what Creevey calls the Whig aristocracy. The Duke of Bedford, however, as I afterwards learnt, had made an arrangement to provide a seat for me, if I were not returned for some other place.

---

[1] The following is the letter from the Rev. William Otter (now Bishop of Chichester). — ED.

"Kinlet, near Bewdley, July 6. 1818.

" My dear Sir,

" I cannot deny myself the pleasure of congratulating you most heartily and sincerely upon the event of the anxious but glorious struggle in which you have been engaged. Nothing, indeed, could be more fitting or more honourable. You are placed precisely in the situation which your public services had merited ; and the electors of Westminster have raised themselves mightily in the opinion of all wise and honourable men. In my own judgment, every thing has turned out exactly as it should have done. It was right that you should be called upon publicly to become a candidate — still better that you should not be supported by the friends of Sir Francis Burdett — and best of all, that you should be at the head of the poll. It is an additional pleasure to infer, from the completeness of your success, that the Whigs are gaining ground in public opinion ; for, although I most sincerely believe that no one but yourself could have achieved for them such a victory, yet I doubt whether even you could have done it a year or two ago. In this county almost all the gentlemen are Tories ; but I have not seen one who did not express a hearty wish for your success.

" I fear that the agitation of this scene has not been favourable to Lady Romilly's disorder ; but joy is a good physician, and I hope it will prove so to her."

Sept. 3d.   Arrived at Cowes.[1]

12th.   Anne went into the sea-bath.

13th.   Taken ill.

14th.   Sailed with Mr. Fazakerley to Southampton.

16th.   Consulted Mr. Bloxam.

19th.   Roget and William arrived, and Mr. Nash.

Oct. 9th.   Slept for the first time after many sleepless nights.

10th.   Relapse of Anne.

[Lady Romilly died on the 29th of Oct. 1818. Her husband survived but for three days the wife whom he had loved with a devotion to which her virtues, and her happy influence on the usefulness of his life, gave her so just a claim. His anxiety, during her illness, preyed upon his mind, and affected his health; and the shock occasioned by her death led to that event which brought his life to a close, on the 2d of Nov. 1818, in the 62d year of his age.]

---

[1] This and the following memoranda are written upon a loose sheet of paper, found in the last volume of this Diary. — ED.

LETTERS TO C.

INTRODUCTION.

THE following portion of this work, which the Editors have entitled "Letters to C.," consists of four unfinished papers by Sir Samuel Romilly, which may be described in his own words as "Observations on his situation in life and future prospects, in the course of which he indulged himself in passing in review some projects for the public benefit."[1] The two first, written in 1801, which are in the form of letters addressed by an imaginary friend to himself, and the third, in 1807, relate to the office of Lord Chancellor. The fourth, written in 1818, which is in the form of a letter addressed by himself to the same imaginary friend, refers to the course of conduct he ought to pursue as a representative for the city of Westminster. Connected with the three first of these letters is a series of papers on the duties of a Lord Chancellor in his character of a Legislator, a Minister, and a Judge. They do not form any regular or complete treatise, but are principally in the nature of sketches to be afterwards filled up, and occasionally little more than memoranda to recall former reflections. The following account of them may serve to show in what manner they are connected together, and what light they throw on the letters themselves : —

One of them is entitled "*Memoranda of things*

[1] Vol. II. p. 234.

to be done on entering into office." It contains a series of resolutions relating to the duties of the Lord Chancellor in his different capacities.

Those which relate to his legislative duties are in these words : — " To reform the Civil Code ;" " To reform the Penal Law ;" and they refer to separate manuscripts bearing the same titles. These contain a list, more or less detailed, of the particular reforms which he contemplated in both these divisions of the law : and a note is attached to each proposition referring to manuscripts, to works, and to reported decisions, which afford information as to the nature and extent of the abuse, and the mode of reforming it ; and, in some cases, to the names of persons who might furnish information or assistance. The following selection from those which are entitled " *The Reform of the Civil Code*" may give a more correct idea of their nature and object : —

1. " To alter the law respecting debtor and creditor ; to make the real estates of a person who dies indebted, assets for the payment of all his simple-contract debts ; to make copyhold estates assets, to make them subject to executions ; to make the estates of tenants in tail assets for the payment of all their debts.

2. " To correct the injustice attending the law as it now stands, with respect to extents and the recovery of debts due to the Crown.

3. " To amend the Bankrupt Law.

4. " To declare that a voluntary conveyance shall not be void, as against a subsequent purchaser, if he had notice of it prior to his purchase.

5. " To abolish certain injurious legal fictions, such as that *lis pendens* is notice to all the world.

6. " To establish a general registry of deeds.

7. " To reform the practice of the Courts, particularly of Courts of Equity; to diminish the delays which now prevail, and to correct the many abuses which notoriously exist in the Masters' offices.

8. " To abolish useless offices in the Court of Chancery, and such as are burdensome to the suitors. The Six Clerks, Cursitors, &c. to reimburse the present possessors of those offices out of the dividends of the unclaimed property in the Court.

9. " That some greater form or solemnity than is now necessary ought to be required in wills of personal estates.

10. " To abolish the common law offences of forestalling, engrossing, and regrating.

11. " To pass an Act declaring that the Court of Justiciary in Scotland shall not have power to transport for common law misdemeanors."

Where, in these lists, any one of the reforms contemplated is stated in very general terms, a paper is commonly to be found bearing the same title, and containing in a similar form an enumeration of changes proposed to be made in that branch of the law. Thus, in the selection already given, the propositions relating to the reform of the Bankrupt Law and the practice of the Court of Chancery are developed in other papers, where some of the proposed alterations are stated; and they are accompanied with the usual references to manuscripts, books, and persons whence assistance might be derived.

The manuscripts to which the notes in these lists refer are sometimes mere sketches of the mode of carrying the proposed reforms into effect; but the greater part of them are essays[1] on the reform of

[1] The following is a list of such of these Essays as are most complete :—

1. On the Promulgation of Laws.
2. On a Written Code of Laws.
3. Project of a New Code.
4. On unauthorised Reports of Judicial Proceedings.
5. On certain Rules of Evidence.
6. On the Imposition of Taxes on Law Proceedings.
7. On Irrevocable Laws.
8. On the Law of Libel.
9. On Apprenticeships.
10. On Bankrupts.
11. On the Poor-Laws.
12. On Divorces among the Poor.
13. On Superstition.
14. On Judicial Superstition.
15. Attempts to Reform Defects and Abuses in Criminal Law.
16. On a Public Prosecutor.
17. On Ignominious Punishments.
18. On Cruel Punishments.
19. On Military Punishments.
20. On the Regard to be had to Sex, Age, and Condition of Life in inflicting Punishment.
21. On Punishments to Children.
22. On Transportation.
23. On Conspiracies to convict innocent Men.
24. On Confession and Denial after Conviction.
25. On Perjury.
26. On the Punishment of Perjury.
27. On Shoplifting.
28. On Petty Treason and Murder.
29. On Appeals of Death.
30. Account of a Criminal Trial in Scotland.
31. On Suicide.
32. On Blasphemy.
33. On Bigamy.
34. On Felony.
35. On the Clergy as amenable to Criminal Law.
36. On Forestalling and Regrating.
37. On Laws against unusual Crimes.
38. On allowing Counsel to Persons accused.
39. On Compensation to Persons wrongfully accused.

specific evils in the law. They were written at various times, and, for the most part, before the writer appears to have indulged in any expectation of becoming Lord Chancellor, but which, when he entertained that idea, he reconsidered, made various additions to, and incorporated in the manner already mentioned, with his reflections on the legislative duties of that office.

A series of propositions relating to the ministerial duties of Lord Chancellor are collected in the papers entitled " *Memoranda of things to be done on entering into office,*" similar to those relating to the reform of the law; but, from the different nature of the subject, they are less developed in accompanying manuscripts, and contain fewer references to extrinsic sources of information. The following are selections from these propositions : —

1. " To keep lists of persons qualified for the different offices in my appointment, and to designate in my own mind who shall succeed upon the first vacancy : to avoid the evil of the offices remaining long vacant, and to prevent solicitation of candidates.

2. " To find out, and bring forward, talents wherever they can be found. In doing this, to

---

40. On the Policy of giving Rewards on Conviction.
41. On frequent Public Executions.
42. Observations on Eliza Fenning's case.
43. Observations on Bentham on Punishment.

It was respecting that portion of these Essays which relates to the Criminal Law, and some other papers not here enumerated, that the direction in a codicil to his Will, mentioned in the Preface to the First Volume, refers.

disregard rank and family and places of education, and, above all, to divest myself of all consideration of personal favour.

3. " Invariably to appoint to offices the men who are most fit to fill them ; to do this in every profession, and in every department of the State.

4. " In the Church, to consider those as best qualified to advance the interests of true religion and of the State who entertain the most liberal opinions ; not those who consider the religious order as a kind of corporation, as a profession which has its own particular interests to consult, and between which and the laity there should be kept up, as it were, a continual struggle.

5. " To promote and improve public education in all orders of society.

6. " To reform the Public Grammar Schools.

7. " To reform the Universities, and establish in them new professorships.

To the 2d of these propositions is attached a short list of names ; and notes to the 6th and 7th refer to books and authorities relating to the powers of visitors, and to the mode in which these powers should be enforced.

The consideration bestowed on the judicial office appears from several papers in which the functions and duties of Judges are described. One of these consists of characters of several Judges before whom Sir S. Romilly had practised, with introductory observations on the qualifications required for the due discharge of the judicial office, and the instructive lessons which succeeding Judges might derive from

the example of the merits and defects of their predecessors. Another is on the manner in which a
person might best qualify himself for the judicial
station, and on the mode in which he ought to discharge its duties. This is in the form of a speech
supposed to be addressed by a Lord Chancellor to a
Chief Justice of the Common Pleas on his appointment, according to the practice which anciently
prevailed in this country. Neither of these papers
is complete; and the latter breaks off just where it
would seem that the writer, after pointing out the
general mode of discharging the judicial duties,
was about to enter into a more detailed examination of them.

This account has been here introduced for the
purpose of showing that the views entertained by
Sir S. Romilly in writing the following letters were
not confined to mere speculation, but that they
were accompanied by much reflection and much
investigation of the modes by which he might best
carry them into effect. As he advanced in life,
and became convinced that he should never have
an opportunity of exercising judicial functions, he
turned his attention to the particular but different
duties which he considered that his station in life
imposed upon him ; and, accordingly, these form
the subject of the fourth of these letters.

Although these communings with himself are of
a peculiarly intimate nature, it has, nevertheless,
been determined by the Editors, conformably with
the motives which have led them to the publication
of this work, not to exclude from it papers which
appear to them to display, in a remarkable manner,

the character of Sir Samuel Romilly's mind; his habits of self-examination; his endeavours to prepare himself for every event; his care to lay down the course of conduct he ought to pursue, under whatever circumstances he might be placed, and (as he himself expresses it) * "to record against himself the obligations by which he was bound."

* In an unpublished paper.

I.

Tenby, 1801.

OUR friendship, my dear C., is of too long standing, and has been proved on too many occasions, for
you to doubt my sincerity, when I assure you that
nothing ever gave me more pleasure than to hear
how very successful you have lately been in your
profession. Though I never entertained any doubt
that the rank of King's Counsel[1] would be of great
advantage to you, I did not foresee that your progress could be so rapid. It was not, indeed, to be
foreseen ; nor could it possibly have happened but
for the late unexpected changes in the Administration, which, by removing the Attorney and Solicitor General[2] from your court, forced a great deal
of business into a new channel.

What satisfaction would it not afford our dear
Roget, if he were now living, to see so much of his
predictions accomplished, to exult in your success,
and to enjoy your reputation! He would be well
entitled to enjoy it, since it is to him, in a great
degree, that you owe it ; for it was his advice and
encouragement which induced you to enter upon a

[1] Sir Samuel Romilly had been appointed King's Counsel on the
6th of November, 1800. — ED.
[2] Sir John Mitford (afterwards Lord Redesdale) and Sir William
Grant ; the former of whom was elected Speaker of the House of Commons, and the latter appointed Master of the Rolls, in April, 1801.
— ED.

career for which you did not venture to think yourself qualified. Do you recollect the conversation which passed between you one night in his garden, in the neighbourhood of Lausanne ?   I shall never forget it.   It was a very short time before the necessity of your return to England separated you from him,—separated you (as the unfortunate state of his health gave you both, at the time, but too much reason to fear, and as the event too fatally proved) for ever.

We were walking together on that fine elevated terrace, which commands one of the noblest views perhaps that the world affords, where the Lake of Geneva is seen spread out in the whole of its extent, with the Alps rising behind it in wild and stupendous masses.   It was a clear serene night of autumn ; there was no moon, but there was not a single cloud ; and on every side the sky was resplendent with stars.   The faint twilight was just sufficient to show the outline of the sublime scene before us, and to leave it to imagination or to memory to finish the picture.   We had been discoursing on literary subjects : the eloquence of the ancient orators was one of our topics ; insensibly the conversation passed to your profession, and from your profession to yourself.   You seemed unconscious of the powers which Roget thought you possessed. I remember his telling you that he was quite confident of your success.   The time, the scenery about us, the awful stillness of the night, the ideas which the former part of the conversation had set afloat in his mind, gave him an unusual degree of animation.   With a warmth of eloquence which surprised me, even in him, he spoke of the great part you were to act as that which was certain, and, in the spirit of prophecy, unfolded to you your future life. God grant, that in what is to come he may prove as true a prophet as in that which is past! If he does, the sublimest enjoyment that human life affords is reserved for you, — that of exercising in an exalted station the noblest faculties of the soul, of improving the condition of mankind, and adding to the happiness of millions who are unborn.

There must be many periods of your past life which you must have great pleasure in recollecting, and in comparing with your present situation and your future prospects : the time, particularly, when the fate of all the persons most dear to you seemed to depend on your single exertions. The success of those exertions was then uncertain ; and even your health, without which no exertions could be made, was precarious. I well remember the anxiety which at the time it was manifest you always felt, and which to me you sometimes expressed. That anxiety is now completely dispelled. Of your family, those who are most advanced in life are enjoying a moderate competence; and the younger members of it have the prospect of being able to support themselves with honour and esteem, in that middle order of society in which happiness is most easily attainable : and, when you contemplate the change which has taken place in their condition and their future views, you have the solid satisfaction of reflecting that you are yourself in a great degree the author of it.

Yet, great as must be the enjoyment which such a retrospect must afford you, I would exhort you not so much to look back to the past as forward to the future. I would have you consider what has been done as little compared with what it remains for you to do. I would have you familiarize yourself with the idea of becoming a benefactor, not to individuals only, but to a whole nation, and to future ages ; in short, I would have you prepare yourself for that eminent station which it is not impossible, or, if I were to express myself as sanguinely as I feel in common with many of your friends, I should say it is not improbable, that you may one day fill. Be assured that not only the event is possible, but that it may happen much earlier than your friends have any expectation of. Only reflect impartially on the political state of the country, on the situation in which you now stand, and on the talents, the politics, and the reputation of the men who are most eminent as lawyers, and of those who are rising into eminence, and say whether you can disguise from yourself the possibility (I will not use a stronger term) of your attaining, before many years have elapsed, the highest dignity of your profession.

It has happened, I believe, to most of those who have filled the great office to which I allude, to have found themselves placed in it without ever having formed any plan, or adopted any principles, to guide them in the discharge of its duties. I should be sorry that, in that respect, you should follow their example. I would have you now, when alone it can be done, finish that self-educa-

tion which I have heard you say is the only one
you ever received, by fitting yourself for the execution of that most important trust which may
perhaps one day be committed to you, in such a
manner as will be the most beneficial to mankind,
and consequently the most honourable to yourself.
Whenever that day arrives, it will be too late to
form plans, or to trace out a line of conduct. You
will find yourself distracted with the hurry, and
overcome by the immense labours, of your office.
Every moment will be occupied with judicial attendances, with measures of temporary expediency,
with private solicitations and conferences, with
audiences which must be given, with the little in-
trigues of party which must be counteracted, and
with all that empty pageantry and solemn trifling
which in stations of the highest dignity are the
most unavoidable. You will retire every night to
rest, having added one day more of splendid but
unavailing fatigue to your existence; and if, in the
course of it, some reflection should have forced
itself on your mind upon the higher duties of that
office which remain to be discharged, you will defer the consideration of them to a period of promised leisure, which, however, will not arrive.
You will live, like your predecessors, only from day
to day; and, like them, you will descend from your
high elevation with no more consoling reflection
than that you have filled a great office without impropriety, that you have decided impartially the
causes which came before you, that you have left
the condition of your countrymen no worse than
you found it, and that you will be known to future

ages as the ancestor of those individuals whom
they will see distinguished from the mass of mankind by nothing but vain titles and large possessions.   Are these the reflections with which you
would wish to quit such a station?   I think, nay,
I am sure, they are not. I am sure that, unless high
dignities should alter and utterly corrupt you, not
only you could derive no consolation from such
reflections, but it would be to you a never-failing
source of the most poignant self-reproach that you
had suffered so glorious an opportunity of doing
good, afforded you by Almighty God, to pass unimproved.

In the present state of society, I know of no
situation in which an individual can have a greater
influence on the happiness of mankind than that
of a Chancellor of England.   To decide justly,
wisely, and impartially, the private contests which
arise between individuals, has been at all times considered as a very momentous duty.   In England
it derives peculiar importance from the circumstance of its being, in a great degree, an unwritten
law that is administered, where every decision
becomes in its turn a precedent; and where it is
impossible, in many cases, to decide as a judge,
without laying down a rule as a legislator.   But it
is not only this subordinate species of legislation
which a Chancellor has to exercise ; he has always
a seat in Parliament, and, in the present order of
things, his situation gives him a degree of weight
and authority in every thing that he proposes,
which no talents or integrity, not invested with
magistracy, can confer.   Whatever great reforms

are to be made in the civil and criminal jurispru-
dence of the country are wholly in the power of a
Lord Chancellor. The almost irresistible authority
which he possesses on such subjects has, indeed,
been hitherto exercised only to prevent reforms;
but there is little doubt that it would be equally
efficacious in promoting them. It is by recollecting the weight which a Chancellor must always
have in the legislation of England,—and that England has, for some time past, in measures of public
policy, as it were taken the lead in the civilised
world,—that we may form an adequate idea of the
extensive influence which he possesses over the
well-being of his fellow creatures. His other
duties — the advice he is to give in the Council
on all measures of temporary expediency, not only
with respect to the domestic government of the
country, but to its relations with foreign states;
and the selection of proper persons to fill the
situations of trust to which, in the exercise of
his extensive civil and ecclesiastical patronage,
he appoints, — are, indeed, when considered by
themselves, of very great importance. I cannot,
however, but consider these, together with his
judicial functions, as matters comparatively of little moment, and as the inferior duties of his
office.

It is, however, those inferior duties of the office
which seem to have principally, if not alone, occupied almost all the persons who have filled it. The
great Bacon alone, of all the Chancellors of England,
seems to have turned his thoughts to the accom-
plishment of important reforms. In his time, in-

deed, and for a considerable period afterwards, the office was regarded in a very different view, and was, indeed, very different in its nature from what it is now become. The judicial duties of it were not then attended with a fiftieth part of the labour which now belongs to them. The rules of equity were then few and simple; they did not form that complicated system, that refined and subtle science, into which they have now branched out; and consequently it was not then thought necessary that a mere lawyer should fill the office. The single circumstance, that for a very long period of time none but practising lawyers have been appointed to the office of Chancellor, may sufficiently account for the manner in which its duties have been discharged. It is not from such a man that we should expect comprehensive reforms or important alterations in the law. His education, his inveterate habits, the society he has lived in, the policy by which he has always regulated his conduct, have all tended to inspire him with a blind reverence for every part of that system of law which he has found established. When we reflect on this,—when we trace the former lives of all the Chancellors of modern times; when we see them, from the moment when they have quitted college, giving up their whole time to the study of one positive science, and cultivating no faculty of the mind but memory, the talent of discovering and pursuing nice and subtle distinctions and forced analogies, and the art of amplifying and of disguising truth; when we see them stunned, as it were, during the best years of their lives, by the continual hurry of business, reading nothing but what relates to the particular cases before them, shutting out all liberal knowledge from their minds, and contracting their views to the little objects with which they are continually occupied ; when we see them, after a time, advanced to the offices of Solicitor and Attorney-General, in which to defend and to extol every provision of the law seems to be considered as a kind of duty, as the test of loyalty, and as an earnest of their fitness for some high judicial office ; when we see them compelled to become politicians because they are the lawyers of the Crown, and acting, in the House of Commons, not the part of liberal and enlightened statesmen, but that of the retained counsel of the King and his Ministers ; not debating for the public, but pleading for their peculiar clients ;—can we be surprised that, stepping from hence into the seat of Chancellor, they do not at once assume a new character ; that their dispositions and their habits are not altered ; but that the same ignorance of every thing but law, the same narrow views, the same prejudices, the same passions, the same little mind, are to be found in the magistrate, as marked before the hired and hackneyed advocate ?

But you will ask, " Is not this satire, rather than instruction and advice ?" Do I not know that you too are a practising lawyer, that your business is very considerable, and that your life passes in the same hurry, and is engrossed by the same occupations, as those whose faculties I represent as being so much injured by them and degraded ? Do I

imagine that you possess some magic charm by
which you can preserve your energy and liberality
of mind unimpaired in situations so dangerous to
others? or would I advise you to give up your
practice, and to devote yourself entirely to the study
of the great principles of philosophy and legislation
which alone can form a statesman in the genuine
sense of that word? Most certainly that is not the
advice which I would give you : you could not
adopt a more effectual expedient for excluding
yourself for ever from the Chancellorship, than
such a course of preparation for it. If ever you
are Chancellor, it will be because you are a lawyer
in great practice : and those parts of your character
and attainments on which I set the highest value
will be only excused in favour of those which appear to me to be comparatively mean and unim-
portant.

Neither do I suppose you possessed of any charm
to preserve your mind untainted by professional
habits, or to render it inaccessible to those prejudices which an advocate, in the course of his practice, usually contracts; but I would have you be
on your guard against them. I would prevent
your so devoting yourself to your present occupations as not to look forward to that higher destiny
which awaits you. I would have the expectation
of that destiny be itself the charm which shall render you proof against all the corruptions of your
present condition; and, as we have seen Chancellors who, though invested with all the dazzling in-
signia of the highest magistracy, were still nothing
more than advocates, so I would have you, while

an advocate, be already, in the extent of your
views and the elevation of your mind, a Chancellor. I would have you keep that high station continually in your thoughts ; not, indeed, as it has possessed the minds of many, serving only as a spur to
their ambition, and prompting them to suffer no opportunity of facilitating their accession to it to pass
unimproved, — but that you may lose no time in
preparing yourself for the discharge of those duties
which you know not how soon may be imposed
upon you; and, perhaps, before you can be enabled
to make the most for mankind of the advantages
which you will possess. Reflect, again and again,
not only on every thing which you are to accomplish, but on all the means by which you are to
accomplish them. Suffer nothing to escape you
which has the least chance of being useful to a
Chancellor, such as you conceive he ought to be ;
and note down every thing which you observe.
Look about amongst your friends and acquaintance
for the men who are likely to be zealous coadjutors
in your designs, and treasure up their qualifications
in your memory, till you can call them into action ;
and in the mean time consider yourself as such a
coadjutor ; as one to whom a Chancellor — anxious
to make his talents, his knowledge, his honours,
his authority, his influence, in short, all the extensive means which God has afforded him, as profitable as he can to his fellow-creatures — has opened
his glorious projects; and endeavour to assist to the
utmost of your power in their execution, by availing
yourself of all the opportunities which a Chancellor
in the execution of his office cannot possess.

It will be an encouragement to you, in the fatigue and irksomeness of your daily practice, to have such an object in view. With this ever present to your mind, a private cause, which in itself would only afford you weariness and disgust,   *   *   *
*   *   *   *

II.[1]

NOTHING that has passed, my dear C., since I last wrote to you, has at all weakened my expectation of seeing you one day in that high station to which I then so anxiously encouraged you to aspire. I do not wish to divert you from such anticipations; nay, on the contrary, I would have you entertain and dwell on them. If, indeed, I could suppose that, in such reveries, the circumstances on which your imagination dwelt with most pleasure were the splendour and magnificence which attend so high an office; the homage which is always paid to the man, be he who he may, before whom the mace and the great seal are borne; the advantage of appearing with high distinction in the brilliant circle of a court; of living in habits of familiarity with those to whom the vulgar look up with awe and veneration; the pride of transmitting a title to your posterity; or even the satisfaction of thinking that it is your own exertions alone which have raised you to such an eminence,—I should fear the indulgence of them would be attended with consequences the most pernicious. Men with whom such things are objects of ambition are seldom very scrupulous about the means by which their ambitious ends may be accomplished; and if they happen to fail of success, the dreams of greatness which they had

---

[1] There is no date to this letter in the original. — ED.

cherished serve only to mortify their pride, and to
embitter their chagrin and disappointment. But
he who sees principally in a high office the enlarged
means of doing good, and the exquisite satisfaction
of discharging well the most important duties ; who
dwells on the delightful vision of a highly improved state of society, in which the evils inseparable from the human . condition are mitigated,
and the errors, the follies, and the vices of mankind are corrected, tempered, and repressed ; and
who can, in these waking dreams, connect himself
with the improvements he contemplates, as being
in some degree the cause and author of them ; — to
such a man, the very reveries which he has entertained are a real good. If ever they should be
realized, he will come into office having well considered, and being matured, and, as it were, exercised
for, its important functions, and ready to improve
and make the most of every moment of his public
life. His enjoyments will be multiplied beyond
what is the common lot even of the most upright
magistrates ; for he will have enjoyed in hope and
in expectation all that it will be his great good
fortune to accomplish. The period of his remaining in office, considering the brevity of human life,
and the late stage of it at which such promotions ever
are attained, cannot be of long duration ; and the
time which may elapse after his magistracy is at an
end, the season of reflection on his past life, cannot,
in the nature of things, be long attended with unimpaired faculties, or with any capacity of such
enjoyments ; but, by anticipating in his reflections the good which he is to do, he will have en-

larged the period of a happy and an honoured existence.

If, on the other hand, his expectations never should be realized — if his honest projects should be disappointed without any fault of his, and he should remain to his death in privacy and obscurity, yet the hopes which he has nourished, and the dreams in which he has indulged, have gilded and enlivened that season of life which, without them, would have been comparatively dull and insipid; they have in his own eyes ennobled his existence, and enlarged and elevated his views and his habits of thinking. He was in an error; but it has been a salutary error. He has amused himself with a fiction; but that fiction has produced substantial benefits. His mind, occupied with such noble subjects of contemplation, has not been so accessible to mean and little and selfish consideration as it would have been if he had been engrossed by frivolous or inferior pursuits.

III.

Cowes, in the Isle of Wight, Sept. 1807.

It is now just six years since I found myself, at the same season of the year, in a situation much resembling that which I am in at present. After very close application to the severe labours of my profession, I had retired for the long vacation to Tenby, in Pembrokeshire, and was indulging myself in the enjoyment of the refreshing breezes of the sea, the beautiful scenery around me, and the perfect quiet and undisturbed leisure which formed so striking a contrast with the course of life from which I had just escaped. Such an interruption of my usual occupations and fatigues led me, at that time, naturally enough, to reflect on my situation, and to meditate on my future prospects. I could not bring to mind the progress which I had made in my profession, and observe the then state of political parties, without thinking it possible that I might, at some time or other, be raised to the highest office of judicature; and I could not, without forgetting all that I had heard from my friends and my acquaintance, but suppose that such an event was even probable. Recollecting what duties that high station would bring with it, and fully sensible of my own inability adequately to discharge them, I applied myself to the consideration of what a Chancellor of Great Britain

ought to be ; of what extensive means he has of
improving the condition of his fellow-creatures ;
and how anxious he should be not to suffer opportunities of beneficence, which are afforded to so
few, to pass unimproved.   I endeavoured to familiarize myself with ideas which would become such
a station; and, while still in privacy and obscurity,
and possessed of the leisure which is requisite for
such undertakings, to prepare myself with the
system of conduct which I ought to adopt, and to
mature plans of reform which I should be desirous to establish.   That I might derive the more
profit from these meditations, I thought of committing them to writing.   When I set about this
task, however, it appeared to me so ridiculous
that a private individual, a mere advocate, distinguished by no honour in his profession except that
of being King's Counsel, a person not in Parliament, and not connected with any political party,
should amuse himself with the idea of becoming
a Lord Chancellor, that I could not trust the
thought to paper, even though it was to be seen
by no eyes but my own.   To accomplish, therefore, my object, and yet escape this ridicule, I began a series of letters, supposed to be addressed
by some intimate friend to a barrister, who might
form expectations of rising to the highest eminence
in his profession, suggesting to him reflections
which I wished myself to indulge, and giving as
advice what I intended to prescribe to myself as
laws.   I had not prosecuted this idea very far when
my leisure was broken in upon by some avocation
or other, and the season of business too speedily

returned. In the next long vacation, I profited by the short peace which this country enjoyed to gratify my curiosity by revisiting Paris; and I have not in any succeeding vacation found myself in a situation so well adapted to the continuation (the renewal, I should rather say) of that self-admonition which I had begun, as at the present moment. With respect to myself, however, circumstances have in this interval very greatly altered.

The expectation of arriving at the highest honours of my profession would perhaps now not be treated with ridicule by any person who heard that I entertained it. I have filled the office of Solicitor-General under that Administration which was formed by a union of Mr. Fox and Lord Grenville, and of all their political friends, and which consisted of all the public men in the kingdom most distinguished for abilities and for enlarged political views. They have been dismissed from their offices under the pretext that a measure of great importance to the tranquillity and safety of the empire, which they had projected, was likely to endanger the Church establishment. The present Ministry, however, can hardly, considering what the crisis is to which public affairs are hastening, be very long in power; and, if those whom they have supplanted should recover their authority, the Great Seal can scarcely be again entrusted to the hands of Lord Erskine : with all his talents (and very great they undoubtedly are) his incapacity for the office was too forcibly and too generally felt for him to be again placed in it : — Piggott, the late Attorney-General, would, probably, decline a situation of so

much fatigue, if it were offered to him ; and there
is no other lawyer, at all connected with any of the
men who would form the administration, who can
aspire to so high a station.

But while the course of public events seems to
have brought this object more within my reach, it
has rendered it to me less, very far less, an object
of desire. The aspect of public affairs has strangely
altered in this short interval. .Who can look at
what has taken place in the rest of Europe, and
think of what may be expected here, and consider
offices of high trust as objects of envy ? What, in
such times as those which are fast approaching, is
a man of high rank, but a person who is destined to
bear a larger portion than others of the public misfortunes ? What a Minister, but a man raised to
eminence, only that he may be responsible for
calamities which it is not, however, in human wisdom to avert ? If there be any mode by which I
could ever render any service to my countrymen,
it could only be by advancing the arts of peace, by
useful laws, and salutary reforms ; by promoting the
diffusion of science, and the improvement of the
public morals : but what room will there be for all
this in the troublous times which we may expect,
and with the dispositions which we see entertained
by those on whose will the success of such things
principally depends?

Deprived of the hope of doing that good which
I had once flattered myself it might be my singular
good fortune to achieve, what motive can I now
have for accepting such an office? If I consult
only my own happiness, or the good of those who

are dearest to me in the world, I can never hesitate a moment to refuse it, under whatever circumstances it may be offered to me.   Not that I pretend to be so free from vanity as not to be highly
gratified at being thought endowed with qualities
worthy of so eminent a station.   I have no claim
to the merit of such philosophy.   On the contrary,
I am sensible to the praises and the admiration of
those with whom I live, to a degree of which I
have reason, perhaps, to be ashamed; but I know
that all such gratifications are of short duration,
and that they are most dearly purchased at the
price of that domestic peace and tranquillity which
must infallibly be sacrificed to obtain them.   To
live without interruption in the bosom of my family;
to enjoy every day, and almost every hour, the
affectionate and endearing society of that most
sensible and most amiable woman with whom I
have the happiness to be united; to watch and
improve the dawnings of reason in the children I
am blessed with; to forget, in poring over the
pages of historians, of poets, and of philosophers,
the evils which are at this moment afflicting the
world; — these are my dearest and fondest enjoyments *: all these must be resigned.   I cannot

* In making these observations on that domestic comfort which I
have the happiness to enjoy, and to feel the value of, I did not sufficiently consider how much of that comfort arises from the public duties
which I here suppose to be so incompatible with it.   Pure as these
enjoyments are, I possibly might not have so strong a relish for them
if they were not interrupted by the occupations of business; and a great
part, undoubtedly, of the satisfaction which I feel in privacy and retirement, arises from reflecting upon what little public good I have been
able to do, and from the public services which I have it in contemplation to perform.   When I observe my sweet children, and please myself
with imagining what in time they will be, I cannot but be desirous that

devote any portion of my time to such objects without betraying my duty.　Every hour must be consumed in the most laborious occupations, or, what is still more hateful to me, in the parade of courts, the giving audiences, and entertaining strangers ; in pomp and show, in unprofitable forms and unmeaning ceremonies.　And what should I reap from this splendid but painful drudgery ? — for the public, nothing : for my own reputation, nothing : and in point of emolument I must even to a great degree be a loser.　It is true that my income would, for the time, be greater than it is at present ; but not so much greater as, allowing for the necessary increase of my expenses in equipages, entertainments, and the decorations of such an office, to afford me the means of laying by every year nearly so large a saving as at present, for my support in old age, and as a provision for

---

they may hereafter reflect without dissatisfaction, nay, with pleasure and pride, upon what their father was, and what he shall have accomplished.

Mackintosh, observing, in one of the lectures which he read at Lincoln's Inn, upon the conduct and the fate of Regulus, very justly remarked that, when his virtue was supposed to have brought on him the greatest misery, and when it might therefore be thought that his was an example ill calculated to prove the expediency of a strict adherence to principles of honour and patriotism, it ought to be recollected what enjoyment those principles and that temper of mind, which made it impossible for him, in the circumstances in which he was placed, not to expose himself to such cruelties, must, in the whole course of his past life, have continually afforded him ; and that, great as the torments were which were inflicted on him, yet, if a just estimate were made of the whole sum of good and evil of his life, it would probably be found that the evil was greatly overbalanced by the good.　In the same manner it would become me, if ever I should find myself harassed and overwhelmed with the duties of my office, and made wretched by the calamities which may attend my public life, to reflect that those sentiments which would have made me think it most dishonourable, through regard to my own individual comfort, to shrink from such trials, will have been the source of that pure and perfect happiness which, in the earlier part of my life, I have enjoyed.

my children : and then that income, instead of being permanent as long as my health and my faculties shall be preserved, will cease the moment of my removal from my office ; and I should then find myself afflicted with a title which would render my eldest son, as well as myself, incapable of gaining a livelihood. The heir to a title, that son would be doomed to idleness for the remainder of his days, and perhaps at the same time to indigence. If my poor boy should ever be condemned to a destiny so calamitous as this, let me at least be sure that it is not through his father's fault that it has been brought upon him ; that his misfortunes are not to be ascribed to the foolish vanity of his father, or to his ill-judging ambition, but to a strong and imperative sense of duty, which would have compelled him to sacrifice his own happiness, and what it would cost him a much sharper pang to risk, in the hope of being able to improve the condition of a large portion of his fellow creatures.

Yes, it would be that hope, that hope alone (and it would be strange indeed if, in thus communing with myself, I could use any disguise), which could induce me, for an instant, to hesitate at renouncing all thoughts of accepting any public station. It behoves me, therefore, most seriously to consider whether there be now any reason for my nourishing any such hope. The prospect before us is that of foreign wars and domestic tumults. We have to expect the long meditated invasion of the most formidable enemy that this country ever knew ; and at the same time to dread

the ill-smothered resentment of a large portion
of our fellow subjects*, who have been long and
most cruelly trampled on, and who are now probably only watching their opportunity to break out
in open rebellion. In the scenes which are likely
to be acted in this country, the laws themselves
will probably be silent; how can it be expected,
then, that the temperate voice of reform should be
listened to?

Nor does the alarming state of public affairs
alone give reason to despair of being able to benefit
mankind by any attempt to serve them. The disposition of all orders of persons in the country
seems adverse to such designs. The influence
which the French Revolution has had over this
nation has been in every way unfavourable to them.
Among the higher orders it has produced a horror
of every kind of innovation; among the lower, a
desire to try the boldest political experiments,
and a distrust and contempt of all moderate reforms. In the very limited attempt which I have
already made to begin to alter and improve those
barbarous and irrational laws, respecting the rights
of creditors over the property and persons of their
debtors, which disgrace this country, I have experienced how indifferent the great body of the
public is to such subjects, and how much power is
attached to a senseless cry of the wisdom of our
ancestors, when it is set up to defend institutions
of which the forms and names have long survived
the spirit and reason. A Chancellor is not all-
powerful : he may, indeed, alone correct the

---

* The Irish.

abuses and reform the practice of his own court ; but, as to any great schemes of public benevolence, it is impossible for him to carry them into execution, without the co-operation of his colleagues, and the support of Parliament. What, therefore, at the present day, could a man, who would be desirous of employing the great means which he would seem to possess to the most advantage for his country, derive from the situation of Chancellor, but the pain of being tantalized with the delusive appearance of accomplishing great objects, which, as he endeavours to reach them, will constantly elude his grasp ?

Indeed, in whatever way I consider the prospects before me, I see no chance of my being able to do any public good. If, indeed, my lot had been cast in days of peace; if it had been my fortune to have met with the support of a frank and beneficent Prince, or with the encouragement of a Parliament actuated by the purest patriotism, and the most earnest desire to promote the welfare of the people, — very different might have been my destiny; but, looking around me, seeing who are the individuals with whom and for whom I am to act, and recollecting what I am, I cannot but be convinced that a life of privacy and obscurity is that for which I am best suited : — I shall pass from off this mortal stage, it is true, without having rendered any public benefit to my country, and without leaving a name worth being remembered ; but I shall have lived as happy as the endearments of domestic life can render any human being ; and my dearest wife and my beloved children will be the happier and the better because such will have been the obscure path in which I shall have journeyed through life.

But while I thus, in a time of calm and of leisure, and at a moment when my judgment is likely to be most sound, renounce all thoughts of acting a part on that great theatre which probably would be open to me, I cannot but sometimes indulge myself with splendid and enchanting visions which float across my mind. In representing to myself the good which might still be done in this country, with some little change of circumstances, and in fancying myself an instrument in accomplishing that good ; — in these my half-waking dreams, I sometimes suppose that season to have arrived when His Majesty, having lived to an extreme old age, shall have yielded to the universal law of nature, and shall have descended into the tomb of his fathers, and when the Prince shall have ascended the throne which he was born to inherit. I suppose him to have delivered the Great Seal into my hands, and to have done it with assurances, and in a manner, which convinced me that I had his entire confidence. I imagine all the persons who have been then newly appointed to the highest offices of the State to be animated with the same zeal for the public good. All jealousy, all apprehensions of a colleague interposing his advice in matters not within his own immediate department, are banished. All are actuated by the same spirit ; all feel the same contempt for the personal advantages to be derived from office, and for the mean homage which attends the exercise of ministerial patronage; all feel alike a sense of the difficulties in which the country is involved, and a conviction that nothing can extricate it, and can raise it in the new order of things which prevails in Europe to the rank which it once held among nations, but to call forth all the strength, the courage, the talents, and the resources of the kingdom.

I imagine myself eagerly and earnestly preparing to discharge all the various and important duties which a Minister, and that Minister a Lord Chancellor, would, in such a situation, find pressing upon him. I am impatient to see executed all the schemes which I had formed for improving the condition of my fellow-creatures; for I cannot persuade myself that, under such circumstances, the perils with which the country is threatened would afford any reason for abandoning, or even for postponing them. If, indeed, a Minister had only to choose between preserving the country from a foreign yoke, or perfecting its laws and its institutions, — if the last of these objects could not be pursued without hazarding the first of them, — no doubt all projects of reform and of improvement should, in such a moment, be renounced altogether. For, although I am strongly impressed with a sense of the public evils and abuses which exist in this country; yet, God forbid that I should for an instant entertain that unnatural and impious sentiment which, though it has been imputed to some men, is perhaps really felt by none, — that things

are so bad with us, that we have nothing which we
ought to wish to preserve ! Much as there is which
loudly calls for reformation amongst us, yet, with
all its defects and oppressions, no wise and virtuous
man would hesitate to sacrifice his life to preserve
our government, even such as it is, for those who
are to come after him. Fortunately, however, Ministers have no such painful alternative offered to
them. Improving our domestic concerns, instead
of weakening us as a nation, would give us renewed
strength and increased resources. To remove all
just causes of complaint in the people ; to give
them new securities for their liberties ; to improve
their condition ; to perfect our laws ; to correct
all abuses ; to purify the administration of justice ;
—to do all this, is to supply us with far better means
of defence than could be acquired by additional
fleets and armies.

Placed in such a situation as I have imagined,
and impressed with these sentiments, the first thing
I should attempt would be to inspire my Sovereign
with the same enthusiasm for the public good
which I felt myself; and to endeavour to make
myself secure, that in the measures to be proposed
I should have his cordial support. The importance of this preliminary step I should feel to be
so great, that I should endeavour to accomplish it
by all the means in my power. To awaken these
generous sentiments in the bosom of the King, it
would be necessary to open to him, without disguise, the whole of my plans ; to place before him
his real situation, as well as that of his people, and

to speak truths which never before have reached his ears. To carry on, then, this romantic vision (for such, no doubt, it is), let me suppose that, taking advantage of a moment most favourable for such a purpose, having obtained an audience of the King, and having first awakened his curiosity by giving him to understand that it was on a subject of deep importance to himself and to the nation, I address him to this effect : —

" The situation, Sir, in which you are placed is one of extreme difficulty. You have succeeded to the throne at a crisis of danger unexampled in the history of your kingdom. The present moment is one which requires the utmost exertions of the State, not to ensure to it a triumph over its enemies, but to enable it to preserve its existence. The popularity of the most beloved Prince that ever reigned over a free people, — the utmost energy of men feeling all the value of the liberties they have inherited, and proud of their pre-eminence amongst nations, — a national enthusiasm of public spirit wrought up to the highest pitch, — all this would not be more than equal to rescue the country from the dangers which threaten it : but, instead of all this, what does your Majesty find? To deceive you, to withhold from you any part of the truth, under circumstances so urgent as the present, would be the basest of treasons. If your Majesty were incapable of hearing and of profiting by the truth — if no one had the courage to speak it to you — the situation of the country would indeed be desperate. To use no disguise, then, your Majesty,

notwithstanding what the voice of adulation may
have told you, enjoys no popularity amongst your
subjects : your youth is supposed to have been
spent in unjustifiable excesses ; political factions
have laboured to exaggerate your indiscretions ;
the utmost industry has been used to give, as ex-
tensively as possible, impressions of you the most
unfavourable, and that industry has been exerted
with but too much success. It is of the highest
importance to your Majesty's happiness, and to
the tranquillity of your reign, that these impressions should be removed as speedily as possible.
There was a time, indeed, when a long line of
royal ancestors gave a prince such perfect security
that he should transmit in peace to his heir the
throne which he had inherited from his father, that
it was unnecessary for him to desire or to deserve
the affection of his subjects : but that time is past.
It is in his own personal qualifications alone that a
prince must now look for his security ; and your
people, Sir, are yet to be convinced that the personal qualifications which will secure a throne are
yours. The first acts of your government will decide
the character of your reign. You have ascended
the throne at a mature period of life ; and, in the
first errors of your reign, if your Majesty should
unfortunately fall into any, your people will not
have the consolation of looking forward to better
times, when the facility or impetuosity of youth
shall have passed away, and their King shall have
profited by the lessons of experience. Though
the policy of your royal father, and the high rank

of the heir-apparent, prevented you heretofore from taking any open part in public affairs, yet your Majesty cannot have remained an inattentive or an unconcerned spectator of what was passing around you.   The moment which has now arrived must have been long anticipated by you in imagination ; and it cannot but be supposed, that the principles of government which will characterise your reign have long been rooted in your mind. Many of those upon whom your Majesty's enemies have most strongly impressed an opinion to your disadvantage, are yet not unwilling to hope that your public opinions may be of a different character from that which, they have been taught to believe, has marked your private conduct; and all persons look forward with eager solicitude to the events of a few months to come, as those which are to declare the fate of this country.

" The happiness of a people must always depend in a considerable degree on the character and disposition of their sovereign ; but never, perhaps, did any monarch before find himself in a situation in which the well-being, not of his subjects only, but of their posterity, more depended on himself, than these now depend on your Majesty.   Those persons, Sir, are strangely deceived who persuade themselves that, in the present state of the world, no great part is left to any of the sovereigns of Europe to act ; and who represent them all as reduced only to struggle to retain a precarious possession of their thrones, — happy, it should seem, if they can but preserve the pageantry of royalty

from the all-destroying ambition of the Emperor of
the French. Listen not to such degrading sugges-
tions. No, Sir; to you it is still allowed to aspire
to the highest glory that ever elevated any human
being above his fellow-creatures. It is true that if
your ambition were to make conquests, — if you
were desirous to impose the yoke of your dominion
on independent and unoffending nations, — those
paths of glory, as they are falsely called, are not
open to you : there you cannot be unrivalled; nay,
it would be gross adulation to say, that you would
not be far surpassed : but there are other and still
nobler attributes of royalty in the exercise of
which you need not fear any rival. Let it be seen
that to make your people happy will be the great,
the only object of your reign : that the most effectual means of accomplishing that end will constantly occupy your thoughts ; that you look at the
regal office, not as affording you means and opportunities of luxurious enjoyment, but as imposing
on you the most important and sacred duties, and
that you are resolved magnanimously to discharge
them.

" When you shall have once impressed your subjects with the belief that these are your sentiments,
— when your Ministers shall have shown that they
are inspired with zeal to serve faithfully, and to
give vigour and efficacy to the beneficent and pa-
ternal views of, their Patriot King,—put arms into
the hands of all your subjects ; make this an armed
nation for its defence. A people that is free ; that
is contented ; that knows the value of its rights,

and the benefits it derives from its laws; that feels,
not a superstitious veneration for the name of King,
but a grateful attachment to the man who seems
to have assumed the cares of royalty only to provide for their security and happiness;—such a people, fighting on their own soil, surrounded by their
fathers, their children, their wives, their kindred,
their friends, and their countrymen, must be invin-
cible.   Let not a false and narrow-minded policy

   *   *   *   *   *   *

IV.

My dear C.   Sept. 5. 1818.

Our correspondence has been long interrupted. It is now more than ten years since I
conferred with you very confidentially on the views
which I then entertained with respect to myself
and to public affairs. I laid my whole mind open
to you. Allow me to do so again; to make you
once more my confessor; and to enter before
you upon the task of self-examination, and to
deliberate with you upon the prospects which lie
before me. These prospects are now greatly contracted. Ten years is a large portion of human life,
at any stage of it; but, at the advanced period to
which I had arrived when I last addressed you, it
might be supposed nearly to comprise the whole
of what then remained. The lapse of those ten
years, however, seems to have left me with undiminished strength and activity, and with the same
power, had I the same prospects, of making myself
useful to others as I had at the commencement of
them. Those prospects, nevertheless, are greatly
altered. I cannot but be sensible that the means
I have left of being serviceable in any way to my
countrymen or my fellow-creatures must, according
to the usual course of human life, be now contracted
into a very narrow space. A few years more of

active life with unimpaired faculties is the utmost I can hope for. When I last addressed you, I looked forward to what then seemed within the probable compass of human events — my being raised to a high judicial station. I was busied in preparing myself for the discharge of its sacred duties ; and, in a happy anticipation, I already exulted in the opportunity which such a station must afford of benefiting the present as well as future generations. From such splendid dreams I have long since awakened.

The time within which, if ever they must have been realized, has passed away, and has not only left me in a state of privacy, but with much less prospect, even if my stock of life had remained undiminished, of ever emerging from it. The monarch who then sat on the throne has since been, in effect, removed from it by mental incapacity. His son, the present Regent, has shown sufficiently by his conduct that those political principles which I have always professed, and with which I shall descend into my grave, must for ever exclude those who act upon them from his favour. The hopes which the nation began to cherish from the rising virtues of the Princess Charlotte have been, by her premature and unexpected death, for ever extinguished. In the Duke of York, and in the other of the King's sons, (with the exception of the Duke of Sussex, who is too far removed from the succession to afford any prospect of its devolving upon him,) are to be found the most narrow and bigoted notions of government. God forbid that my public conduct should ever recommend me to the fa-

vour of any of these princes. Still, however, though
destined never to fill any public office, and though
few must be the years that remain for me, I am
not without the means of rendering some services
to mankind ; and I still feel a strong impulse to
employ these means to the best advantage. The
faculties, indeed, which I possess, and the influence
which I have in Parliament, are not sufficient to
enable me to carry there any important measures ;
yet it remains for me to propose what I think
right ; to resist what is pernicious ; to support my
opinions by sound arguments, and on generous
principles ; and to leave to the world an example
in public life of honesty, independence, and patriotism. In following this course, I shall not have
lived in vain ; and, little as those who breathe the
same air with myself may profit by my exertions,
it is possible that the happiness which those who
are to come after me, nay, which a remote posterity may enjoy, may, in some degree, be attri-
butable even to my unsuccessful efforts, and rejected
motions.

The honour which has lately been conferred on
me, that of being elected to represent the city of
Westminster in Parliament, has, in some respects,
added to my means of being useful. It has drawn
upon me an additional portion of public attention ;
it has placed me, as it were, in a more conspicuous
theatre ; and has given some importance to my
actions, and even to my speeches. It has, however, at the same time, brought with it some difficulties to which I was not before exposed. I seem
to be not quite so much the master of my own

conduct as I used to be. Chosen by popular election to represent the metropolis which on all great
questions of public interest has, of late years, taken
the lead in supporting the claims and pretensions of
the people, it will be expected of me, that I shall
maintain such pretensions more strenuously than
I have ever done before ; that I should pay my
court to the people, and be ever ready to attend
the call of those who shall think proper, as they
have been accustomed to do, to summon popular
meetings on great public questions as they may
occur. I feel, however, no inclination to act any
such part. I am the servant of the people, but I
am determined not to be their slave ; and I should
think the proud distinction which has been conferred on me had lost half its value, if it had been
obtained, or was to be preserved, by acting the part
of a factious demagogue. I do not say that I
will attend no popular meetings, but I will attend
them only on extraordinary occasions ; and, when
these occur, I will endeavour to temper the violence and to remove the prejudices which I may
find prevailing there. No conduct can, in my eyes,
be more criminal than that of availing one's self of
the prejudiced clamours of the ignorant or misin-
formed, to accomplish any political purpose, however good or desirable in itself. If I use strong
language, and take a bold part for the people,
it shall be in the House of Commons, not in Palace
Yard. If I cannot serve those of my fellow-
citizens who are in the humblest situations of life,
at least I will not injure them. I will be careful
not, by inflaming their passions, and encouraging

them to enter upon courses of which the danger would exclusively be theirs, to draw ruin upon their heads.

Recollecting what frequently passes at popular meetings, I cannot but think that those who often attend them generally lose by such attendance much of the weight and dignity which may have belonged to their characters; whatever may belong to mine I will endeavour to preserve undiminished. Though it be now evident that I shall never be raised to any high office, yet I am resolved so to conduct myself, as if I knew that the highest dignity was my certain destination. Upon the hustings, in Covent Garden, at election dinners, and at tavern meetings, when I am obliged to be present at them, I will always endeavour to speak and act like one who bears in mind that the time is approaching when he is to fill the highest seat of justice. What, indeed, is it which, in a private station, can give to any man weight and influence with others, but the independence and dignity of his character? It is by these alone that he can be enabled to stand up against all the power and authority which rank, and office, and court favour must always confer. It is by a dignified conduct, and an unsullied reputation, much more than even by arguments or eloquence, that he may gain over supporters to the people's cause, and check, and restrain, and intimidate an insolent and corrupt administration, and counteract their mischievous designs. A representative of Westminster who would effectually serve his constituents, must, above all things, be attentive not to debase his character by pursuing mean and unworthy objects, or even by exposing it to undeserved contempt or ridicule. He must be careful not to throw away or spoil in Palace Yard the most formidable weapons with which he can fight the battle of his constituents in Parliament.

APPENDIX.

No. I. (See p. 224.)

Letters and Papers from Mons. Gallois.

Paris, Dec. 31. 1815.

My dear Sir,

Je profite du retour de M. B—— pour vous envoyer les brochures dont je vous avais parlé. Vous les trouverez bien médiocres, et vous aurez raison. Mais enfin vous jugerez par là de l'état de notre presse. Nous pouvons dire maintenant d'elle ce que Bossuet disait de votre Princesse Henriette : *Là voilà telle que la mort nous l'a faite.* Nous avons la licence de la presse, nous n'en avons pas la liberté ; nous en avons la licence pour le profit de la faction qui veut dominer, nous n'en avons pas la liberté pour les intérêts de la nation. Il faut que je vous raconte sur ce sujet un trait qui vous donnera une idée des caractères et des sentiments élevés de la plus grande partie des hommes qui ont de la réputation dans ce pays, et qui se sont formés à la politique dans l'école de l'ancien gouvernement, transportée par ces messieurs dans le nouveau. Vous avez entendu parler de la nouvelle loi des Cours Prévôtales. Ces Cours Prévôtales ne se bornent pas comme les anciennes aux simples actes de violence à mains armées par des rassemblements d'individus ; elles sont aussi établies contre les rassemblements, dont l'espèce est déterminée par la loi. Croiriez-vous qu'un membre de l'Institut, un des hommes qui ont le plus de réputation en France dans les sciences physiques, *M. Cuvier*, maître des requêtes sous Bonaparte, conseiller d'état sous Louis XVIII., chargé par

le Roi en sa qualité de conseiller d'état de venir défendre
ce projet de loi à la Chambre des Députés, a osé dire cette
phrase-ci. : " Je conviens, Messieurs, que les *juges prévôtaux*
pourront devenir les *juges de la littérature.* Je conviens,
Messieurs, qu'on écrira moins de livres de politique, que les
libraires en vendront moins ; mais vous conviendrez bien,
Messieurs, qu'il n'y a pas au fond un trop grand malheur à
cela ? " Il est bien sûr que comme ce digne homme n'écrit
que sur les mollusques et l'anatomie comparée, les ossements
fossiles, &c., et qu'il jouit pour ces grands travaux si utiles à
la prospérité de la nation de 30 milles livres de rente, il
n'aura pas grand chose à craindre des Cours Prévôtales,
et que si l'on ne peut plus s'occuper des sciences politiques
et morales, il faudra en revenir, pour faire quelque chose
aux insectes et aux os fossiles, ce qui sûrement mettrait fort
à leur aise les vampires qui voudraient exploiter la France
pour leur profit particulier. —— Nos journaux et papiers
publics sont principalement dans un état déplorable ; pas une
vérité utile à la nation, pas un fait important à connaître ;
tout l'art de ceux qui les composent sous la surveillance de
la police, est de cacher tout ce qu'il importerait au public
de savoir, et de lui donner les plus fausses impressions des
faits qu'on lui présente. Quand le funeste empire de
Bonaparte à été détruit, je n'ai que trop pressenti que
nous souffririons encore longtemps de la pernicieuse influence de ses pratiques de gouvernement, et des hommes
pervers qui s'étaient formés à son école ; que l'esprit de
son administration, ses commis et ses agents, transplantés
dans le gouvernement nouveau, ne feraient qu'aggraver le
danger et les maux qui naissaient naturellement de ces
circonstances nouvelles. Au milieu de tout cela, la nation
reste debout, et marche dans la direction de l'esprit des
temps et de la raison universelle : elle vit sur ces foules
d'idées et de sentiments qui sont le patrimoine commun
de l'Europe, et dont aucun accident politique ne pourra
jamais priver les nations : elle n'a rien de commun avec
tous ces sycophantes politiques qui, dans leur journaux,

leurs discours publics, ou les actes de leur administration, prétendent stipuler pour elle, parcequ'elle sait très-bien que ce qu'ils demandent pour elle, elle ne le veut pas attendre, qu'ils ne demandent que ce qui peut servir leurs intérêts et leurs passions contre son intérêt véritable.

Je vous envoye sur l'affaire des Protestants deux écrits; l'un est leur défense imprimée, écrite par l'un des ministres Protestants du département du Gard. Les personnes impartiales et bien instruites des faits disent, que cet écrit ne renferme rien que de vrai; mais la police en a empêché la circulation, de sorte que cet écrit est devenu très-rare. L'autre écrit que je vous envoye est manuscrit; il a été rédigé par un Protestant, *Royaliste très-prononcé*, que je connais beaucoup : ainsi vous voyez que sous ce rapport cet écrit n'a rien de suspect. Ces deux écrits vous donneront une idée exacte de la nature de ces évènements. Je joins ici les détails, que vous me demandez dans votre dernière lettre du 19. de ce mois que j'ai reçue par M. Delessert, relativement aux conférences des plénipotentiaires Français avec le Duc de Wellington.

Quand j'aurai pris tous les renseignements qui me manquent encore sur les élections dernières, je vous les enverrai.

Agréez je vous prie les nouvelles assurances de tous les sentiments avec lesquels je suis, Votre, &c.

Immédiatement après l'abdication de Bonaparte, les deux chambres nommèrent un gouvernement provisoire.

Ce gouvernement envoya des plénipotentiaires vers les souverains alliés pour *traiter de la paix*, puisque ces alliés avaient constamment déclaré que c'était à Bonaparte seul qu'on faisait la guerre, et que Bonaparte seul faisait obstacle à la paix.

Pendant que ces plénipotentiaires, revenus de Manheim à Hagueneau, cherchaient inutilement à pénétrer vers les ministres de ces souverains, qui ne répondaient que par des évasions et des retards, les armées du Duc de Wellington et de Blücher s'avançaient vers Paris.

Le gouvernement provisoire sentit alors la nécessité d'envoyer vers ces deux généraux des plénipotentiaires dont l'unique objet était d'obtenir un *armistice qui donnât le temps aux plénipotentiaires, alors à Hagueneau, de continuer à traiter de la paix.*

Ces plénipotentiaires furent MM. Flaugergue, Boissy d'Anglas, Valence, Andréossy, et la Bernardière. Ils furent chargés de se rendre d'abord directement au quartier général de Blücher, qui était près de Senlis. Arrivés aux avant postes, celui-ci leur fit répondre qu'il n'avait rien à leur dire, et qu'ils pouvaient s'addresser au Duc de Wellington. Ils vinrent alors auprès de celui-ci, qui était près du Pont St. Maxence, et lui firent part de l'objet de leur mission, *l'armistice.* Le Duc répondit qu'il verrait Blücher, qu'il ne pouvait traiter de rien sans lui à l'égard de cet armistice. Mais les circonstances s'arrangèrent toujours de telle manière, que les deux généraux ne purent jamais se rencontrer, ni probablement s'écrire; les jours s'écoulèrent ainsi. En attendant, les armées s'approchaient toujours de Paris autant qu'elles pouvaient. Au bout de quelques jours, le Duc de Wellington annonça aux plénipotentiaires qu'il allait partir pour St. Cloud, où devait être signée, avec de nouveaux commissaires arrivés de Paris, la convention relative à l'occupation de la capitale par les armées alliées. Il fut évident que Blücher et Wellington n'avaient jamais voulu traiter la question de *l'armistice;* qu'ils l'écartaient sans cesse, tantôt sous un prétexte, tantôt sous un autre; qu'ils voulaient absolument, et à quelque prix que ce fût, entrer à Paris, y faire entrer le roi à leur suite, et que les choses s'arrangeassent ensuite, comme elles le pourraient, entre le roi, la nation, et les puissances alliées. L'objet unique des plénipotentiaires étant *l'armistice,* les cinq ou six jours qu'ils passèrent auprès du Duc de Wellington furent tout-à-fait perdus quant à l'objet principal : il n'y eut entre eux que des conversations étrangères à l'objet dont ils étaient chargés, quoiqu'elles fussent relatives à la situation et aux affaires de la France.

Dans la première de ces conversations, le Duc de Wellington leur dit qu'on ne faisait point la guerre pour Louis XVIII., qu'on la faisait uniquement contre Bonaparte, parceque l'indépendance de l'Europe et la tranquillité du monde étaient incompatibles avec lui. Sur cette observation l'un des plénipotentiaires lui dit, que dans ce cas la guerre n'avait donc plus d'objet, que Bonaparte n'était plus le chef du gouvernement, que son existence politique était finie. Le Duc leur répondit, qu'il fallait le leur livrer; les plénipotentiaires répliquèrent que cela était impossible, et par deux raisons; la première, parceque cet acte serait de la part du gouvernement un acte de cruauté et d'infamie qui ferait horreur à la France, et dont le gouvernement était incapable; la seconde, qu'ils étaient certains qu'il allait se rendre à Rochefort pour s'y embarquer, qu'ils avaient même quelque raison de croire qu'il était déjà parti de Paris. A quoi le Duc répondit, ' Il n'en sera pas plus avancé; s'il s'embarque, nos frégates sauront bien le prendre, et il sera bientôt amené prisonnier en Angleterre.'

Alors un des plénipotentiaires lui dit, en riant : — Mais, Mylord, puisque vous avez tant d'envie de tenir Bonaparte, pourquoi ne le teniez-vous pas mieux, pourquoi ne l'avez-vous pas mieux gardé, lorsqu'il était à l'île d'Elbe? C'était, répondit le Duc, c'était à votre gouvernement à le garder mieux qu'il n'a fait; il avait en croisière trois bâtimens pour cela.

Dans l'une de ces conversations, le Duc de Wellington dit que les vertus personnelles, le caractère connu du Roi Louis XVIII. étaient regardés par toutes les puissances comme la meilleure garantie que la France pouvait leur offrir en ce moment. Si les Français, ajouta-t-il, voulaient un autre roi, le Duc d'Orléans par exemple, ce serait un usurpateur, *bien né* sans doute, mais enfin ce serait toujours un usurpateur : alors la France aurait besoin de donner de plus grandes garanties. Si l'on voulait le petit Napoléon, mais (dit-il, en s'interrompant, et comme rejettant loin de lui cette idée) cela est impossible; mais, enfin, si l'on voulait le petit Napoléon, alors il faudrait de bien plus grandes garanties encore, peut-être une grande partie du territoire de la France.

Il revint ensuite à l'idée que Louis XVIII. était le roi qui convenait le mieux à la France en même temps qu'à l'Europe; il rejeta fort loin la prétention de la part des Français de proposer au roi aucune condition; dit qu'il fallait s'en rapporter uniquement à lui, à ses bonnes intentions, et à ses principes éprouvés.

L'un des plénipotentiaires avait dit, dans l'une de ces cinq ou six conversations qui eurent lieu, que le roi devait, en entrant à Paris, prendre la cocarde tricolore ou nationale, à laquelle tout le peuple Français portait affection, et qui se rattachait à tant d'idées et de sentiments chers à la nation, que cette condescendance de la part du roi, qui était conseillée au roi même par des hommes considérables dans l'armée et dans le civil, en qui le roi avait toute confiance, que cette condescendance serait en ce moment un des plus puissants moyens de réunion et de paix, et préviendrait peut-être de nouvelles tempêtes politiques pour l'avenir. Le Duc de Wellington se récria beaucoup, et même avec une chaleur masquée, contre cette idée de cocarde nationale; il dit que cela était impossible, improposable; que la cocarde tricolore était une invention, un signe toujours visible, de la révolution; que le roi ne devait pas la prendre, qu'il ne la prendrait certainement pas. L'un des plénipotentiaires lui fit observer, que la cocarde tricolore ne serait pas plus un signe visible de la révolution, que ne pouvoit l'être l'habit de l'armée Française, et de toute la garde nationale de France, qui était aussi aux trois couleurs.

Du reste, les plénipotentiaires furent très-satisfaits de sa politesse simple et franche, de ses égards, et de l'espèce de confiance avec laquelle il leur parla. Voici, par exemple, un des traits de cette franchise et de cette confiance qui est assez curieux:— Un jour qu'il était à causer avec eux, on lui apporta un paquet de M. de Metternich; après en avoir pris lecture, il leur dit, Savez-vous ce que c'est? Ce sont ces Messieurs qui m'écrivent qu'ils viennent d'être avertis que le gouvernement provisoire envoye des plénipotentiaires vers moi pour traiter, qu'ils désirent que je ne les reçoive pas, et que je n'aye aucun rapport avec eux. Parbleu! je ferai moi ce qu'il me plaira. Je n'ai pas besoin que ces Messieurs me souscrivent leurs ordres; nous continuerons donc de nous voir tout comme auparavant. Voilà les détails que vous m'avez demandé, et que je vous donne, *d'après ce que vient de me dire*, il y a deux jours, l'un de ces plénipotentiaires, sur l'exactitude duquel je crois que l'on peut tout-à-fait compter.

SUR LES DERNIÈRES ÉLECTIONS. (See p. 224.)

Ce qu'on a imprimé sur ce sujet dans le *Morning Chronicle* du 28 Décembre est parfaitement exact. Voici ce que je crois pouvoir y ajouter pour vous. Talleyrand et ses collègues arrivèrent à Paris au retour du Gard, tellement effrayés de l'esprit de la dernière *Chambre des Représentants*, et de la disposition des assemblées électorales qui les avaient nommés, qu'ils crurent qu'il fallait recourir à quelque *moyen extraordinaire* pour y faire dominer l'esprit de royalisme, qu'ils croyaient ne pouvoir être que le royalisme constitutionel; mais en recourant à ce *moyen extraordinaire*, ils ne surent mettre dans l'exécution, ni habileté, ni prévoyance, ni même le moindre dégré de l'attention la plus commune.

Ils choisirent d'abord, sans le moindre discernement, et sur la présentation qui leur en fut faite par des gens plus habiles qu'eux, des hommes dont la très-grande majorité était connue pour être opposée aux principes de la révolution, et nommèrent ces hommes présidents, des 368 collèges d'arrondissements, et des 83 collèges des départements. Ils firent rendre ensuite par le roi une ordonnance qui adjoignait 10 nouveaux membres à chaque collège, et 20 à chaque collège de département. Ces nouveaux membres devaient être choisis par chaque préfet parmi les *citoyens qui ont rendu des services ;* c'était environ 60 électeurs que chaque préfet avait droit de nommer. Il faut remarquer, que d'après la loi sur cette matière (du 4 Août, 1802), le nombre des électeurs d'arrondissement ne peut excéder 200, ni être au-dessous de 120, et le nombre des électeurs de département ne peut excéder 300, ni être au-dessous de 200. Quand l'ordonnance fut rendue, et que les présidents eurent été nommés, le Prince de Talleyrand abandonna toute l'affaire à *la grâce de Dieu.* Pendant ce temps-là, les ultra-royalistes surent bien mettre à profit l'insouciance, la léthargie, l'incapacité du ministère. Ils entourèrent de leurs parents, de leurs amis, les préfets, sous-préfets, et présidents des collèges ; tous les moyens de séduction et de menaces furent employés pour faire nommer leurs créatures et eux-mêmes *adjoints* de ces collèges. Ainsi, à l'insçu du ministère, et à l'instant même où, dans la plus parfaite confiance dans le succès de sa mesure, il se livrait sottement à l'espérance d'avoir une assemblée nouvelle toute nommée dans son sens, les ultra-royalistes préparaient l'assemblée qui devait chasser cet inepte ministère qui n'a su jamais montrer quelque habileté, que lorsqu'il a marché à la suite de Bonaparte et de ses 500,000 hommes.

Les adjoints une fois formés dans chaque assemblée, et formés dans le même esprit, s'unirent fortement entre eux, et firent leurs listes des députés ; ils se réunirent tout naturellement par les mêmes choix aux autres royalistes des collèges qui n'avaient pas paru dans la dernière élection de la *Chambre des Représentants* sous Bonaparte ; ils détachèrent de l'autre parti beaucoup d'hommes ou indifférents ou effrayés de l'ascendant qu'ils voyaient que les *ultra-royalistes* allaient prendre dans le gouvernement, et dont ils

ne voulaient point s'exposer à être victimes; ils en atti-
rèrent aussi d'autres par la promesse d'être récompensés par
le gouvernement de leur dévouement à sa cause. Pendant
que le parti ultra-royaliste se grossissait ainsi, l'autre parti
diminuait par la raison contraire: un grand nombre d'électeurs qui avaient voté pour la nomination de la dernière
Chambre des Représentants n'osèrent point se présenter,
ou ne le voulurent pas, persuadés d'avance de l'espèce des
choix qui allaient être faits.

Dans plus d'un département il y eut des provocations
et des menaces de la part des *ultra-royalistes* contre ceux qui
avaient voté pour *l'acte additionnel;* et vous savez que le
nombre de ces votants a été de plus de 1,300,000. En
général, comme le petit nombre d'ultra-royalistes était re-
gardé comme ayant le gouvernement en sa faveur, et qu'on
appréhendait de la part du gouvernement des réactions et
des vengeances, les autres craignaient en les heurtant de
se faire désigner par eux aux persécutions dont d'ailleurs
ces Messieurs ne se faisaient aucun scrupule de se vanter,
surtout dans les départements de l'ouest et du midi.

D'autres circonstances se sont jointes encore à celles-là;
dans plusieurs départements, les cultivateurs, riches fermiers,
et autres, dont les maisons étaient occupées par les troupes
ennemies, n'ont point osé les quitter et abandonner ainsi
leurs familles à la discrétion de tels hôtes, pour se rendre
aux assemblées électorales; ainsi l'on peut dire, avec vérité,
que dans plusieurs départements cette partie, très-nom-
breuse de propriétaires, n'a pas concouru à l'élection; et c'est
ainsi, que par la circonstance de l'occupation militaire en-
nemie, la classe très-considérable en France des petits propriétaires ruraux n'a pu contrebalancer avec succès, comme
elle l'aurait fait, l'influence du parti nobiliaire. Quant
au fait particulier de M. D'Argenson dont vous me
parlez, voici comme on m'a assuré qu'il s'était passé.
Les troupes Allemandes établies dans le département du
Haut Rhin, dont le chef lieu est *Colmar,* empêchaient toute
communication entre l'arrondissement de *Belfort* et celui de

Colmar, où se tenait l'assemblée électorale du département. Elles ne voulaient point en conséquence laisser passer les électeurs de Belfort qui demandaient à se rendre à Colmar. Le Général le Courbe qui commandait la portion de l'armée Française que était de ce côté, obtint du Général allemand des permissions pour envoyer a Colmar des commissaires Français relativememt aux subsistances de son armée. Les choses s'arrangèrent de manière qu'on choisit pour commissaires des *électeurs*, et ceux-ci emmenèrent, sous le titre de domestiques et d'agents inférieurs, d'autres électeurs de Belfort. Ils se trouvèrent ainsi réunis à Colmar au nombre de 40, dans le même sens, et firent le choix qu'ils avaient voulu.

Il se passa dans l'un des arrondissements de ce même départment un fait assez curieux. Un président de collège eut la simplicité de lire publiquement dans son assemblée une lettre, par laquelle le préfet lui écrivait de faire tous ses efforts pour qu'on ne nommat point tel individu qu'il lui désignait. Cette balourdise fit un grand effet dans l'assemblée, et mit le préfet en fureur contre le président. Il n'est que trop vrai que, dans les départements du midi, on a expulsé par la force ou empêché d'arriver par la crainte tous ceux qu'on croyait s'être trop prononcés autrefois en faveur de la révolution.

Dans le département du Gard, en particulier, les Protestants ont été menacés de la vie s'ils osaient paraître dans ces assemblées. Aucun d'eux ne s'y est montré, et ils forment le tiers de la population.

Dans le mémoire qui vient de paraître sous le nom de *Pozzo di Borgo*, et que celui-ci n'a pas fait démentir par un seul mot de sa part jusqu'à présent, vous trouverez quelques autres faits qui sont très-certains sur le même sujet. Vous en trouverez aussi, dans le 7ᵉ vol. du *Censeur*, qu'on m'a assuré avait été envoyé d'ici à *Brougham*. Vous pouvez lui demander cet ouvrage, qui est très-curieux, et très-digne d'être lu. La police l'a fait saisir ici avant qu'on le mit en vente, en violation même de la loi très-

restrictive sur la presse qui a été rendue l'année dernière.
Du reste, rien n'est plus précieux en ce genre que la
déclaration qu'a fait sur ce sujet le nouveau ministre de
l'intérieur, *Vaublanc*, en présentant à la Chambre des Députés son nouveau projet de loi sur les *élections*, projet de
loi qui est bien la chose la plus comique qu'on ait jamais
imaginé sur cette matière. C'est le 18 Décembre dernier
qu'il parlait ainsi, et vous trouverez ce curieux passage dans
le *Moniteur* du 20. Le voici, remarquez bien que c'est
à ces Messieurs qu'il dit cela en face ; aussi je vous assure
qu'ils ont été fort choqués de cette ingénuité.

" *Dans les dernières élections, vous avez vu que l'on a été
obligé* D'EMPLOYER DES MOYENS EXTRAORDINAIRES *pour
balancer l'influence que pouvait avoir eue sur les collèges électoraux l'esprit dans lequel ils avaient été formés, mais ces
mesures,* AUTORISÉES PAR LES CIRCONSTANCES, *ne pourraient
plus se renouveller : il faut donc une loi nouvelle.*" Je ne crois
pas que vos ministres soient aussi *candides* que celui-là ; —
cela ferait trop de plaisir à vous et à vos amis. Chaque
mot de ce singulier passage mérite d'être pesé. Quant à
cette loi nouvelle, je vous dirai en deux mots qu'elle propose
sérieusement d'avoir des collèges électoraux composés
d'archévêques, d'évêques, de curés, de vicaires, juges de paix,
présidents des tribunaux de justice, des tribunaux de
commerce, des procureurs du roi, &c. Vous voyez qu'avec
ce digne homme nous serions bien à l'abri des dangers du
suffrage universel. Du reste, ce projet de loi prétendue a
excité une risée si universelle, qu'il dit maintenant qu'il
ne tient pas à son projet, et qu'il ne demande pas mieux
que d'en voir proposer un autre ; et cependant, grâce à la
précieuse prérogative de l'initiative royale ! cette ridicule
extravagance a été présentée à la Chambre des Députés,
précédée de la formule d'usage, *Louis par la grâce de Dieu
Roi de France et de Navarre*, et terminée par *l'an de grâce*,
1815, *et de notre règne le* 21ᵉ.

Les ultra-royalistes n'en veulent pas, parcequ'ils disent
que ces collèges électoraux n'étant que des collèges d'hommes

publics, seraient des collèges révolutionnaires. Les autres n'en veulent pas non plus, parcequ'ils disent que ces collèges seraient toujours sous la main du gouvernement, puisqu'ils ne seraient presque compris que de ses agents.

Voilà le dégré de déraison où l'on est parvenu en ce pays c'est à dire, où sont parvenus les hommes qui veulent gouverner une nation accoutumée depuis 25 ans à des opinions et à des sentimens si différents. Quant à ces dernières élections dont je viens de vous parler, je vous assure que si l'on pouvait rire en si triste matière, ce serait du désappointement de cet habile ministère précédent, qui, comme nous le disons en français, n'a su que préparer les verges pour se faire fouetter, et qui a été tellement épouvanté de son propre ouvrage, qu'il s'est hâté de déménager, sans attendre qu'on le chassât.

Ce dernier ministère se trouve placé maintenant entre deux partis qui le haïssent et le méprisent également. On prétend que le chef cherche à se faire reporter à sa place par l'influence de votre illustre Duc, mais je crois que celui-ci se contentera de la gloire et de l'habileté d'y avoir, en arrivant, fait placer son ancien collègue, *Fouché*.

No. II.

(See Vol. II. p. 310. and Vol. III. pp. 293. 299.)

In a codicil to Sir Samuel Romilly's will is the following passage : — " I leave to Rev. Dr. Samuel Parr, as a token of my respect and affection for him, my copy of Aristophanes, *Editio princeps*. I likewise bequeath to him all the plate which he some time ago very generously presented to me. It was a testimonial of his approbation of my conduct which I was justly proud of; he had originally left it to me by his will, and afterwards thought proper to discharge the legacy in his lifetime. I will, however, consider it but as a legacy to me ; and therefore, if I do not survive him, I return it to him by this my will." On being informed of these bequests, Dr. Parr, on the 11th Nov. 1818, wrote a letter to Mr. Whishaw, Sir S. Romilly's executor, of which the following is an extract: —

" I thank you again and again for the contents of your letter, and for the friendly spirit which pervades it; and now, dear Sir, I address myself to you and your brother-executor. I set a just value upon the motives which induced my dear friend to bequeath the plate to me. First, I shall accept it as given by him, and I will send a receipt to the executors. But no earthly consideration will induce me to keep possession of it. I must entreat you, at a proper time, to convey to the eldest son of Sir Samuel my earnest wish that he would have the goodness to accept the whole service of plate, as a mark of my unfeigned good-will to himself, and of my unaltered esteem, affection, and veneration for the dear and sacred name of his father."

The present thus offered was accepted; and the following is the concluding letter from Dr. Parr on this subject: —

Hatton, Jan. 17. 1819.

Dear Mr. Romilly,

The heart which now glows with kindness towards yourself and those who are dearest to you will ere long cease to beat, and the hand which subscribes this letter will be mouldering in the grave. Till that season arrive, I shall ever take a solicitous and affectionate interest in the health and welfare of those who bear your most honoured name. It has derived that appellation, dear Sir, from talents, from literary attainments, from professional knowledge, from spotless integrity, from benevolence unfeigned and unwearied, such as rarely adorn the sons of men; such as procured, for the possessor, from me esteem, reverence, unbounded confidence, and regard more than brotherly; such as are written in characters quite indelible on the tablets of my memory; such, too, as will ever exercise, and will ever improve, and ever consecrate, the purest and noblest feelings of my soul. He that stands, as I do, upon the brink of eternity, will anxiously look back to those examples which have made him a wiser and a better man, and he will lift up his hope to another and a happier state, in which all tears will be wiped away from all eyes, and the pangs of separation will be dreaded no more.

When your letter reached me, I gazed upon it eagerly; I grasped it with agony; I could by no effort summon fortitude sufficient to open it. I laid it by till my spirits should be more composed. I opened it fearfully; I read it most attentively; I was soothed with the matter, and the language, and the spirit. I shall preserve it carefully to the latest moment of my life, and I shall direct those who come after me to place it among the most precious and sacred memorials of friendship.

Mr. Romilly, I entreat you to accept my sincerest and most thankful acknowledgments for the honour which you have conferred upon me in permitting me to transfer for your use the plate. May Heaven grant you long life, uninterrupted health, and undisturbed spirits to avail yourself of my well-intended and well-accepted offer! Surely there will be some day, and some place, in which I shall have an opportunity to shake you by the hand. Come, I beseech you, and see me, and bring with you any of your brothers. In the mean time, you and they will accept my most sincere and most serious blessing.

I have the honour to be, dear Sir,
Your real Friend and respectful obedient Servant,
SAMUEL PARR.

INDEX.

THE END.

LONDON:
Printed by A. SPOTTISWOODE,
New-Street-Square.